IMU, ICM, Medals, Prizes, and Laureates

IMU, ICM, Medals, Prizes, and Laureates

Ravi P. Agarwal

MDPI

Basel • Beijing • Wuhan • Barcelona • Belgrade • Novi Sad • Cluj • Manchester

Author
Ravi P. Agarwal
Department of Mathematics
and Systems Engineering
Florida Institute of Technology
Melbourne, FL, USA

Editorial Office
MDPI AG
Grosspeteranlage 5
4052 Basel, Switzerland

For citation purposes, cite as indicated below:

(ACS) Author 1; Author 2. *Title*; MDPI: Basel, Switzerland, Year. *Or* (APA) Author 1, & Author 2. *Title*. MDPI. *Or* (Chicago) Author 1, and Author 2. Year. *Title*. Basel: MDPI.

ISBN 978-3-7258-4616-0 (Hbk)
ISBN 978-3-7258-4615-3 (PDF)
doi.org/10.3390/books978-3-7258-4615-3

This book did not undergo peer review. The opinions expressed in the book are the author's own and do not reflect the view of the publisher.

Dedication

Dedicated to my wife Sadhna Agarwal.

Contents

Abbreviations

AAAS	American Academy of Arts and Sciences
ACM	Association for Computing Machinery
AMS	American Mathematical Society
APS	American Philosophical Society
BBVA	Banco Bilbao Vizcaya Argentaria
DMV	Deutsche Mathematiker-Vereinigung
EC	Executive Committee
EECS	Electrical Engineering and Computer Science
EMS	European Mathematical Society
ENS	École Normale Supérieure
ETH Zurich	Eidgenössische Technische Hochschule Zürich
FAS	French Academy of Sciences
FRS	Fellow of the Royal Society
FIT	Florida Institute of Technology
IAS	Institute for Advanced Study
ICM	International Congress of Mathematicians
ICMI	International Commission on Mathematical Instruction
ICSU	International Council of Scientific Unions
ICTP	International Centre for Theoretical Physics
IHES	Institut des Hautes Études Scientifiques
IIT	Indian Institute of Technology
IMPA	Instituto de Matemática Pura e Aplicada
IMU	International Mathematical Union
IRC	International Research Council
KUIAS	Kyoto University Institute for Advanced Study
KIAS	Korean Institute of Advanced Studies
LMS	London Mathematical Society
MIT	Massachusetts Institute of Technology
MPIM	Max Planck Institute for Mathematics
MSRI	Mathematical Sciences Research Institute
NAS	National Academy of Sciences
NUS	National University of Singapore
NASL	Norwegian Academy of Science and Letters
RAS	Russian Academy of Sciences
RIMS	Research Institute for Mathematical Sciences
RSAS	Royal Swedish Academy of Sciences
RSE	Royal Society of Edinburgh
SASTRA	Shanmugha Arts, Science, Technology & Research Academy
SIAM	Society for Industrial and Applied Mathematics
UC	University of California
UCLA	University of California, Los Angeles
ULB	Université Libre de Bruxelles

Preface

In our joint book *Creators of Mathematical and Computational Sciences (2014)*, we alluded that mathematics is a unique aspect of human thought, and its history differs in essence from all other histories. Only in mathematics is there no significant correction—only extensions. Each great mathematician adds to what came previously, but nothing needs to be uprooted. We recorded the essential discoveries of more than 400 mathematicians in chronological order, following the birth of ideas on the basis of prior ideas ad infinitum and contemporary events occurring side by side in different countries or cultures, reflecting some of the noblest thoughts of generations; documented the winding path of mathematical scholarship throughout history and, most importantly, the thought process of each individual that resulted in the mastery of their subject; derived information from records from several locations, some of which have been unearthed only in recent years, throwing light on the very humanity of mathematicians who have very often been reduced to a theorem in a school textbook; addressed the nature and character of every mathematician as we try to understand their visible actions; and added amusing anecdotes and after-dinner jokes that have been taken from the published literature, while noting that it is difficult to vouch for the authenticity of most of them—but still interesting because they reveal the human nature of mathematicians, who are very often believed to be eccentric individuals. In the book *Mathematics Before and After Pythagoras (2024)*, I focused on the intellectual contributions of Pythagoras, providing a global and historical perspective by discussing the mathematical developments before his time and touching upon a variety of significant problems that have engaged, and continue to engage, many of the most gifted scientific minds of later generations up to the present.

The present book supplements the two books above. I shall discuss the formal establishment of the International Mathematical Union (IMU) and its purpose of promoting international cooperation in mathematics (especially with developing countries) by supporting and assisting the International Congress of Mathematicians (ICM) every four years and other international scientific meetings/conferences. The IMU also encourages and helps other international mathematical activities considered likely to contribute to the development of mathematical science in any of its aspects, whether pure, applied, or educational. We shall present the most important features of each ICM (from 1897 to 2022, with two interruptions during World War I and II), including the following: the participation of leading mathematicians (in thousands) from almost all over the world; the host countries with the names of the cities and the duration of the Congress; the list of the dedicated members of the various important committees, who do not leave anything to chance; opening and closing ceremonies; and the number of 1 h, 45 min, and short 10 min lectures. Since 1936, the ICM has also acknowledged outstanding research contributions to mathematics through scientific medals and prizes: the Fields Medals (2 to 4 awarded per Congress since 1936, so far 64 with two female recipients); the IMU Abacus Medal (previously known as the Rolf Nevanlinna Prize, awarded since 1986, so far 11); the Carl Friedrich Gauss Prize (awarded since 2006, so far 5); the Chern Medal (awarded since 2010, so far 4); and the Leelavati Award (awarded since 2010, so far 4). Although the prestigious

Abel Prize (awarded yearly since 2003, so far 27 with one female recipient) and Ramanujan Prize (awarded yearly since 2005, so far 20) are not a part of the ICM, the IMU also strongly supports these prizes. For each medal and prize listed above, I shall justify the name of the mathematician after whom it is labelled by providing his biographical data and foundational contributions to mathematics. For each medal and prize winner awarded during ICMs, I shall provide his/her family background, education right from the elementary level, the name of the institution from where their doctorate degree was obtained, with the year and title of the thesis, the name of the thesis supervisor(s), a short description of the work that led to the award, a history of academic jobs, research conducted after receiving the award, and the list of further honors and awards. The book ends with some details of the author's own achievements.

To write this book I have consulted hundreds of articles, parts of all the ICM proceedings, several books[1], and several websites, especially en.wikipedia.org and mathshistory.st-andrews.ac.uk. It is written for every researcher and graduate student of mathematics. After reading this book the reader might perceive that several prize winners from the IMU were born at least with some of the following opportunities: born in a wealthy and/or educated family, being a prodigy, admitted to recognized primary and secondary schools, had inspiring teachers, took part in mathematical activities such as national and international olympiads, being accepted at a recognized university for graduate studies, and had an eminent doctoral advisor. However, the strict criteria for securing a Fields Medal (IMU Abacus Medal) are as follows: at least one major breakthrough in any branch of mathematics (computer science) that has the potential for future achievement, an individual can only be awarded one medal, and the recipient must be under 40 years old; for the Gauss Prize the essential requirements are as follows: the scientist's work must have had a notable impact in fields such as engineering, business, or everyday life, essentially an impact outside of mathematics; for the Chern Medal the obligations are outstanding lifelong achievements of the highest level in the field of mathematics; and for the Leelavati Award the candidate must have a very high recognition and great appreciation for outstanding contributions to increasing public awareness of mathematics as an intellectual discipline and the crucial role it plays in diverse human endeavors. Since very few qualify even to be considered for a prize by the IMU, we should be satisfied with what we have achieved in life and not be demoralized, but rather continue to work to become better mathematicians. After all, there were no medals or prizes during the time of Euler, who is considered "Master of Masters", Gauss, who ranks as "The Best Mathematician World Has Ever Produced", and according to Hermite "Abel left mathematicians enough to keep them busy for five hundred years". The only prize Ramanujan "The Mathematical Genius from India" received in his lifetime

---

[1] *International Mathematical Congresses: An Illustrated History 1893–1986; Mathematicians of the World Unite! The International Congress of Mathematicians a Human Endeavor; Mathematics Without Borders: A History of the International Mathematical Union; Modern Mathematics in the Light of the Fields Medals; Mathematics Unbound: The Evolution of an International Mathematical Research Community, 1800–1945; The Origin and History of the Fields Medals; Framing Global Mathematics: The International Mathematical Union between Theorems and Politics; The Origin and History of the Fields Medals.*

was the K. Ranganatha Rao prize for mathematics from his school's headmaster, Krishnaswami Iyer. I firmly believe this book will convey an excellent survey of mathematics research throughout the last century and be a very useful reference.

I am thankful for the inspiring comments/corrections/deletions/additions on this manuscript provided by Presidents of the IMU Hiraku Nakajima (2023–2026), Carlos Eduardo Kenig (2019–2022), Shigefumi Mori (2015–2018), László Lovász (2007–2010), John Macleod Ball (2003–2006), and David Bryant Mumford (1995–1998); Vice-President Ulrike Tillmann (2023–2026); and Laureates Elliott Hershel Lieb (2022), Hugo Duminil-Copin (2022), Barry Charles Mazur (2022), James Alexander Maynard (2022), Mark Braverman (2022), Masaki Kashiwara (2018), Constantinos Costis Daskalakis (2018), Ali Nesin (2018), Stanley Joel Osher (2014), Phillip Augustus Griffiths (2014), Subhash Khot (2014), Yves François Meyer (2010), Curtis Tracy McMullen (1998), Avi Wigderson (1994), Edward Witten (1990), Shigefumi Mori (1990), Vladimir Gershonovich Drinfeld (1990), Leslie Gabriel Valiant (1986), Simon Kirwan Donaldson (1986), Shing-Tung Yau (1982), Pierre René Deligne, (1978), Charles Louis Fefferman (1978), David Bryant Mumford (1974), and especially Jean-Pierre Serre (1954). I am also grateful to Junko Ito (daughter of Kiyosi Ito) for pointing out a few changes in Section 35.6; Xavier Cabre Vilagut and Yan Yan Li (doctoral students of Louis Nirenberg) for reviewing Section 38.7; Curtis Tracy McMullen and Jan Vondrák (husband of Maryam Mirzakhani) for suggesting a few changes in Section 39.4; Martin Grötschel (president of the 1998 ICM and IMU secretary 2007–2010 and 2011–2014) for his admiration; and Steve George Krantz for his continual support.

My apologies, to save space, I have not put the designation Professor in front of any name, but each one of them is/was a Distinguished Professor.

Ravi P. Agarwal
Author

1. International Mathematical Union (IMU)

The first steps towards the formation of the IMU were taken in 1919 in Brussels at the Constitutive Assembly of the International Research Council (IRC). Formally, it was founded in 1920 as a truly international non-governmental and non-profit scientific organization, with the purpose of promoting international cooperation in mathematics (especially with developing countries); supporting and assisting the International Congress of Mathematicians (ICM) and other international scientific meetings/conferences; acknowledging outstanding research contributions to mathematics through the awarding of scientific prizes, the Fields Medals (two to four awarded per Congress since 1936), the IMU Abacus Medal (previously known as the Rolf Nevanlinna Prize; awarded since 1986), the Gauss Prize (since 2006), the Chern Medal (since 2010), and the Leelavati Award (since 2010); and encouraging and supporting other international mathematical activities considered likely to contribute to the development of mathematical science in any of its aspects, whether pure, applied, or educational. The IMU was dispersed in September 1932 but reconstituted in 1950 at the Constitutive Convention in New York in law on 10 September 1951, when ten (member) countries (Austria, Denmark, France, Germany, Great Britain, Greece, Italy, Japan, the Netherlands, and Norway) had become members. Five more countries joined in 1951: Australia, Canada, Finland, Peru, and the United States. The IMU has existed in its current form since 1951. In 1952, the General Assembly met in Rome to inaugurate its activities and establish the first Executive Committee (EC): the President (Marshall Harvey Stone, 1903–1989, USA), two Vice-Presidents (Félix Édouard Justin Émil Borel, 1871–1956, France, and Erich Kamke, 1890–1961, Germany), the Secretary, and six Members-at-Large. In 1952 the IMU was also readmitted to the International Council for Science (former name, International Council of Scientific Unions [ICSU]). Every four years, the IMU membership gathers in a General Assembly, which consists of delegates appointed by the Adhering Organizations and the present members of the EC. All important decisions are made at the General Assembly, including the election of the new officers (which includes the Former President as a member), the establishment of commissions, the approval of the budget, and any changes to the statutes and by-laws. The EC is responsible for all policy matters and for tasks such as choosing the members of the ICM Program Committee and various prize committees. To preserve its history, the IMU maintains an archive containing important correspondence and documents. The archive keeps, in particular, the correspondence of all IMU prize selection committees. The EC of the IMU decided that all material related to IMU prizes must be kept confidential. The IMU archive was at Eidgenössische Technische Hochschule Zürich (ETH Zurich) for a long period of time until it moved to the University of Helsinki in 1994. On the 16th meeting of the General Assembly in Bangalore (current name, Bengaluru), India, in August 2010, Berlin was chosen as the location of the permanent office of the IMU, which was opened on 1 January 2011 and was hosted by the Weierstrass Institute for Applied Analysis and Stochastics (WIAS), named after Karl Theodor Wilhelm Weierstrass (1815–1897, Germany). This institute of the Gottfried Wilhelm Leibniz (1646–1716, Germany) scientific community has about 120 scientists engaging in mathematical research applied to complex problems in industry and commerce. Currently, the IMU has 83 (full) member countries and two Associate Members from mathematically developing countries (Bangladesh and Paraguay). Each member country represents at least one Adhering Organization, which may be its principal academy, a mathematical society, its research council or some other institution or association of institutions, or an appropriate agency of its government. For example, America and India, respectively, represent the American Mathematical Society (AMS) and Indian National Science Academy. For the years 2023–2026, the President of the IMU is Hiraku Nakajima, born in 1962, Japan, and the Vice-Presidents are Ulrike Tillmann (she), Germany–UK, and Tatiana Toro (she), born 1964, Colombia–USA. Every two months the IMU publishes an electronic newsletter, *IMU News*, that aims to improve communication between the IMU and the worldwide mathematical community by reporting on decisions and recommendations of the Union, major international mathematical events and developments, and other topics of general mathematical interest. The *IMU Bulletins* are published annually with the aim of informing the IMU's members about the Union's current activities. For complete details of the establishment of the IMU, see the exceptional book of Schappacher [1], which was introduced to the author by Carlos Eduardo Kenig (born 1953, Argentina–USA).

2. International Congress of Mathematicians (ICM)

Georg Ferdinand Ludwig Philipp Cantor (1845–1918, Russia–Germany) was one of the first to press for international mathematical conferences. In 1888 he proposed a meeting between German and French mathematicians, and later, between 1894 and 1896, he contacted several leading mathematicians proposing an international conference. He had support from Felix Christian Klein (1849–1925, Germany), Heinrich Martin Georg Friedrich Weber (1842–1913, Germany), Émile Michel Hyacinthe Lemoine (1840–1912, France), and several others. Cantor proposed that a trial conference be held in 1897, either in Switzerland or Belgium. He realized that neutral options were necessary to get both French and German mathematicians to attend. He suggested that the first actual conference be in Paris in 1900. It quickly became clear that of the two options, Switzerland or Belgium, Switzerland was favoured because of its international reputation. Deutsche Mathematiker-Vereinigung (DMV) and the French Mathematical Society approved these ideas and agreed to contact Carl Friedrich Geiser (1843–1934, Switzerland) in Zurich.

3. First ICM

As Cantor suggested the first international conference was held in Zurich (Switzerland) during 9–11 August 1897, with 208 participants (including 4 women) from 16 countries. The organizing committee included several prominent mathematicians such as Antonio Luigi Gaudenzio Giuseppe Cremona (1830–1903, Italy), Felix Klein, Magnus Gustaf Mittag-Leffler (1846–1927, Sweden), and Andrei Andreyevich Markov (1856–1922, Russia); however, Geiser and Ferdinand Rudio (1856–1929, Germany–Switzerland) were the main coordinators of the conference. The conference proved to be so successful that, rather than considering it a trial conference, it became the first candid International Congress of Mathematicians. Adolf Hurwitz (1859–1919, Germany–Switzerland) in his most welcoming speech on Sunday 8 August 1897, 21:00 in Tonhalle, Zurich's concert hall, said "It is true that the great thoughts of our science were created and developed in a scholar's quiet room in most cases; no other science, with the exception of philosophy, has such a brooding and hermitic character to it as mathematics. But still, a mathematician also feels the need to communicate and discuss with their peers. Surely each one of us has already experienced what an inspiring power is inherent in personal scientific communication". The main resolutions set out at this Congress, which continue to influence the style of the congresses, were as follows:

1. Henceforth, international mathematical congresses shall be held in intervals of 3–5 years and in due consideration of the various countries.
2. In the closing ceremony of each Congress, the dates and place of the next Congress as well as its organising and inviting bodies shall be designated.
3. Should any circumstances make it impossible to hold a Congress on the designated dates and in the designated place, the Executive Committee of the previous Congress is authorized to make the necessary arrangements for calling a new Congress, as may be the case. For this purpose, it will also contact the bodies defined in resolution 2.
4. For tasks of an international nature, whose solution requires a fixed organization, each Congress may nominate a permanent sub-committee, whose period of office lasts until the next Congress. The responsibilities and liabilities of such sub-committees shall be determined every time such a sub-committee is nominated.
5. The next Congress shall be held in Paris in 1900 (Cantor's recommendation). The Société mathématique de France is commissioned with its preparation and organization.

4. Second ICM

As was resolved in the first ICM, the second ICM was held in Paris, France, during 6–11 August 1900. The Congress was attended by 250 full members (with 6 women) from 26 countries. Jules Henri Poincaré (1854–1912, France) was appointed as the President of the conference, and the ten Vice-Presidents were Emanuel Czuber (1851–1925, Austria), Paul Albert Gordan (1837–1912, Poland–Germany), Alfred George Greenhill (1847–1927, England), Ernst Leonard Lindelöf (1870–1946, Finland), Carl Louis Ferdinand von Lindemann (1852–1939, Germany), Mittag-Leffler, Eliakim Hastings Moore (1862–1932, USA, absent), Matvei Aleksandrovich Tikhomandritskii (1844–1921, Russia now Ukraine), Vito Volterra (1860–1940, Italy), and Hieronymus Georg Zeuthen (1839–1920, Denmark). The conference began with a short speech from the President, who thanked the assembly and proposed to appoint Charles Hermite (1822–1901, France) as an Honorary President. This was followed by two plenary lectures by Moritz Benedikt Cantor (1829–1920, Germany) and Vito Volterra, both in French. On Wednesday, 8 August, at 9.00 am, David Hilbert (1862–1943, Germany) gave his lecture *On the Future Problems of Mathematics*, which is considered as the most influential speech ever given to mathematicians, given by a mathematician, or given about mathematics. It is sometimes described as a plenary lecture and sometime it is not. He presented a list of 23 open problems (now termed Hilbert's problems) with the intension of enlightening the future of mathematics in the twentieth century. Due to limited time, Hilbert presented only ten problems. These problems appeared in the 1902 translation in the *Bulletin of the AMS*. Some of these were solved within a short time, and others were discussed throughout the 20th century, but a few are now assumed to be too open-ended to come to closure. Some remain a challenge for mathematicians to this day. In any case, such a large body of new mathematics has arisen from Hilbert's problems that we can say that the problems he posed became the backbone for mathematical research in the 20th century. The solution of one of Hilbert's problems provides instant recognition in the mathematical community. Hilbert's address is still important and should be read by anyone interested in pursuing research in mathematics. We list here the following problems with their current status:

1(a). *Georg Cantor's problem of the cardinal number of the continuum.* (Is there a transfinite number between that of a denumerable set and the numbers of the continuum?) For this problem Kurt Friedrich Gödel (1906–1978, Czech Republic–USA) in 1938 and Paul Joseph Cohen (1934–2007, USA) in 1963 showed that the answer depends on the particular version of set theory assumed. Consistent set theories may either include it or deny it.

1(b). *Can the continuum of numbers be considered a well-ordered set*? With or without the axiom of choice (for any indexed collection of nonempty sets, there exists a choice function), this has been shown to be impossible to prove or disprove within Zermelo–Frankel (Ernst Friedrich Ferdinand Zermelo, 1871–1953, Germany, and Abraham Fraenkel, 1891–1965, Germany–Israel) set theory.

2. *The compatibility of the arithmetical axioms.* (Can it be proven that the axioms of logic are consistent?) There is no consensus on whether the results of Gödel and Gerhard Karl Erich Gentzen (1909–1945, Germany) give a solution to the problem as stated by Hilbert. Gödel's second incompleteness theorem, proved in 1931, shows that no proof of its consistency can be carried out within arithmetic itself. Gentzen proved in 1936 that the consistency of arithmetic follows from the well-foundedness of the ordinal ϵ_0.
3. *The equality of the volumes of two tetrahedra of equal bases and equal altitudes.* (Give two tetrahedra that cannot be decomposed into congruent tetrahedra directly or by adjoining congruent tetrahedra.) Max Wilhelm Dehn (1878–1952, Germany) in 1902 showed this could not be achieved by inventing the theory of Dehn invariants, and Venyamin Fedovović Kagan (1869–1953, Russia) obtained the same result in 1903, independently.
4. *Problem of the straight line as the shortest distance between two points.* (Find geometries whose axioms are closest to those of Euclidean geometry if the ordering and incidence axioms are retained, the congruence axioms weakened, and the equivalent of the parallel postulate omitted.) This problem was shown by Georg Karl Wilhelm Hamel (1877–1954, Germany) to be too vague as stated, as there are several interpretations of the original statement of this problem. However, in 1901, he furnished its proof.
5. *Lie's concept of a continuous group of transformations without the assumption of the differentiability of the function defining the group.* This problem was solved by John Louis von Neumann (1903–1957, Hungary–USA) in 1930 for bicompact groups and the abelian case, and the solvable case was addressed by Deane Montgomery (1909–1992, USA) and Leo Zippin (1905–1995, USA) in 1952, followed by Hidehiko Yamabe (1923–1960, Japan–USA) in 1953.
6. *Mathematical treatment of the axioms of physics.* This problem is partially solved, in particular by Constantin Carathéodory (1873–1950, Greece–Germany) in 1909 in thermodynamics, Richard Edler von Mises (1883–1953, Austria–USA) in 1919, Andrey Nikolaevich Kolmogorov (1903–1987, Russia) in 1933 in probability theory, von Neumann in quantum mechanics in 1930, and George Hamel in 1927 in mechanics.
7. *Irrationality and transcendence of certain numbers.* (Is a^b transcendental for algebraic $a \neq 0, 1$, and irrational algebraic b?) The affirmative answer was given by Alexander Osipovich Gelfond (1906–1968, Russia) in 1934 and Theodor Schneider (1911–1988, Germany) in 1935, independently, now known as the Gelfond–Schneider theorem. Here irrationality of b is necessary.
8. *The Riemann hypothesis.* (The *Riemann zeta function* after George Friedrich Bernhard Riemann, 1826–1866, Germany, is $\zeta(s) = \sum_{n=1}^{\infty} 1/n^s$, $s = \sigma + it$, $\sigma > 1$. In 1859, Riemann claimed that on the Argand diagram for s, the non-trivial zeros of the zeta function lie on the line $\sigma = 1/2$; here, trivial zeros are at $-2, -4, -6 \cdots$). This conjecture has been neither proved nor disproved.
9. *Find the most general reciprocity law for the norm residues of k-th order in a general algebraic number field, where k is a power of a prime.* A special case of this problem was resolved by Teiji Takagi (1875–1960, Japan) in 1920. Then in 1927, a partial solution was given by Emil Artin (1898–1962, Austria–Germany) by establishing the Artin reciprocity law, which deals with abelian extensions

of algebraic number fields. (After a lecture by Artin someone asked "Your talk was most interesting. But of what use is such work anyway?" Artin's reply was, "I make my living at it!") Then Teiji Takagi and Helmut Hasse (1898–1979, Germany) used the more general Hasse reciprocity law, which led to the development of class field theory, realizing Hilbert's program in an abstract fashion. Certain explicit formulas for norm residues were later found by Igor Rostislavovich Shafarevich (1923–2017, Ukraine–Russia) during 1948–1950.

10. *Determination of the solvability of a Diophantine equation.* (Find an algorithm to determine whether a given polynomial Diophantine equation with integer coefficients have an integer solution.) In 1970, the impossibility of this was shown by Yuri Vladimirovich Matiyasevich (born 1947, Russia). It was later independently solved by Gregory Volfovich Chudnovsky (born 1952, Ukraine–USA) at the age of seventeen. In appreciation, Matiyasevich described Chudnovsky's method as the right approach to solve this problem. In 1970, Roger Penrose (born 1931, England) proved that this problem has no solution. Penrose held appointments at many academic institutions, including Cambridge University, Princeton University, the University of Texas, and the University of Oxford. He is also famous for his contributions to recreational mathematics.
11. Quadratic forms with any algebraic numerical coefficients. In 1924, Helmut Hasse devised a theory of quadratic forms over the rational numbers and later extended this solution to any algebraic number field.
12. *Extension of Kronecker's theorem (after Leopold Kronecker, 1823–189, Poland–Germany) on abelian fields to any algebraic realm of rationality.* This problem is unresolved. It calls for the construction of holomorphic functions in several variables that have properties analogous to the exponential function and elliptic modular functions.
13. *Impossibility of solution of the general equation of the 7th degree by means of functions of only two arguments.* The continuous variant of this problem was solved by Vladimir Igorevich Arnold (1937–2010, Ukraine–France) in 1957 based on work by Kolmogorov, but the algebraic variant is unresolved.
14. *Proof of the finiteness of certain complete systems of functions.* This problem was resolved with the answer no, by a counterexample, by Masayoshi Nagata (1927–2008, Japan) in 1959.
15. *Rigorous foundations of Schubert's enumerative calculus (after Hermann Cäsar Hannibal Schubert, 1848–1911, Germany): precisely determine the limits of the validity of the numbers that Schubert had determined on the basis of the principle of special position by means of his enumerative calculus.* This problem has been partially solved, but no general theory has been developed.
16. *Problem of the topology of algebraic curves and surfaces: in particular, developing Carl Gustav Axel Harnack's (1851–1888, Germany) methods and Poincaré's theory of limited cycles.* The Shimura–Taniyama Conjecture (after Yutaka Taniyama, 1927–1958, Japan, and Gorō Shimura, 1930–2019, Japan) postulates just this connection. This problem is unsolved.
17. *Expressions of definite forms by squares.* Artin showed in 1927 that a positive definite rational function is the sum of squares.

18. *Building up of space from congruent polyhedra.* This problem has been resolved by Karl August Reinhardt (1895–1941, Germany) and Thomas Callister Hales (born 1958, USA). However, Penrose found non-periodic solutions.
19. *Are the solutions of regular problems in the calculus of variations always necessarily analytic?* This problem was solved in the affirmative by Ennio de Giorgi (1928–1996, Italy) in 1955 and independently by using different methods by John Forbes Nash Jr. (1928–2015, USA) some months later.
20. *The general problem of boundary values.* This problem has been resolved most likely by Hilbert himself and Leonida Tonelli (1885–1946, Italy). This was a significant area of research throughout the 20th century, which culminated in solutions for the nonlinear case.
21. *Proof of the existence of linear differential equations with a prescribed monodromic group.* Several special cases proving their existence have been solved, but a negative solution was found in 1989 by Andrei Andreevich Bolibrukh (1950–2003, Russia–France).
22. *Uniformization of analytic relations by means of automorphic functions.* This problem was solved by Paul Koebe (1882–1945, Germany) in 1907.
23. *Further development of the methods of the calculus of variations.* This problem is too ambiguous to be stated resolved or not.

Hilbert originally included 24 problems in his list, but decided against including 1 of them in the published list. The "24th problem" (in proof theory, on a criterion for simplicity and general methods) was rediscovered in Hilbert's original manuscript notes by the historian Rüdiger Thiele (born 1943, Germany) in 2000.

In 1974 a symposium was held at Northern Illinois University on the mathematical developments arising from Hilbert problems. Some prominent mathematicians discussed progress on each problem and how work on the problem has influenced mathematics. The two-volume proceedings of the symposium were edited by Felix Earl Browder (1927–2016, Russia–USA) and published by the AMS in 1976.

The concluding session opened on Saturday, 11 August at 9.00 am, under the chairmanship of Poincaré. It was unanimously accepted that the next Congress would take place in Germany in 1904 and it would be organized by the DMV, and the society would choose the city and the time later. This was followed by two general addresses by Mittag-Leffler and Poincaré. Immediately after these lectures, the Chairman dismissed the Congress with the words "La séance est levée, le congrés est clos" (The session is adjourned; the congress is closed).

5. Third ICM

The third Congress was held in Heidelberg, Germany, during 8–13 August 1904. There were 336 full members (with 2 women) from 19 countries. DMV in 1901 itself elected Heinrich Weber the President of the Congress, and in 1902 decided to have the Congress in Heidelberg. DMV also decided to commemorate the century of the birth of Carl Guslov Jacob Jacobi (1804–1851, Germany). On Tuesday, 9 August, during the opening ceremony the Chairman Heinrich Weber called to mind with brief words of characterization some of the eminent mathematicians who were no longer among the living since the first Congress—Weierstrass, Charles Hermite, James Joseph Sylvester (1814–1897, England), George Salmon (1819–January 1904, Ireland), Marius Sophus Lie (1842–1899, Norway), Francesco Brioschi (1824–1897, Italy), Cremona, Elwin Bruno Christoffel (1829–1900, Germany–France), and Lazarus Immanuel Fuchs (1833–1902, Poland–Germany). Heinrich Weber also referred to certain general lines of present mathematical progress. This was followed by the lecture of Leo Königsberger (1837–1921, Poland–Germany) on the life of Jacobi. His lecture was printed and given as a gift to all the participants at the Congress. During the lecture the presence of the daughters of Jacobi lent an additional element of personal interest. An interesting feature of the Congress was a lecture by Gyula König (1849–1913, Hungary) where he claimed that Georg Cantor's famous continuum hypothesis (the set of real numbers has minimal possible cardinality that is greater than the cardinality of the set of integers) was false. An error in König's proof was discovered by Ernst Zermelo soon thereafter (some have claimed the next day). Another attraction of the Conference was the lecture "The modern problem of the integration of differential equations" (in French) given by Paul Painlevé (1863–1933, France). On Saturday, 13 August, Vito Volterra proposed, on behalf of the Italian Members of the Mathematics Section of the Accademia dei Lincei, and in agreement with the Presidency of the Circolo Matematico di Palermo, that the Fourth Congress should meet in Rome in the spring of 1908, which was accepted with applause. Vito Volterra also informed the Congress that Giovanni Battista Guccia (1855–1914, Italy) had made available to the Circolo Matematico di Palermo the sum of 3000 francs for an international prize that, under the name of the Guccia Medal, would be awarded during the next Congress to a dissertation making essential progress in the theory of algebraic space curves. The commission that would judge the competition was composed of Max Noether (1844–1921, Germany), Poincaré, and Corrado Segre (1863–1924, Italy). Alfred George Greenhill's request to hold the fifth ICM in England was not accepted since the venue of an ICM could only be decided at the previous Congress. The meeting was then closed.

6. Fourth ICM

The fourth Congress was held in Rome, Italy, during 6–11 April 1908. There were 535 full members (with 10 women) from 22 countries. Pietro Blaserna (1836–1918, Italy) was appointed as the President of the conference, he was then also the President of the Accademia dei Lincei, and the eleven Vice-Presidents were Valentino Cerruti (1850–1909, Italy), Enrico D'Ovidio (1843–1933, Italy), Andrew Russell Forsyth (1858–1942, Scotland–England), Gordan, Marie Ennemond Camille Jordan (1838–1922, France), Hendrik Antoon Lorentz (1853–1928, Netherlands), Franz Carl Joseph Mertens (1840–1927, Poland–Austria), Mittag-Leffler, Simon Newcomb (1835–1909, Canada–USA), Vassiliev, and Zeuthen. On Monday, 6 April, Pietro Blaserna, during the opening ceremony, initiated with the remark "Anyone who cultivates a science, easily realises that two lovers of the same subject, even if distant and belonging to different nations, are closer to each other, than two other scholars of different sciences even if they live in the same city". Vita Volterra summarized in his lecture Mathematics in Italy in the second half of the nineteenth century that the major change in the 1908 Congress from the previous three was the greater emphasis on applied mathematics. Another innovation at this Congress was the award (first and the last) of an international mathematical prize, the Guccia Medal, to Francesco Severi (1879–1961, Italy). The Rome Congress also adopted a new resolution: creating an *International Commission on Mathematical Instruction* (ICMI) with the initial mandate of making a comparative study on the methods and plans of teaching mathematics at secondary schools. In 1952, the ICMI was reconstituted, and it became an official commission of the IMU. Although the ICMI follows the general principles of the IMU and ICSU, the organization has a large degree of autonomy. The founding President of the ICMI was Felix Klein, for whom mathematics education was a deep and career-long interest. His promising words "great progress in our science is often obtained when new methods are applied to old problems" will always remain true. He remained as President of the ICMI from 1908 to 1920. Later ICMI Presidents and their terms are as follows: David Eugene Smith (1860–1944, USA), 1928–1932; Jacques Salomon Hadamard (1865–1963, France), 1932–1940; Albert Châtelet (1883–1960, France), 1952–1954; Henri Fehr (1870–1954, Switzerland) was Honorary President for the period 1952–1954; Heinrich Adolph Louis Behnke (1898–1979, Germany), 1955–1958; Marshall Harvey Stone, 1959–1962; André Lichnerowicz (1915–1998, France), 1963–1966; Hans Freudenthal (1905–1990, the Netherlands), 1967–1970; Michael James Lighthill (1924–1998, Britain), 1971–1974; Shokichi Iyanaga (1906–2006, Japan), 1975–1978; Hassler Whitney (1907–1989, USA), 1979–1982; Jean-Pierre Kahane (1926–2017, France), 1983–1990; Miguel de Guzmán (1936–2004, Spain), 1991–1998; Hyman Bass (born 1932, USA), 1999–2006; Michéle Artigue (born 1946, France), 2007–2009; Bill Barton (New Zealand), 2010–2012; Ferdinando Arzarello (born 1947, Italy), 2013–2016; Jill Adler (born 1951, South Africa), 2017–2020; and Frederick Koon-Shing Leung (born 1937, Hong Kong), 2021–2024. Another hallmark of the conference was to resolve the agenda to publish all the works of Leonhard Euler (1707–1783, Switzerland), which was approved by a unanimous vote. For the fifth ICM Andrew Forsyth recalled the desire already expressed in Heidelberg by him to have it in England. He then formally proposed that the Cambridge Philosophical Society invite the ICM to hold their fifth meeting in 1912 in Cambridge. This invitation was supported by the London Mathematical Society (LMS). The proposal was approved by the assembly in a unanimous vote and with lively applause. Then, Mittag-Leffler made the following statement: As a Swedish mathematician and editor of the Acta Mathematica, I have the honour of inviting the ICM to meet in Stockholm in 1916. After that the President Pietro Blaserna declared the Congress closed.

7. Fifth ICM

The fifth Congress was held in Cambridge, UK, during 22–28 August 1912. There were 574 full members (with 38 women) from 28 countries. On the motion of Mittag-Leffler and seconded by Abramo Giulio Umberto Federigo Enriques (1871–1946, Italy), the President of the Cambridge Philosophical Society George Howard Darwin (1845–1912, England) was elected President of the Congress. On Darwin's motion Lord Rayleigh (John William Strutt, 1842–1919, England) was made Honorary President of the Congress. The following thirteen Vice-Presidents were elected: Walther Franz Anton von Dyck (1856–1934, Germany), Lipót Fejér (1880–1959, Hungary), Rikitaro Fujisawa (1861–1933, Japan), Hadamard, Johan Ludwig William Valdemar Jensen (1859–1925, Denmark), Percy Alexander MacMahon (1854–1929, Malta–England), Mittag-Leffler, Eliakim Moore, Ferdinand Rudio, Pieter Hendrik Schoute (1846–1913, the Netherlands), Marian Smoluchowski (1872–1917, Austria–Poland), Vladimir Andreevich Steklov (1864–1926, Russia), and Vito Volterra. The President George Darwin in his opening address said "Both the pure and the applied mathematician are in search of truth, but the former seeks truth in itself and the latter truths about the universe in which we live". "The Science of Mathematics is now so wide and is already so much specialised that it may be doubted whether there exists today any man fully competent to understand mathematical research in all its many diverse branches. I, at least, feel how profoundly ill-equipped I am to represent our Society as regards all that vast field of knowledge which we classify as pure mathematics. I must tell you frankly that when I gaze on some of the papers written by men in this room, I feel myself much in the same position as if they were written in Sanskrit". In his lecture he delivered an emotional eulogy to Henri Poincaré, who died just five weeks before. No doubt, Poincaré [was] the last man to take practically all mathematics, pure and applied, as his province... Few mathematicians have had the breadth of philosophic vision that Poincaré had, and none in his superior in the gift of clear exposition. Following the previous Congress in Rome, there was a strong emphasis on applications of mathematics. However, Edmund Georg Hermann (Yehezkel) Landau (1877–1938, Germany) listed the following four basic problems about prime numbers, which are still unresolved:

1. Goldbach's conjecture: Can every even integer greater than 2 be written as the sum of two primes? (due to Christian Goldbach, 1690–1764, Prussia–Russia)
2. Twin prime conjecture: Are there infinitely many primes p such that $p + 2$ is prime? (due to Alphonse de Polignac, 1826–1863, France),
3. Legendre's conjecture (after Adrien-Marie Legendre, 1752–1833, France): Does there always exist at least one prime between consecutive perfect squares?
4. Are there infinitely many primes p such that $p - 1$ is a perfect square? In other words, are there infinitely many primes of the form $n^2 + 1$? (initiated by Euler in 1752)

This Congress also witnessed the first communication presented by a woman; it was "On Binodes and Nodal Curves" by Hilda Phoebe Hudson (1881–1965, England).

During the closing ceremony Mittag-Leffler enunciated "On behalf of the members of the third class of the Royal Swedish Academy of Sciences (RSAS), on behalf of the Swedish editorial staff of the Journal Acta Mathematica and all the Swedish mathematicians, I have the honour to invite the ICM to meet in Stockholm in the year 1916". Emanuel Beke (1862–1946, Hungary) presented an invitation "On behalf of Hungarian mathematicians, I have the honour to invite the Seventh ICM to come and take place in 1920 in Budapest, the capital of Hungary". Cyparissos Stephanos (1857–1917, Greece) also expressed the hope that the Congress would meet in Athens in 1920 or 1924. On the motion of the President George Darwin, the invitation to Stockholm was accepted unanimously. He also said the place of the next Congress (after that of 1916) would probably be in Stockholm.

8. World War I

For four years, from 28 July 1914 to 11 November 1918, World War I raged across Europe's Western and Eastern fronts, including Germany, France, Russia, Italy, Belgium, Austria–Hungary, Serbia, the Ottoman Empire against Great Britain, the United States, the Middle East, Africa, the Pacific, and parts of Asia. While the real reason is still a mystery, it has been claimed that the assassination in 1914 of Austrian Archduke Franz Ferdinand (1863–1914) at the hands of a Bosnian revolutionary led to the outbreak of World War I. Austria–Hungary declared war on Serbia, and other countries involved themselves either in support or to defend the war. In 1919, in Paris, thirty nations participated; however, the "Big Four" David Lloyd George (1863–1945, Britain), Vittorio Emanuele Orlando (1860–1952, Italy), Georges Benjamin Clemenceau (1841–1929, France), and Woodrow Wilson (1913–1921, USA) dominated the proceedings that led to the formulation of the *Treaty of Versailles*, a treaty that ended World War I. This treaty held Germany responsible for starting the war and imposed harsh penalties on the Germans, including loss of territory, massive reparation payments, and demilitarization. By the time the war was over more than 20 million people—soldiers and civilians alike—were dead and 21 million wounded. World War I's aftermath had a tremendous impact on all aspects of cultural, economic, and social life. Consequently, the ICM Congress in 1916 could not be held.

9. Strasbourg ICM 1920

In 1919, the IRC decided that the next Congress would be held in Strasbourg, France, and not Stockholm, as had been proposed in 1912. This was a highly political decision made to 'celebrate' France regaining Strasbourg from Germany. However, even today, Strasbourg has a unique blend of French and German culture; in fact the cuisine, language, and architecture fall somewhere in the middle, and street signs are written in both German and French. Strasbourg ICM 1920 was held during 22–30 September. There were only 200 full members from 27 countries. This was the lowest number of participants in the history of all ICMs. The main reason for this was the exclusion by the IRC of mathematicians from the former Central Powers: Germany, Austria–Hungary, Bulgaria, and Turkey. However, many felt that mathematics should not be subjected to political pressures but should welcome equally mathematicians of all nations. In particular, Godfrey Harold Hardy (1877–1947, UK) and Mittag-Leffler opposed their exclusion and did not participate in the Congress. On 25 January 1919, Mittag-Leffler wrote to Hardy "I agree with you that we as mathematicians need to be at the head in "the task of reestablishment of friendly relations" between the men of science of all countries". Charles Jean de la Vallée Poussin (1866–1962, Belgium) was selected as the President of the Congress, and Jordan, Horace Lamb (1849–1934, England), Charles Émile Picard (1856–1941, France), and Vito Volterra were nominated as Honorary Presidents. The following five Vice-Presidents were elected: Paul Emile Appell (1855–1930, France), Luigi Bianchi (1856–1928, France), Leonard Eugene Dickson (1874–1954, USA), Joseph Larmor (1857–1942, Ireland), and William Henry Young (1863–1942, England–Switzerland). In his lecture Émile Picard said "Gentlemen, it is one of the objects of Congresses, to establish personal relationships between researchers who cultivate the same or neighbouring sciences. After the appalling turmoil of recent years, which has broken so many ties, reconciliations are necessary between scholars who esteem themselves and who, without any ulterior motive, have no other concern than the selfless worship of truth". He also pronounced that many concepts created by mathematicians have not yet found applications in the study of physical phenomena, but the history of science shows that it is reckless to assert that such and such a notion will not be used one day. Geometers like to recall the words of Joseph-Louis Lagrange (1736–1813, Italy–France), who, one day comparing mathematics to an animal of which we eat all the parts, said "Mathematics is like pork, everything is good". Émile Picard also hoped that pure mathematics and applied mathematics would continue a fruitful collaboration. In the closing ceremony it was decided that the ICMs would take place every four years. For the next Congress in 1924, two proposals were simultaneously put forward by the Belgians and the Americans. Finally, to avoid the difficult European atmosphere, Dickson's proposal was accepted to hold the 1924 ICM in New York and the next in Belgium. However, the ICM 1924 had to be moved to Toronto after the AMS withdrew its invitation to host the Congress in protest against the exclusion rule. It is interesting to note that the number "six" appears nowhere in connection with the Strasbourg Congress—not even in the speeches.

10. John Charles Fields (1863–1932, Canada)

He was born in Hamilton, Canada West, to Henrietta (Harriet) Bowes and John Charles Fields (Senior), who had a leather shop. John Charles Fields (Senior) died when his son was eleven years old. Fields attended Hamilton Collegiate Institute, where he proved to be a remarkable student, received several scholarships, and graduated in 1880. Then, he entered the University of Toronto to study mathematics. Unfortunately, when he was 18, in the middle of his university course, his mother also died. In spite of this tragedy, he received his bachelor's degree in mathematics from the University of Toronto in 1884, winning the gold medal for mathematics. Fields then went to the United States to study at Johns Hopkins University in Baltimore, Maryland. He received his Ph.D. degree in 1887. His thesis, entitled *Symbolic Finite Solutions and Solutions by Definite Integrals of the Equation* $d^ny/dx^nn = x^my$ was published in the *American Journal of Mathematics* in 1886. After receiving his degree Fields taught for two years at Johns Hopkins and then joined the faculty of Allegheny College in Meadville, one of the oldest colleges in Pennsylvania. In 1891, Fields left for Europe, staying mainly in Berlin, Göttingen, and Paris, where he associated with the best mathematical minds of the time, including Weierstrass, Felix Klein, Ferdinand Georg Frobenius (1849–1917, Germany), and Max Karl Ernst Ludwig Planck (1858–1947, Germany). He also began a lifelong friendship with Mittag-Leffler. In 1902, Fields was appointed as a Lecturer at the University of Toronto, where he remained until his death, although he frequently visited Europe, where he was acquainted with many national leaders. He became an Associate Professor in 1905, Full Professor in 1914, and Research Professor in 1923. The work of Fields on algebraic functions must be regarded as the development and organization of ideas on the subject that he happened to have at the turn of the century. He published 38 mathematical articles and a very influential book *Theory of the Algebraic Functions of a Complex Variable.* Fields was elected a Fellow of the Royal Society of Canada in 1907 and, in 1913, he was elected a Fellow of the Royal Society (FRS) of London. He also held the position of President of the Royal Canadian Institute (opened in 1914) from 1919 to 1925. He was also elected a member of the Russian Academy of Sciences (RAS) and of the Institute of Coimbra (Portugal). The Italian Government wanted to honor Fields with the title "Commander of the Crown of Italy", but following Canadian Government laws, he had to decline this honor. The Fields Institute, named in his honor, was founded in 1992 at the University of Waterloo, and it was relocated to the University of Toronto in 1995. He never married; as a young man he loved various sports and walking, music was a great joy to him, and he avoided tea, coffee, and alcohol.

11. Toronto ICM 1924

After the refusal to hold the ICM 1924 in New York, in 1922 Fields proposed to the IMU to have it in Toronto, Canada. Although Fields accepted the stricture on participation in mathematicians from the former Central Powers, he persuade many opponents of the Union to attend the Toronto Congress and have it succeed. For this, he spent several months in Europe, raised CAD 70,000 from the Ontario and Canadian governments to offset the cost of travel for mathematicians from abroad, and increased the scope of the Congress by broadening the definition of mathematics so that practical users in areas such as engineering, insurance, and meteorology could be included. Finally, Toronto ICM 1924 was held during 11–16 August. There were 444 participants from 28 countries. Hardy boycotted the Congress as a protest against the exclusion policy. During the opening session Vallée Poussin nominated Fields to be the President and main organizer of the Congress, which was approved unanimously. The following thirteen Vice-Presidents were elected: Bohumil Bydžovský (1880–1969, Czechoslovakia), Francisco Miranda da Costa Lobo (1865–1945, Portugal), Dickson, Senator Fernand Faure (1853–1929, France), Henri Fehr, Lars Edvard Phragmén (1863–1937, Sweden), Salvatore Pincherle (1853–1936, Italy), Erik Schou (Denmark), Clément Joseph Servais (1862–1935, Belgium), Fredrik Carl Mlertz Størmer (1874–1957, Norway), Willem van der Woude (1876–1974, the Netherlands), William Young, and Stanislaw Zaremba (1863–1942, Poland). During the opening ceremony Vallée Poussin, then President of the IMU, remarked about Strasbourg ICM 1920 as follows: "It was not just a scientific Congress that was about to open; it was a symbol and it was a feast, that of the deliverance of Alsace and also, as I said then, that of the liberation of science that sacrilegious hands had enslaved for too long with criminal designs". He also commented that "The peace we dream of among the peoples is the very peace that reigns here among us. This is based on justice, good faith and love of the truth. Mathematicians find one of their great enjoyments is in admiring the work of others and their greatest desire is to give back to each one what is due to him. It is probably a pipe dream to want nations to be as disinterested as mathematicians, but whatever we want, peace with all that it entails for humanity of hope of happiness and promises of progress, that peace can only be based on justice". On 13 August, an honorary D.Sc. degree was conferred by the University of Toronto to Vallée Poussin, Francesco Severi, Gabriel Xavier Paul Koenigs (1858–1931, France), Vladimir Steklov, William Henry Bragg (1862–1942, England), and Charles Algernon Parsons (1854–1931, UK). The same day, William Young in his lecture "Some characteristic features of Twentieth Century pure mathematical research" said "...at abstraction within a science which is concerned with abstractions, and with abstractions of abstractions, seems indeed peculiarly appropriate and the more necessary that, even after more than a quarter of a century of Congresses, we mathematicians still resemble the workers at the Tower of Babel, trying to construct one and the same edifice, but speaking different mathematical tongues". On 15 August, USA delegates proposed to the IMU that the American Section of the IMU request the IRC to consider whether the time was ripe for the removal of restrictions on membership now imposed by the rules of the Council.

The motion was supported by Italy, Denmark, the Netherlands, Sweden, Norway, and Great Britain. During the same session the IMU elected Pincherle as the new President of the IMU as well as of the Italian Mathematical Union. During the closing ceremony on 16 August, Fields stated that throughout the Congress applications of mathematics were even more strongly in evidence, with only two sections on pure mathematics topics and five on applications. The decision on the venue of the next Congress was not taken.

After the Congress Fields had health problems, which delayed the publication of the Proceedings of the Toronto Congress, which could appear only after four years in 1928, and accounts of the Congress could be closed only on 24 February 1931. The Committee of the International Congress, still chaired by Fields, reported that there was a balance of CAD 2700—a sizable sum in those days. Fields proposed that out of this money two medals be presented to young mathematicians (to stimulate others to compete for the prize) on the occasion of successive ICM gatherings. Fields' health began to fail in May of 1932 when he suffered heart problems. A few days before his death on 9 August 1932, he drew up a will, with his friend and colleague John Lighton Synge (1897–1995, Ireland) at his bedside, including an amount of CAD 47,000 to be added to the funds for the medals.

12. Bologna ICM 1928

The IRC in the session of 29 June 1926 had decided to lift any restrictions on admission, among the unions belonging to it, of the hitherto non-acceding States and had invited Germany, Austria, Bulgaria, and Hungary to participate in the Council. The next Congress was held in Bologna, Italy, during 3–10. However, German mathematicians did not accept the invitation and preferred to stay away from the Congress. Pincherle then put the Congress under the patronage of the University of Bologna, thus avoiding the IMU's control and maintaining the open invitation for attending. He was able to gather 836 full members (with 72 women) from 36 countries. Hilbert's entrance into the 1928 Congress leading the German delegation of 76 was met by a standing ovation. Here Hilbert's golden quotes are necessary to mention: "It makes me very happy that after a long, hard time all the mathematicians of the world are represented here. That is as it should be and as it must be for the prosperity of our beloved science. Let us consider that we as mathematicians stand on the highest pinnacle of the cultivation of the exact sciences. We have no other choice than to assume this highest place, because all limits, especially national ones, are contrary to the nature of mathematics. It is a complete misunderstanding of our science to construct differences according to peoples and races, and the reason for which this has been done are very shabby ones. Mathematics knows no races... For mathematics, the whole cultural world is a single country". Another exciting event of this Congress was the delegation from the Soviet Union with 27 participates. During the opening session Giuseppe Belluzzo (1876–1952, Italy) quoted "Mathematics is a formidable weapon that penetrates the areas in the shadow of knowledge and illuminates them; it is a powerful weapon that with physics and chemistry strives to demolish the wall behind which lies the mystery of creation, slowly and tenaciously conquering new positions, opening new vast horizon to experimental investigations. ... it is certainly because mathematical discoveries only give intimate satisfaction and moral rewards that among mathematician of the same nation and among those of different nations there exists a solidarity and a spirit of collaboration that is not always the rule in branches of applied science". The following twelve Vice-Presidents were elected: Vallée Poussin, Hadamard, Hilbert, William Young, Fields, Oswald Veblen (1880–1960, USA), Henri Fehr, Esteban Terradas (1883–1950, Spain), Waclaw Sierpiński (1882–1969, Poland), Harald August Bohr (1887–1951, Denmark), Nikolai Nikolaevich Luzin (1883–1950, Russia–Ukraine), and Sōichi Kakeya (1886–1947, Japan). The main enthusiastic hallmark on the opening day was the lectures of Hilbert on "Probleme der Grundlegung der Mathematik" (Problems of the foundation of mathematics), and of Hadamard "Le développement et le rôle scientifiqu du Calcul fonctionnel" (The development and scientific role of functional computing). In the closing session of the Congress, Pincherle declined to continue as President and elections were not held, so the IMU had no President for a year. In 1929 the Bureau elected William Young to assume the presidency for the years 1929–1932. The next venue, Zurich, and year, 1932, of the ICM were unanimously approved by the Congress participants. Karl Rudolf Fueter (1880–1950, Switzerland) declared acceptance of this decision and invited the mathematicians to Zurich in 1932, the same site of the first Congress after 35 years.

13. Zurich ICM 1932

This Congress was held during 5–12 September. There were 667 full members (with 34 women) from 35 countries. Rudolf Fueter opened the Congress as President of the Organizing Committee. In his address he announced that Geiser, despite his almost ninety years, did not miss being with them that day. On Pincherle's proposal, Rudolf Fueter was elected President of the Congress by acclamation. He then proposed eleven Vice-Presidents: Alf Victor Emanuel Guldberg (1866–1936, Norway), Hadamard, Hilbert, Nikolay Mitrofanovich Krylov (1879–1955, Russia), Pincherle, Takagi, Vallée Poussin, Oswald Veblen, Wilhelm Wirtinger (1865–1945, Austria), William Young, and Zaremba. There were 22 planned plenary lectures: Ludwig Georg Elias Moses Bieberbach (1886– 1982, Germany) had opposed German participation in the 1928 Congress but was a plenary speaker in the 1932 Congress; Hardy could not deliver his lecture *Recent work in additive theory of numbers* despite being at the Congress; Sergei Natanovich Bernstein's (1880–1968, Ukrain–Russia) lecture was read by Bohuslav Hostinský (1884–1951, Czechoslovakia); and the first woman who gave an ICM plenary lecture was Amalie Emmy Noether (1882–1935, Germany–USA)—the second ICM plenary talk by a woman would have to wait another 58 years. At the opening of the Congress, Hermann Klaus Hugo Weyl (1885–1955, Germany) said "We attend here to an extraordinary improbable event. For the number of n, corresponding to the just opened ICM, we have the inequality $7 \leq n \leq 9$; unfortunately our axiomatic foundations are not sufficient to give a more precise statement". As a consequence of this controversy, from the Zurich Congress onward, the ICMs are not numbered. In fact, the Strasbourg and Toronto ICMs are not considered true ICMs. One of the highlights of the Congress was the proposal of John Fields (who had died a month before the Congress began) to institute an award for brilliant young mathematicians. The Congress committee agreed to consider his proposal and announced its decision at the closing session of the Congress: The International Congress of mathematicians held in Zurich accepts with thanks the offer made by the late Professor Fields of two medals (then nameless) to be awarded to two mathematicians at intervals of four years by the International Congress. The Fields committee chosen at the Congress to name the recipients of the medals to be awarded in 1936 was composed of Francesco Severi as the Chairman, George David Birkhoff (1884–1944, USA), Carathéodory, Élie Joseph Cartan (1869–1951, France), Francesco Severi, and Takagi. Initially no age limit was imposed, but gradually the tradition that the recipient be at most forty years of age took shape to be consistent with Fields' wish that the award be an encouragement to further work by the recipients. In the closing ceremony Hermann Weyl explained why Switzerland is dear to mathematicians: It is the birthplace of some of our greatest heroes, such as the Bernoulli family and master of master's Euler. He also requested to make the following pledge: we never want to betray each other again as people and as mathematicians for the sake of political struggle. In spite of world-wide financial crisis following the Depression of 1929, the organizers left nothing to chance, and Zurich ICM 1932 turned out to be an extraordinary event. Finally, for the next ICM the Congress (not the union) accepted the invitation of Alf Victor Emanuel Guldberg to hold it in Oslo. As in 1912, there was a proposal from Athens for the following Congress.

14. The Fields Medal

Since 1901, the celebrated *Nobel Prize* has been awarded in the fields of physics, chemistry, physiology or medicine, literature, and peace, and a memorial prize in economic sciences was added in 1968 by Sweden's central bank. However, there is no Nobel Prize in mathematics. A legend for this most noticeable omission is that Mr. Alfred Bernhard Nobel (1833–1896, a Swedish chemist, inventor of dynamite, engineer, entrepreneur, businessman, and author), after whom the prestigious award is named, wanted to retaliate against Mittag-Leffler, a likely winner at the time of the inception of the prize, who was reported to be having an affair with his wife. No doubt the gossip about a love affair aroused the interest of mathematicians, but the catch is that Nobel never married. Another version of this gossip claims that Mittag-Leffler, a man of considerable wealth, antagonized Nobel. It is generally believed that Nobel was more interested in practical fields whose inventions and discoveries have a direct impact on humankind. In 1931–32, Fields' proposal of two medals was perhaps to fill the gap left by Alfred Nobel. In spite of his frail health, he consulted widely on the design of the medal, particularly about the inscriptions on both its sides, and in 1932 corresponded with Robert Tait McKenzie (1867–1938, Canada–USA), a physician and sculptor. It is not certain whether Fields saw a preliminary sketch or a prototype of McKenzie's model; however, John Synge completed Fields' arrangement with McKenzie and with the IMU, which accepted the medal in October 1932 and announced it during the Zurich ICM. The earliest known facsimile of the medal, cast in bronze and dated 1933, is held at the Fields Institute. To fulfill Fields' wishes to award the medals on the occasion of successive ICM gatherings to two young mathematicians whose work has been recognized, completed, and has the potential for future achievement, the age limit 40 years on 1 January of the year in which the medal is awarded was imposed (with this restriction there are many cases where outstanding mathematicians who succeed in resolving complex mathematical problems miss the chance of receiving the Fields Medal). Further, an individual can only be awarded one Fields Medal. As decided by Fields the medal is made of pure gold—it is 7.5 cm in diameter; the face side of the medal consists of a picture of the Greek mathematician Archimedes of Syracuse (287–212 BC, Greece) together with a quotation attributed to him in Latin: *Transire suum pectus mundoque potiri* (To pass beyond your understanding and make yourself master of the universe); and the reverse side bears the following inscription in Latin: *Congregati ex toto orbe mathematici ob scripta insignia tribuere* (The Mathematicians having congregated from the whole world awarded because of outstanding writing). There is also carved, on the background, an Archimedes sphere inscribed in a cylinder. The name of the recipient of the award is engraved on the rim of the medal. In the beginning besides the gold medal the receiver was also given a cash prize of CAD 1500, which continued until 1983, but since 2006, it has been increased to CAD 15,000. The Fields Medal is regarded as one of the highest honors a mathematician can receive and has been described as the Nobel Prize of mathematics, although there are several major differences, including the frequency of the award, number of awards, age limits, monetary value, and award criteria.

The front of the Fields Medal.

The back of the Fields Medal.

15. Oslo ICM 1936

This Congress was held in Oslo, Norway, during 14–18 July. There were 487 full members (with 35 women) from 36 countries. The main reason for poor attendance was that the Italian government prohibited mathematicians from attending the ICM in protest of the sanctions Norway had imposed on Italy following their invasion of Ethiopia. Further, no mathematicians from the Soviet Union attended. Alf Guldberg, who was successful in having this Congress in Norway, passed away just five months before on 15 February 1936. The Congress was opened in the presence of King Haakon VII of Norway. Rudolf Fueter proposed that Carl Størmer be elected President of the Congress, a proposal which the assembly approved by acclamation. The President then selected twelve Vice-Presidents: Harald Bohr, Torsten Carleman (1892–1949, Sweden), Matsusaburo Fujiwara (1881–1946, Japan), Gaston Maurice Julia (1893–1978, Algeria–France), Solomon Lefschetz (1884–1972, Russia–USA), Ernst Lindelöf, Karl Menger (1902–1985, Austria–USA), George Pólya (1887–1985, Hungary–USA), Erhard Schmidt (1876–1959, Estonia–Germany), Jan Arnoldus Schouten (1883–1971, the Netherlands), Waclaw Sierpiński, and Edmund Taylor Whittaker (1873–1956, UK). In the opening session Carl Størmer said "The scientific discoveries made by the scientists of one country can be immediately used all over the world. This particularly applies to mathematics. Mathematical truths are indeed universal and its means of expression international. As a result, collaboration across borders should be more natural for mathematicians than for all other scholars". "Mathematics is a field apart, so full of wonderful surprises for those who enter it, that considerations of utility [often asked by hoi polloi] become secondary compared to the joy of discovery that one feels in solving problems, and to see the light of truth shine on areas of wonderful beauty". Since Francesco Severi was prevented from coming to the Oslo Congress, Élie Cartan took the chair of Fields committee and announced a new feature of the Congress, the awarding of the two Fields Medals (despite the wish of Fields that they should not bear anyone's name) to Lars Valerian Ahlfors (1907–1996, Finland–USA) and Jesse Douglas (1897–1965, USA). Although Douglas was in Oslo, he had no prior information, so he was absent during the ceremony. His medal, in his name, was collected by Norbert Wiener (1894–1964, USA). Carathéodory highlighted the works of the winners of the two Fields Medals. He declared Lars Ahlfors "one of the most brilliant representatives of the famous Finnish school of function theory, founded by Ernst Lindelöf," and praised his work on the Rolf Herman Nevanlinna (1895–1980, Finland) theory for meromorphic functions. For Douglas, he explained his "absolutely original method, which uses very few elements of the existing theory which allowed him to obtain far reaching and unexpected consequences" for the solution of Plateau's problem: finding the surface with minimal area determined by a fixed boundary. This is the mathematical model for soap films, where nature tries to minimize the area of a soap film spanning a wire contour. This problem was posed by Euler and Lagrange in 1760, and was extensively studied by the Belgian physicist and mathematician Joseph Antoine Ferdinand Plateau (1801–1883), from whom it received its name. For the next Congress the Fields committee was Hardy as the Chairman, Pavel Sergeyevich

Alexandrov (1896–1982, Russia), Erich Hecke (1887–1947, Germany), Gaston Julia, and Tullio Levi-Civita (1873–1941, Italy), and also substitutes Solomon Lefschetz and Rolf Nevanlinna. However, Hardy in a letter of 7 August 1936 informed the Secretary General that he could not accept this task, and then Solomon Lefschetz took his place. This Congress is perhaps most famous for being the first at which Fields Medals were presented, and this became an important feature of all futures congresses. During the closing ceremony the following remarkable statement was made by S. Gann (Director of Squares and Markets Representative of the Municipality of Oslo), a non-mathematician: "...the greatest progress that has been made in mathematics, is the result of an imaginative impulse, of the incomprehensible genius of intuition, of these living, intensive thoughts which are in the realm of inspiration". Finally, Luther Pfahler Eisenhart (1876–1965, USA) along with George Birkhoff, Hans Frederick Blichfeldt (1873–1945, Denmark–USA), Lefschetz, Harold Calvin Marston Morse (1892–1977, USA), Virgil Snyder (1869–1950, USA), Oswald Veblen, and Wiener invited the Congress to come to the United States in 1940, the choice of city being left to the AMS. This invitation was accepted by acclamation.

15.1. Lars Valerian Ahlfors

He was born in Helsinki, Finland. His father Karl Axel Mauritz Ahlfors (1874–1961, Finland) was first an engineer and then a Professor of mechanical engineering at the Polytechnical Institute in Helsinki. Tragically, his mother died when Lars was born. The Lars Ahlfors family was Swedish-speaking, so he was educated at a private Swedish-language high school, Nya Svenska Samskolan. He learnt Finnish later in life. Lars' father wanted him to become an engineer but, realizing that his son was vehement about mathematics and unable to master anything mechanical, when Lars was about 15 years old his father predicted that he would become a Professor of mathematics. Lars entered Helsingfors University at the age of 17, and there he was taught by Ernst Lindelöf and Rolf Nevanlinna. Lars graduated in 1928. Lars assisted Nevanlinna in 1929 with his work on Arnaud Denjoy's (1884–1974, France) conjecture of 1907: the number of asymptotic values attained by a non-constant entire function of order ρ on curves going outwards toward infinite absolute value is less than or equal to 2ρ. In 1929, Lars published the first proof of this conjecture, now known as the Denjoy–Carleman–Ahlfors theorem. He completed his doctorate at the University of Helsinki in 1930. During 1930–1932, Lars made several visits to Paris, in 1933 he joined the University of Helsinki as an Associate Professor and married Erna Martha Liesbeth Lehnert (1902–2001, Austria–Finland), and during 1935–1938, he visited Harvard University, Cambridge, Massachusetts (USA). In 1936, Lars received a Fields Medal at the ICM in Oslo for his research on covering surfaces related to Riemann surfaces of inverse functions of entire and meromorphic functions. In 1938, Lars returned to Finland and joined the University of Helsinki as a Professor. In 1945, he joined the Swiss Federal Institute of Technology, and in 1946 he returned to work at Harvard, where he remained until his retirement in 1977. He received many honors, including the Wolf Prize in Mathematics in 1981 (after Ricardo Wolf, 1887–1981, Germany–Israel), and served as the Honorary President of the ICM in 1986 at Berkeley, California, in celebration of his 50th year of the award of his Fields Medal. He received honorary degrees from Boston University (1953), the University of Zurich (1977), and the University of London (1978). Among his several books *Complex Analysis: An Introduction to the Theory of Analytic Functions of One Complex Variable* of 1953 retains its popularity even today (the author followed this book in 1969). He is remembered for the Denjoy conjecture, geometric derivation of the Nevanlinna theory, generalization of the Karl Hermann Amandus Schwarz (1843–1921, Germany) lemma, theories of Riemann surfaces, quasi-conformal mappings, Paul Julius Oswald Teichmüller (1913–1943, Germany) spaces, and the finiteness theorem for Kleinian groups.

15.2. Jesse Douglas

He was born in New York City, the son of Louis Douglas and Sarah Kommel. After graduation from high school, Jesse attended the City College of New York and won the Belden Medal for excellence in mathematics in his first year at the College. He graduated with honors in mathematics in 1916 and entered Columbia University and earned his Ph.D. in 1920 under the supervision of Edward Kasner (1878–1955, USA). The title of his thesis was *On Certain Two-Point Properties of General Families of Curves; The Geometry of Variations*. During 1920–1926, Jesse continued to study differential geometry while teaching at Columbia College. In 1926, he secured a four-year National Research Fellowship and spent time at Princeton University (1926–1927), Harvard University (1927), Chicago (1928), Paris (1928–30), and Göttingen (1930). Throughout this period, he worked on the Plateau problem. This problem also attracted the attention of several leading mathematicians such as Riemann, Weierstrass, Hermann Schwarz, and Henri Léon Lebesgue (1875–1941, France). In a series of papers from 1927 to 1931, Jesse detailed the complete solution of Plateau's problem, culminating in his 1931 paper in the *Transactions of the AMS*. In recognition of this work, Jesse was awarded a Fields Medal at the ICM in Oslo. He subsequently held appointments at the Massachusetts Institute of Technology (MIT), 1930–1936, and the Institute for Advanced Study (IAS) at Princeton, 1938–1939. He received Guggenheim Foundation Fellowships in 1940 and 1941. Jesse married Jessie Nayler in 1940. In 1942, he returned to New York and joined Brooklyn College until 1954, when he left to teach at Columbia University. In 1943, he was awarded the Bôcher Memorial Prize by the AMS for his memoirs on the Plateau problem. Jesse was elected to the United States National Academy of Sciences (NAS) in 1946. His wife, Jessie Douglas, died in 1955, the same year he was appointed Professor of mathematics at the City College of New York, where he remained until his death in 1965. At the CCNY sophomores (and freshmen with advanced placement) were fortunate to receive their introduction to real analysis from a Fields medalist.

16. World War II

On 18 July 1936, the last day of the ICM in Oslo, a military *coup d'état* started the Spanish Civil War, on 7 July 1937 Japan invaded China, and during 1 March 1932–16 September 1939 the Soviet–Japanese Border War occurred—these were frightening preparations for World War II. This war was in several respects a continuation, after an uneasy 20-year interruption, of the remaining controversies of World War I. Conflict that involved virtually every part of the world started on 1 September 1939 and continued until 2 September 1945, when Japanese officials signed the surrender documents aboard the battleship USS Missouri at Tokyo Bay, Japan. The main belligerents were the Axis powers—Germany, Italy, and Japan—and the Allies—France, Great Britain, the United States, the Soviet Union, and to some extent China. Almost all other countries of the world fought as part of these military alliances. It is estimated that in World War II about 75 million people died, which includes about 20 million military personnel and 40 million civilians, many of whom died because of deliberate genocide, massacres, mass bombings, disease, and starvation. The main episodes of World War II are as follows: on 1 September 1939 Nazi Germany, under Adolf Hitler (1889–1945, Austria–Germany), invaded western Poland, and two days later France and the United Kingdom declared war on Germany; on 17 September 1939 Soviet forces invaded eastern Poland; on 9 April 1940 German forces invaded Denmark and Norway; in May 1940 Germany attacked France and conquered Luxembourg, the Netherlands, and Belgium; prompted by these victories, on 10 June 1940 Italian dictator Benito Amilcare Andrea Mussolini (1883–1945) joined forces with Hitler; on 22 June 1940 Germany took control of much of Western Europe, including France; on 10 July 1940 the German Luftwaffe launched an air war, known as the Battle of Britain, against the United Kingdom; on 27 September 1940, the *Tripartite Pact* was signed in Berlin by Germany, Italy, and Japan, and later expanded to include Hungary, Romania, and Bulgaria, thus yielding the Axis powers; on 7 December 1941 Japan's naval air force attacked the American fleet based at Pearl Harbor, Hawaii; on 8 December 1941 the USA President Franklin Delano Roosevelt (1882–1945) signed the United States' declaration of war on Japan; on 11 December 1941 Germany and Italy declared war on the United States, and within hours the United States declared war on Germany and Italy; during 4–7 June 1942 the USA Navy defeated the Japanese Navy at the *Battle of Midway*; on 9 July 1942 Allied forces invaded Sicily; on 8 September 1943 Italy surrendered to the Allies, but German forces occupied northern Italy; on 6 June 1944 Allied forces landed on the beaches of Normandy, France, marking D-Day (the largest seaborne invasion in history); on 25 August 1944 the Allies took control of Paris; on 16 December 1944 the Germans counterattacked in northern France, Belgium, and Luxembourg, known as the *Battle of the Bulge*; on 19 February 1945 the United States Marine Corps and United States Navy landed on and eventually on 26 March 1945 captured the island of Iwo Jima from the Imperial Japanese Army; on 22 March 1945, the United States Third Army, under the command of Lieutenant General George Smith Patton Jr. (1885–1945), crossed the Rhine River at Oppenheim, south of Mainz; on 1 April 1945 more than 60,000 soldiers and US Marines of the US Tenth Army stormed ashore at Okinawa, in the final island battle before an anticipated invasion of mainland Japan; on 25 April 1945, eight Russian armies completely encircled Berlin, linking up with the USA First Army patrol, first on the western bank of the river Elbe and later at the town Torgau, and then Germany was for all intents and purposes Allied territory; on 28 April 1945 Mussolini was summarily executed by an Italian partisan, and his death *The New York Times* characterized as "A fitting end to a wretched life"; on 30 April 1945 Hitler committed suicide after being hunted by Soviet troops storming Berlin; on 8 May 1945 Germany surrenders to the Allies, marking V-E Day (Victory in Europe Day); on 6 August 1945 the USA dropped world's first atomic bomb on Hiroshima, Japan (the explosion immediately killed an estimated 80,000 people and tens of thousands more would later die of radiation exposure); on 9 August 1945 the USA dropped another atomic bomb on Nagasaki, Japan (killing an estimated 40,000 people); on 15 August 1945 Japans' Emperor Hirohito (1901–1989) announced his country's unconditional surrender in a radio address, citing the devastating power of "a new and most cruel bomb"; and on 2 September 1945 Japan formally surrendered to the Allies, marking V-J Day (Victory over Japan Day). Later, President Harry S. Truman (1884–1972) announced Japan's surrender and the end of World War II. It left much of Europe and Asia in ruins, ravaged by starvation and economic collapse. Millions of people did not have a home or a country after the war. Expelled from their former nations, many were unable to return. The only nation to emerge stronger right after the war was the United States, while the Soviet Union had suffered catastrophic losses. Several museums and concentration camps and hundreds of books keep on reminding us of the cruelty of men against men during World War II and encourage peace in the world. As a consequence of World War II, the next IMC could take place only in 1950.

17. Cambridge (MA) ICM 1950

Because of World War II, ICM meetings were not held for 14 years. It was only in 1950 that an ICM meeting was held again at Harvard University under the auspices of the AMS during 30 August to 6 September. Unlike World War I, the Congress was open to mathematicians of all countries. The Congress was attended by 1700 full members from 40 countries, although there were no participants from the Soviet Union. It was the largest gathering of persons ever assembled in the history of the world for the discussion of mathematical research. At the proposal of Carl Størmer (actually his representative Thoralf Albert Skolem, 1887–1963, carried the proposal from Oslo), Oswald Veblen was nominated for President of the Congress unanimously. There were three Honorary Presidents: Guido Castelnuovo (1865–1952, Italy), Hadamard, and Vallée Poussin; all three were over 84 years old. Garrett Birkhoff (1911–1996, USA) was elected Chairman of the Organizing Committee, and William Ted Martin (1911–2004) as vice chairman. The other members of this committee were as follows: Abraham Adrian Albert (1905–1972, USA), Joseph Leo Doob (1910–2004, USA), Griffith Conrad Evans (1887–1973, USA), Theophil Henry Hildebrandt (1888–1980, USA), Einar Carl Hille (1894–1980, USA), John Robert Kline (1891–1955, USA), Lefschetz, Leslie Saunders Mac Lane (1909–2005, USA), Marston Morse, von Neumann, Oswald Veblen, Joseph Leonard Walsh (1895–1973, USA), Hassler Whitney, David Vernon Widder (1898–1990, USA), and Raymond Louis Wilder (1896–1982, USA). On 30th August the Congress was officially opened by Garrett Birkhoff. As the President of the Congress, Oswald Veblen explained that for American mathematics, "the colonial period was ending" and "We are approaching the end of another epoch. I mean the period during which North America has absorbed so many powerful mathematicians from all over the world that the indigenous traditions and tendencies of mathematical thought have been radically changed as well as enriched. These American gains have seemed to be at the cost of great losses to European mathematics. But there are so many signs of vitality in Europe that it is now possible to hope that the losses will be only temporary while the American gains will be permanent". He added "Mathematics is terribly individual. Any mathematical act, whether of creation or apprehension, takes place in the deepest recesses of the individual mind. Mathematical thoughts must nevertheless be communicated to other individuals and assimilated into the body of general knowledge. Otherwise, they can hardly be said to exist. But the ideal communication is to a very few other individuals" and "To our non-mathematical friends we can say that this sort of a meeting, which cuts across all sorts of political, racial, and social differences and focuses on a universal human interest will be an influence for conciliation and peace". The committee to select the winners of the 1950 Fields Medals was as follows: Harald Bohr (Chairman), Lars Ahlfors, Karol Borsuk (1905–1982, Poland), René Maurice Fréchet (1878–1973, France), William Vallance Douglas Hodge (1903–1975, Scotland–England), Kolmogorov (he did not participate in the committee's work), Damodar Dharmananda Kosambi (1907–1966, India), and Harold Calvin Marston Morse. The medals were awarded to Laurent Moïse Schwartz (1915–2002, France) and Atle Selberg (1917–2007, Norway–USA). Harald

Bohr summarized the work of Laurent Schwartz on distributions and of Atle Selberg on the Riemann zeta function and his elementary proof (without involving functions of a complex variable, it is "elementary"—though not easy) of the celebrated prime number theorem ($\pi(x)$, which represents that the number of primes less than or equal to a given number x is asymptotically equal to the ratio $x/\ln x$), and also his generalization of the Eratosthenes (around 276–194 BC, Greece) sieve method.

It is interesting to note that Laurent Schwartz and Hadamard, who were both viewed by the US authorities as communist sympathizers, were only able to obtain US visas after the personal intervention of President Harry Truman. An interesting complement to the scientific program was a lecture by Howard Hathaway Aiken (1900–1973, USA) on computing machines. He was the designer of the series of electromechanical devices known as the Harvard Mark computing machines. During the closing ceremony on 6 September, Johannes Gaultherus van der Corput (1890–1975, the Netherlands), on behalf of the delegation from the Netherlands, presented a cordial invitation to the International Congress to hold its next meeting in the Netherlands in 1954. The Congress unanimously voted to accept the gracious invitation of Dutch colleagues.

17.1. Laurent Moïse Schwartz

He was born in Paris. While he attended Lycée Louis-le-Grand to enter the École Normale Supérieure (ENS), in 1934 he met Marie-Héléne Lévy (1913–2013, France) and fell in love with her. She was the daughter of the famous probabilist Paul Pierre Lévy (1886–1971, France). Marie-Héléne herself was a mathematician, who contributed to the geometry of singular analytic spaces and taught at the University of Lille. During World War II they had to hide and change their identities. Schwartz worked for the University of Strasbourg under the name Laurent-Marie Sélimartin, while Marie-Héléne used the name Lengé instead of Lévy. Schwartz spent one year in Grenoble in 1944, and then he joined the University of Nancy, where he spent seven years. He was an influential researcher and teacher. He joined the science faculty at the University of Paris in 1952, and in 1958 he became a teacher at the École Polytechnique. During 1961–1963 the École Polytechnique refused him the right to teach because he had signed the Manifesto of the 121, a document that criticized the Algerian war. Schwartz and Marie had two children, a son and a daughter. Their son committed suicide in 1971. Schwartz is considered as the "father of distributions", which are generalizations of the concept of functions. They resolve the problem of derivation. His theory clarified the mysteries of the Dirac Delta function (after Paul Adrien Maurice Dirac, 1902–1984, England) and the Heaviside step function (after Oliver Heaviside, 1850–1925, England). It helped to extend the theory of Fourier transforms (after Jean Baptiste Joseph Fourier, 1768–1830, France) and is now of great importance to the theory of partial differential equations. In recognition of his contribution, in 1950 he was awarded the Fields Medal. Schwartz became a Corresponding Member of the French Academy of Sciences (FAS) in 1973 and a full member in 1975. Besides the Schwartz distribution, the Schwartz kernel theorem, Schwartz space, and the Schwartz–Bruhat (François Georges René Bruhat, 1929–2007, France) function are named after him. He also promoted public appreciation and understanding of science and mathematics. He said "What are mathematics helpful for? Mathematics are helpful for physics. Physics helps us make fridges. Fridges are made to contain spiny lobsters, and spiny lobsters help mathematicians who eat them and have hence better abilities to do mathematics, which are helpful for physics, which helps us make fridges which. . . ". Schwartz passed away at the age of 87 in Paris.

17.2. Atle Selberg

He was born in Langesund, Norway, to Ole Michael Ludvigsen Selberg (1877–1950) and Anna Kristina Brigtsdatter Skeie (1874–1971). They had nine children, five boys and four girls, Atle being the youngest of them. Atle's father as well as his three brothers were also mathematicians. His father's collection of mathematics books sparked Atle's interest in mathematics when he was a young boy, and he was able to grasp methods for solving equations. While he was still at school, he was influenced by the work of Ramanujan and he found an exact analytical formula for the partition function as suggested by the works of Ramanujan; however, this result was first published by Hans Adolph Rademacher (1892–1969, Germany–USA). In 1935, Atle graduated from high school in Gjovik and matriculated at the University of Oslo. While still an undergraduate, he attended the Scandinavian Mathematical Congress in Helsinki in 1938, where he gave a 20-minute talk. He graduated from the University of Oslo with a master's degree in mathematics in 1939. In 1943, Atle defended his doctorate thesis *On the zeros of Riemann's zeta–function* (Riemann hypothesis) and the University of Oslo awarded him a Ph.D. degree. In 1947, he married the engineer Hedvig Liebermann (1919–1995) in Stockholm. Soon after the marriage Alte went to the United States and joined the IAS, Princeton. After one year Paul Erdös (1913–1996, Hungary) also joined the IAS, Princeton. By July 1948, Alte and Paul Erdös arrived at an elementary proof of the prime number theorem (which sparked bitter confrontation between them; in Hungary the proof is known as the Erdös–Selberg proof, whereas in Princeton it is known as the Selberg–Erdös proof). For his fundamental accomplishments during the 1940s, Selberg received the 1950 Fields Medal. The following year he spent as Associate Professor of mathematics at Syracuse University, returning to the IAS, Princeton, in 1949 as a permanent member. In 1951, Atle was promoted to Professor at Princeton, and in 1987 to Professor Emeritus. He is remembered from the many mathematical terms that bear his name: the Selberg Trace Formula (the most famous and influential of his results), the Selberg Sieve, the Selberg Integral, the Selberg Class, the Rankin–Selberg L–Function, the Selberg Eigenvalue Conjecture, and the Selberg Zeta Function. In 1986, he was awarded Wolf Prize in Mathematics, and in 2002 the honorary Abel Prize (before the awarding of the regular prizes began in 2003). Atle was elected to the Norwegian Academy of Science and Letters (NASL), the Royal Danish Academy of Sciences and Letters, and the American Academy of Arts and Sciences (AAAS).

18. Amsterdam ICM 1954

This Congress was held in Amsterdam, the Netherlands, during 2–9 September 1954, under the auspices of the Wiskundig Genootschap, the Netherlands Mathematical Society. The year 1954 was the centenary of the birth of Poincaré. There were 1553 full members (with 117 women) from 51 countries. This included five mathematicians from the the Soviet Union. During the opening ceremony at the proposal of Oswald Veblen, Jan Schouten was elected President of the Congress with applause. Hendrik Douwe Kloosterman (1900–1968, the Netherlands) was selected as the Vice-President. In his presidential address Jan Schouten said "...the place of mathematics in the world has changed entirely after the second world war. Before, mathematics had an honourable place among the sciences because of its central position, its history and its traditions, but there were in those times not many mathematicians and most people had only some bad memories from their school years and the comforting idea that in real life they would meet mathematics never more. Even some older engineers propagated the idea that the mathematical training of technical students was only a kind of quasi-scientific ornament that could be dropped before long for the greater part because technical methods themselves had by now developed into real sciences! During and after the war it became obvious to every one that nearly all branches of modern society in war and in peace need a lot of mathematics of all kinds, from the simplest school arithmetics up to the highest developed theoretical parts". The members of the Fields Medal Committee were Hermann Weyl (Chairman), Enrico Bompiani (1889–1975, Italy), Florent-Joseph Bureau (1906–1999, Belgium), Henri Paul Cartan (1904–2008, France), Alexander Markowich Ostrowski (1893–1986, Russia–Switzerland), Ake Vilhelm Carl Pleijel (1913–1989, Sweden), Gábor Szegö (1895–1985, Hungary–USA), and Edward Charles Titchmarsh (1899–1963, UK). Hermann Weyl in his address to the Congress announced the two names of the Fields Medals winners as Kunihiko Kodaira (1915–1997, Japan) for his work in algebraic geometry and the theory of complex manifolds and Jean-Pierre Serre (born 1926, France) for his contributions to the homotopy theory of spheres "with the wealth of its surprisingly numerical results". Along with two gold medals, each one of them was also given an honorarium of CAD 1500. Then the Secretary of the EC Bompiani of the IMU announced the office bearers for the period 1 January 1955–31 December 1958 as follows: Heinz Hopf (1894–1971, Germany–Switzerland) as President, Denjoy as the first Vice-President, Douglas Hodge as the second Vice-President, Bompiani as Secretary, and Komaravolu Chandrasekharan (1920–2017, India–Switzerland), Jurjen Ferdinand Koksma (1904–1964, the Netherlands), and Mac Lane as Elected Members. Since then, the ICMs have been held under the auspices of the IMU. An important feature of the Congress was the demonstration of electronic devices, such as IBM electronic calculators 604 and 626, the electronic computer ARRA built in the Mathematical Centre of Amsterdam, and the electronic computer Miracle built by Ferranti. In the closing ceremony Kolmogorov gave a plenary lecture *Théorie générale des systémes dynamiques et mécanique classique* (General theories of dynamical systems in classical mechanics). For the next Congress Douglas Hodge's proposal to hold the 1958 ICM in Edinburgh (sponsored by the City of Edinburgh, the University of

Edinburgh, the RSL and the Royal Society of Edinburgh (RSE)) was recommended and received with great applause. The proposal by the Department of Mathematics of the Hebrew University for the ICM 1962 was forwarded to the next Congress.

18.1. Kunihiko Kodaira

He was born in Tokyo, Japan. He showed a fascination with numbers from a young age, loved counting beans, and, when he was ten years old, he conducted an experiment to confirm that dogs cannot count. Kodaira completed his primary education in 1927 and entered middle school. He graduated from the University of Tokyo in 1938 with a bachelor's degree in mathematics and in 1941 with a bachelor's degree in physics. By 1941 he already had ten papers published. He worked as an Associate Professor at the Imperial University of Tokyo in 1941, as an Associate Professor in the Department of Mathematics of Tokyo Bunri University in 1942, and as an Associate Professor at the Imperial University of Tokyo during 1944–1951. In 1943 he married Seiko, the sister of Shokichi Iyanaga. Kodaira obtained his doctorate degree in mathematics under the supervision of Shokichi Iyanaga in 1949 by submitting a thesis that appeared in the *Annals of Mathematics*, 50 (1949), 587–665, under the title *Harmonic fields in Riemannian manifolds (generalized potential theory)*. This paper caught the attention of Hermann Weyl, who brought Kodaira, in the fall of 1949, to the IAS, Princeton. He was a Visiting Professor at Johns Hopkins University from September 1950 to June 1951, when he returned to the IAS, Princeton, as an Associate Professor, and was promoted to a Full Professor there in September 1955. In 1961, Kodaira accepted a visiting professorship at Harvard University for a year. In 1962, he accepted a professorship at Johns Hopkins University, where he remained until 1965 when he accepted a professorship at Stanford University. Then, he returned to Japan, and to the University of Tokyo, in 1967. Kodaira had an impressive number of excellent students. After retiring from the University of Tokyo in 1975, he was appointed as Professor in the Faculty of Science of Gakushuin University, a highly rated private university. He taught for ten years at this university. The last ten years of his life were ones during which he battled against health problems. He suffered from respiratory problems and also became very deaf, which sadden him greatly since he could not enjoy music, which had meant so much to him throughout his life. Kodaira's wife, Seiko, died in January 2000, two and a half years after her husband. He was the founder of the Japanese school of algebraic geometers. He made original contributions in several different fields, including algebraic geometry, complex manifolds, and Hodge theory. He wrote around 40 academic books and 350 academic papers. Kodaira received many honors for his outstanding research: the Fields Medal in 1954, the Japan Academy Prize from the Academy of Japan in 1957, the Fujiwara Prize in 1975 (after Ginjirō Fujiwara, 1869–1960, Japan), and the Wolf Foundation Prize in Mathematics in 1984. He was honorary member of several academies and learned societies throughout the world, including the Göttingen Academy of Sciences (1974), the United States NAS (1975), the AAAS (1978), and the LMS (1979). In the mathematical world he is remembered for the Kodaira vanishing theorem, Kodaira–Spencer mapping, the Kodaira dimension, the Kodaira surface, the Kodaira embedding theorem, Kodaira's classification of singular fibers, the Bochner–Kodaira–Nakano identity, the Enriques–Kodaira classification, and Weyl–Titchmarsh–Kodaira theory.

18.2. Jean-Pierre Serre

He was born in Bages, Pyrénées-Orientales, France. In 1932, Jean-Pierre began his primary school education at the École de Vauvert. In 1937 he moved to study at the Lycée Alphonse-Daudet in Nîmes, and then from 1945 to 1948 he attended the ENS in Paris. Jean-Pierre married Josiane Heulot (1922–2004, France) in 1948. At this time he became the youngest member of the "Monsieur Nicholas Bourbaki" group (established in 1939, the founding members included Henri Cartan; Claude Chevalley, 1909–1984; Jean Coulomb, 1904–1999; Jean Delsarte 1903–1968; Jean Dieudonné, 1905–1992; Charles Ehresmann, 1905–1979; René de Possel, 1905–1974; Szolem Mandelbrojt, 1899–1983; and André Weil, 1906–1998) of French mathematicians. From 1948 to 1954 he held positions at the *Centre National de la Recherche Scientifique* (CNRS) in Paris. Serre obtained his doctorate at the Sorbonne in 1951 under the supervision of Henri Cartan. The title of his thesis was *Homologie singulière des espaces fibrés*. It was about loop spaces viewed as fibered spaces (a simple but new idea), with applications to homotopy groups, e.g., those of spheres. For two years, 1954–1956, he worked at the University of Nancy. He was then elected Professor at the Collège de France, where he remained until his retirement in 1994, when he became an Honorary Professor. Jean-Pierre spent time at Harvard University (in 1957, 1964, 1974, 1976, 1979, 1981, 1985, 1988, 1990, 1992, 1994, 1995, and 1996) and the IAS, Princeton (in 1955, 1957, 1959, 1961, 1963, 1967, 1970, 1972, 1978, 1983, and 1999). Another of Serre's important works was spectral sequences, which he applied in 1951 to his study of the relations between the homology groups of fibre, total space, and base space in a fibration. Based on this work and his work on complex variable theory in terms of sheaves, Serre was awarded a Fields Medal at the age of 27 (youngest winner to date) at the ICM in 1954. Besides more than 400 research papers, he has published many highly influential texts covering a wide range of mathematics. Among these texts, which show the variety of topics that Serre has worked on, are *Homologie singulière des espaces fibrés* (1951), *Faisceaux algébriques cohérents* (1955), *Groupes algébriques et corps de classes* (1959), *Corps locaux* (1962), *Cohomologie Galoisienne* (1964), *Abelian l-adic representations and elliptic curves* (1968), *Cours d'arithmétique* (1970), *Représentations linéaires des groupes finis* (1971), *Arbres, amalgames, SL2* (1977), *Lectures on the Mordell–Weil theorem* (1989), *Topics in Galois theory* (1992), *Collected Papers I–IV* (2003), *Lectures on $NX(p)$* (2012), *Rational Points on Curves over Finite Fields* (2020), and *Finite Groups: an Introduction* (2022). In the literature he is often cited for Bass–Serre theory, Serre duality, Serre's multiplicity conjectures, Serre's property FA, the Serre spectral sequence, the Serre fibration, the Serre twist sheaf, and the thin set in the sense of Serre. In addition to the Fields Medal, Serre has received numerous other prizes and awards: the Prix Gaston Julia (1970), the Balzan (Eugenio Balzan, 1874–1953) Prize (1985), the Leroy S. Steele Prize (1995), the Wolf Prize (2000), and the Abel Prize (2003). He has been elected to the scientific academies of France, Sweden, the United States, the Netherlands, and the RSL. Serre has been awarded the highest honors in France, the Grand Cross of the Legion of Honour and Grand Cross of the Legion of Merit. He has been awarded honorary doctorates degrees by the University of Cambridge (1978), the University of Stockholm (1980), the University of Glasgow (1983), the University of Harvard (1998), and the University of Oslo (2002).

19. Edinburgh ICM 1958

This Congress was held in Edinburgh, Scotland, during 14–21 August 1958, sponsored by the City of Edinburgh, the University of Edinburgh, the RSL, and the RSE. There were 1658 full members. During the opening ceremony Koksma, on behalf of Jan Schouten (who could not participate on the grounds of his health), read his wish for Douglas Hodge to be the President of the Congress, which was accepted by acclamation. Douglas Hodge in his lecture memorialized Edmund Whittaker (who had passed away two years before) and emphasized the importance of getting together the leaders in "all branches of mathematics" so that they may discuss their common problems and exchange ideas about them. He also mentioned the significance of the newly developed science of computing, and history and education in mathematics. The eight members of the Fields Medal Committee of the ICM in Edinburgh set up by the Organizing Committee consisted of the following: Chandrasekharan, Kurt Otto Friedrichs (1901–1982, Germany–USA), Philip Hall (1904–1982, England), Heinz Hopf (Chairman), Kolmogorov, Laurent Schwartz, Carl Ludwig Siegel (1896–1981, Germany), and Oscar Zariski (1899–1986, Belarus–USA). Heinz Hopf announced that the Committee had decided to award two Fields Medals to Klaus Friedrich Roth (1925–2015, Poland–Scotland) for solving a famous problem in number theory, namely, the determination of the exact exponent in the Thue–Siegel inequality (Axel Thue, 1863–1922, Norway), and to René Frédéric Thom (1923–2002, France) for creating the theory of "Cobordisme", which has, within the few years of its existence, led to the most penetrating insight into the topology of differentiable manifolds. In the Congress there were 19 one-hour addresses by invitation, 37 half-hour addresses by invitation, and 604 fifteen-minute short communications. Two important features of the Congress were a lecture "Teaching Mathematics on Television" by Carl Barnett Allendoerfer (1911–1974, USA) and an interesting exhibition on the mathematical typography arranged by the Monotype Corporation at Heriot-Watt College. In the closing session Douglas Hodge made an unusual announcement to the Congress: I am authorized by the Committee to say that while for reasons of a technical nature it is not possible to make any announcement today of the name of the host country for 1962, the prospects of holding a Congress in that year amount to a certainty. He also made a brief report on the work conducted at the Assembly of the IMU, which had met at St Andrews from 11 to 13 August 1958. Finally, Douglas Hodge declared the Edinburgh Congress closed.

It seems the uncertainty regarding the venue of the 1962 Congress was due to too many competing proposals from several countries. Finally, the IMU conveyed the decision of the committee in charge for Swedish mathematicians to hold the next ICM. On 28 October 1958 the Swedish National Committee for Mathematics decided to accept the invitation. Then on 30 November 1958, the Swedish Mathematical Society confirmed that it would hold the ICM in Stockholm. Thus, Mittag-Leffler's dream to hold the ICM in Stockholm came true 42 years after he presented the first proposal in 1908.

19.1. Klaus Friedrich Roth

He was born to a Jewish family in Breslau, Germany (now Wroclaw, Poland). His parents settled with him in London to escape Nazi persecution in 1933. His father, a solicitor, was exposed to poison gas during World War I and died while Klaus Roth was still young. Klaus Roth attended St Paul's School in London from 1939 to 1943. He then went to Peterhouse, Cambridge, where he was awarded a Bachelor of Arts degree in 1945. On the recommendation of Harold Davenport (1907–1969, England), he was accepted in 1946 to a master's program in mathematics at University College London, where he worked under the supervision of Theodor Estermann (1902–1991, Germany–England). He was awarded his master's degree in 1948 and the same year was appointed to an assistant lecturer position. In 1950, he received his doctorate for the dissertation *Proof that almost all Positive Integers are Sums of a Square, a Positive Cube and a Fourth Power*, which was written under the supervision of Estermann; the same year he was promoted to Lecturer. In 1955, Klaus Roth married Mélék Khaïry (died in 2002) and published what is now known as Roth's theorem: every irrational algebraic number α has a Liouville number (after Joseph Liouville, 1809–1882, France) equal to 2, i.e., for each $\epsilon > 0$ the inequality

$$\left|\alpha - \frac{p}{q}\right| < \frac{1}{q^{2+\epsilon}}$$

can only have a finite number of solutions using coprime numbers p and q. On the occasion of the Fields Medal awarding ceremony at the Edinburgh ICM 1958, Davenport hailed Roth's theorem as the "greatest achievement". He taught at University College London until 1966, becoming a reader in 1956 and then a Professor in 1961. Then, Klaus Roth took a chair at Imperial College London and retired in 1988. In that year he went to University College London as a Visiting Professor, a position he held until 1996. Then, he returned to the north of Scotland. Klaus Roth dedicated the bulk of his estate, over GBP one million, to two health charities and sent the Fields Medal with a smaller bequest to Peterhouse. His most significant contributions are as follows: Diophantine approximation, progression-free sequences, discrepancy theory, and the theory of integer sequences. Besides the Fields Medal, he was elected FRS of London in 1960, Honorary Fellow of the RSE, Fellow of University College London, Fellow of Imperial College London, and Honorary Fellow of Peterhouse. He received the De Morgan Medal (after Augustus De Morgan, 1806–1871, India–UK) of the LMS in 1983 and the Sylvester Medal of the Royal Society in 1991. Klaus Roth was known as a problem-solver in mathematics rather than as a theory-builder.

19.2. René Frédéric Thom

He was born in Montbéliard, Doubs, France. From 1931, Thom attended primary school in Montbéliard itself and showed his academic potential by winning a scholarship. Then he moved to Collége Cuvier again at Montbéliard and received his baccalauréat in elementary mathematics in 1940. After the German invasion of France (9 May–22 June 1940), Thom took refuge in Switzerland and then in Lyon, where he continued his education and received a baccalauréat in philosophy in June 1941. Soon after, he moved to Paris to attend Lycée Saint-Louis (post-secondary school). In 1942, Thom applied to enter the ENS but was unsuccessful; he applied again in 1943 and this time he was successful and became agrégé in 1946. In 1951, he defended his doctorate thesis entitled *Espaces fibrés en sphères et carrés de Steenrod* (Spaces fibered into Steenrod spheres and squares), which was written under the supervision of Henri Cartan. During 1951–1952, he was on a fellowship at Princeton University Graduate College; during 1953–1954, he became Maître de conférences (Assistant Professor) at the University of Grenoble; during 1954–1963, he taught at the University of Strasbourg, where in 1957 he was promoted to a Professor; and during (1964–1990) he worked at the Institut des Hautes Études Scientifiques (IHES) at Bures-sur-Yvette. During the last twenty years of his life, Thom worked mainly in philosophy and epistemology, and he undertook a reevaluation of Aristotle's writings on science. Thom is best known for his work on topology, in particular on characteristic classes and singularity theory, of which catastrophe theory is just one aspect. He is also remembered for the Thom transversality theorem, Thom spaces, the Thom–Mather (John Norman Mather, 1942–2017, USA) isotopy theorem, and the Thom conjecture (now theorem). In 1958, Thom was awarded the Fields Medal at the Edinburgh ICM for the foundations of cobordism theory, which had already appeared in his doctorate thesis. He was awarded the Brouwer Medal (after Luitzen Egbertus Jan Brouwer, 1881–1966, the Netherlands) in 1970, the Grand Prix Scientifique de la Ville de Paris in 1974, and the von Neumann Lecture Prize in 1976. In 1973, he became the first President, together with Louis Eugène Félix Néel (1904–2000, France), of the newly established Fondation Louis-de-Broglie. In 1976, he was elected member of the Académie des Sciences of Paris. In 1990, Thom was made an Honorary Member of the LMS.

20. Stockholm ICM 1962

This Congress was held in Stockholm, Sweden, during 15–22 August 1962. The Congress was attended by 2107 full members from 57 countries. The opening ceremony took place on 15 August, under the patronage and in the presence of His Majesty the King Gustav VI Adolf (1882–1973) of Sweden. Otto Albin Frostman (1907–1977, Sweden), the Chairman of the Organizing Committee, welcomed the audience. He emphasized "...the development of mathematics itself which is proceeding so rapidly that no man can survey but a part or parts of the front line, and total coverage can only be achieved by joint work on an international basis". Rolf Nevanlinna, the President of the IMU, declared the Congress open. He asserted that "...theoretical and general mathematical insight throws light on practical questions, and forms, in fact, the basis of applications in many different fields: in natural science, in technology and, in recent times, in many branches of social and economic life. The astonishing development of electronic computers has contributed enormously to the applicability of mathematical methods". The Fields Medal Committee consisted of the following: Rolf Nevanlinna (Chairman), Alexandrov, Emil Artin, Shiing-Shen Chern, Claude Chevalley, Hassler Whitney, and Kōsaku Yosida (1909–1990, Japan). The medals were awarded to Lars Valter Hörmander (1931–2012, Sweden) and John Willard Milnor (born 1931, USA). The medals were presented to the awardees by the King. Lars Garding (1919–2014, Sweden) spoke on the "outstanding work in partial differential equations" of Lars Hörmander, and Hassler Whitney explained that "differential topology is a strong young field ... its vitality is largely due to the fine achievements of Willard Milnor". There were 16 one-hour invited addresses (none from Sweden), 57 half-hours invited addresses delivered within the sections, and 745 short ten-minute communications. Important features of the Congress were the lecture of Kiyosi Ito (1915–2008, Japan) on how to combine differential geometry and stochastic analysis, which led to major advances in the 1960s and 1970s; a special report by Sergei L'vovich Sobolev (1908–1989, Russia) on the use of electronic computers for deciphering the Mayan language; and an exhibition arranged by IBM, Facit, and Ericsson, which was aimed at participants interested in numerical methods and applied mathematics. During the closing ceremony on 22 August, the President Rolf Nevanlinna of the IMU announced the new EC of the IMU for the years 1963–1966: Georges de Rham (1903–1990, Switzerland) as President, Henri Cartan and Kazimierz Kuratowski (1896–1980, Poland) as Vice-Presidents, Chandrasekharan as Secretary, and John Charles Burkill (1900–1993, England), Friedrich Ernst Peter Hirzebruch (1927–2012, Germany), Mikhail Alekseevich Lavrentev (1900–1980, Russia), Deane Montgomery, Beniamino Segre (1903–1977, Italy), and Rolf Nevanlinna as members. For the next Congress in 1966 in the Soviet Union, Lavrentev's proposal (in Russian, translated to English by Alexandrov) was carried by acclamation. Finally, Rolf Nevanlinna declared the ICM in Stockholm closed.

He was born in Mjällby, a village in Blekinge in southern Sweden. Lars was the youngest of his parents' five children. He attended his first school in Mjällby, then he commuted daily by train to attend realskola (secondary school) in a larger nearby town, and for the gymnasium (high school) he had to move to Lund, where he graduated in 1948. There Lars was influenced by his enthusiastic mathematics teacher Nils Erik Fremberg (1908–1952, Sweden), who encouraged him to study university-level mathematics. Lars then began his studies at the University of Lund, acquiring a bachelor's degree in 1949 and a master's degree in 1950. In 1951, he was awarded a licentiate degree for the thesis *Applications of Helly's theorem to estimates of Chebyshev type*, written under the supervision of Marcel Riesz (1886–1969, Sweden). In 1953, he married Viveka Sonesson (1925–2017, Sweden). The University of Lund offered Lars a doctorate degree in 1955 for the thesis *On the Theory of General Partial Differential Operators*. His official thesis advisor was Lars Gòrding (1919–2014, Sweden); however, he worked independently, finding his own problems and solving them. The thesis was published in the Journal *Acta Mathematica* in 1955. After the award of his doctorate, he left for the United States and spent time at the universities of Chicago, Kansas, and Minnesota, and the Institute for Mathematical Sciences (now the Courant Institute). Then, he returned to Sweden and on 1 January 1957 joined the University of Stockholm as a Professor. In his honor the University of Stockholm's student newspaper, *Gaudeamus*, published an article headed "26-year-old mathematics professor solemnly installed". Hörmander won the Fields Medal at the Stockholm ICM 1962 for his work on partial differential equations. On this accomplishment, Lars Gòrding wrote "Many people have contributed but the deepest and most significant results are due to Hörmander". Lars spent the summers 1960–1961 at Stanford University as an invited professor. Then, he received an offer to come to the IAS, Princeton, as a permanent member and Professor, which he accepted, but stayed there only from 1964 to 1968, and returned to Lund University as a Professor from 1968 until 1996, when he retired with the title of Professor Emeritus. After 1968, Lars made several visits to the United States. He visited the Courant Institute in 1970, the IAS, Princeton, in 1971, Stanford in 1971, 1977, and 1982, and the University of California (UC), San Diego, in winter 1990. Lars was briefly director of the Mittag-Leffler Institute in Stockholm between 1984 and 1986. His five-year compilation of the four-volume monograph *The Analysis of Linear Partial Differential Operators* (published by Springer-Verlag in 1963 as part of the Grundlehren Series) is considered a foundational work on the subject. His well-recognized text *An Introduction to Complex Analysis in Several Variables* (published by North Holland in 1966) is based on lecture notes of a course that he gave at Stanford in 1964. Lars also wrote the books *Lectures on Nonlinear Hyperbolic Differential Equations* (published by Springer-Verlag in 1987) and *Notions of Convexity* (published by Birkhäuser Verlag in 1994). He supervised sixteen doctoral students; among them Germund Dahlquist (1925–2005, Sweden), Christer Oscar Kiselman (born 1939, Sweden), and Vidar Thomée (born 1933, Sweden) have contributed to mathematics significantly. Hörmander was awarded the Wolf Prize in 1988 and Steele Prize in 2006. He was made a member of the RSAS in 1968. In 2012, he was selected as a Fellow of the AMS, but died on 25 November 2012, before the list of Fellows was released. Before his death Lars often used to say that he was content with his life, that it had been a good life.

20.2. John Willard Milnor

He was born in Orange, New Jersey, USA. Milnor was an undergraduate at Princeton University. He was named a Putnam Fellow (after Elizabeth Lowell Putnam, 1862–1935, USA) as a top scorer in the Putnam competition in mathematics in 1949 and 1950. In 1950, he published his first paper *On the Total Curvature of Knots* in the journal *Annals of Mathematics*, which was accepted for publication 1948, when Milnor was only seventeen years old. He graduated with a Bachelor of Arts (B.A.) in mathematics in 1951 after completing a senior thesis, titled *Link Groups*, under the supervision of Ralph Hartzler Fox (1913–1973, USA). He remained at Princeton to pursue graduate studies. In 1953, before completing his doctoral studies, he was appointed to the faculty at Princeton. The same year, he wrote four research papers, including *Sums of Positional Games*. In 1954, he defended his 44-page doctorate thesis *Isotopy of Links*, which was also written under the supervision of Ralph Fox. During 1955–1959, Milnor continued on the staff at Princeton as an Alfred Pritchard Sloan (1875–1966, USA) Foundation Fellow. He was promoted to Professor in 1960; then, in 1962, Milnor was appointed to the Henry Putman chair. At the Stockholm ICM 1962, Milnor was awarded a Fields Medal for his proof in 1956 that a seven-dimensional sphere can have several differential structures, which marked the beginning of a new field—differential topology. He continued at Princeton University until 1967. Then, he had brief positions at UC Los Angeles (UCLA) and MIT. Milnor was a Professor at the IAS, Princeton, from 1970 to 1989; then he became the first Director of the Institute for Mathematical Sciences at Stony Brook University in New York, and later its Co-director. In 1984, Milnor married Margaret Dusa Waddington McDuff (born 1945). She is a Professor of mathematics at Barnard College and is known for her work in symplectic topology. He worked on several different fields, including differential topology, algebraic K-theory, and low-dimensional holomorphic dynamical systems. Milnor has written several very influential books: *Morse theory* (1963); *Lectures on the H-cobordism theorem* (1965); *Topology from the differentiable viewpoint* (1965); *Characteristic classes* (1974) with James Dillon Stasheff (born 1936, USA); *Singular points of complex hypersurfaces* (1968); *Introduction to algebraic K-theory* (1971); *Dynamics in one complex variable* (1999); and *Symmetric bilinear forms* (1973) with Dale Husemöller (born 1933, USA). Milnor's research papers have been published in five volumes by the AMS. He was an editor of the *Annals of Mathematics* for a number of years after 1962. He supervised eighteen doctoral students, including Tadatoshi Akiba (born 1942, Japan), Jon Hal Folkman (1938–1969, USA), John Mather, Laurent Carl Siebenmann (born 1939, Canada), Michael David Spivak (1940–2020, USA), and Jonathan David Sondow (1943–2020, USA). Milnor is known for exotic spheres, the Fáry-Milnor theorem (István Fáry, 1922–1984, Hungary–USA), Hauptvermutung, Milnor K-theory, microbundles, Milnor maps, the Milnor number, Milnor fibration, Milnor–Thurston kneading theory (William Paul Thurston, 1946–2012, USA), plumbing, the Milnor–Wood inequality (John Wood, USA), surgery theory, the Kervaire–Milnor theorem (Michel André Kervaire, 1927–2007, Poland–France), isospectral non-isometric compact Riemannian manifolds, and the Švarc-Milnor lemma (Albert Solomonovich Švarc, born 1934, Soviet–USA). Milnor is the recipient of several honors: the National Medal of Science (1967), Steele Prize (1982, 2004, and 2011), Wolf Prize (1989), and Abel Prize (2011). Reacting to the Abel Prize Milnor told the *New Scientist* "It feels very good", adding that "[o]ne is always surprised by a call at 6 o'clock in the morning". Milnor was elected as a member of the AAAS in 1961, the United States NAS in 1963, and the American Philosophical Society (APS) in 1965 and a Fellow of the AMS in 2013. In 2020, Milnor received the Lomonosov Gold Medal (after Mikhail Vasilyevich Lomonosov, 1711–1765, Russia) of the RAS.

21. Moscow ICM 1966

This Congress was held in Moscow, Russia, during 16–26 August 1966. The Congress was attended by 4280 participants (more than double the size of Stockholm) from 54 countries. This Congress provided an excellent opportunity for the Soviet system to show, in front of the worldwide scientific community, its achievements after the de-Stalinization process. In fact, it also gave a new significance to the ICM that continues through the present time. In the opening ceremony the President of the Academy of Sciences of the USSR (and chief theoretician of Soviet cosmonautics in the 1960s) academician Mstislav Vsevolodovich Keldysh (1911–1978, Latvia-Russia) said "Mathematics, which is the oldest of all sciences, at the same time remains an eternally young, rapidly developing science, constantly expanding the field of its knowledge, developing its connections more widely not only with the natural sciences, but also with the most diverse areas of human activity. I think that the value of mathematical theories is greater, the more closely their roots are associated with the phenomena of the world in which we live, and at the same time, the greater we achieve a degree of abstraction and a common point of view. The success of a theory largely depends on whether we find a degree of generality and a degree of abstraction that are adequate to the phenomenon under study. The value of the theory is determined by the extent to which general provisions allow us to understand specific phenomena and solve specific problems. General mathematical theories allow us to deeply understand the relationship between phenomena. The introduction of mathematical methods transforms the fields of knowledge and not only puts them at the highest level of logical thinking, but opens up new possibilities, new statements of problems, and allows us to look at phenomena in a new way. It is enough to recall what revolutionary, fundamental shifts in the development of natural science were made by the analysis of the infinitely small, the theory of probability, the theory of operators, and, finally, the rapidly developing knowledge of logical processes. The development of such abstract areas of mathematics as set theory and topology, algebra, functional analysis, etc. that have recently arisen has led not only to the creation of theories of extraordinary beauty, but also to the creation of powerful new methods in all of mathematics. It seems to me that we are experiencing an era when the mathematical method is especially rapidly conquering ever new areas of knowledge. Along with physics, the spirit of mathematical thinking is becoming increasingly important in chemistry, biology, and geology, and it penetrates widely into social sciences, and first of all, into economic science. Studying the fundamentals of logical processes and the theory of operations, methods of discrete mathematics, creating electronic computing devices prepared the foundations for the new greatest scientific and technological revolution in the whole life of mankind, a new level of understanding of many processes in nature and life, and a new stage in the automation of processes that until recently times were considered an area of exclusively intellectual human activity, as well as in the implementation of mathematical processes that we considered feasible only in abstract thinking. Let me express the hope that the upcoming Congress will be of great importance in mathematical life. The field of mathematics has become so wide that mathematicians speak not only the languages of different nations, but also different mathematical languages and their language is not yet accessible to many scientists of other specialties, but it is precisely because of the breadth and strength of the mathematical method that this Congress will be of great importance for all science and the development human culture". Then, Ivan Georgievich Petrovsky (1901–1973, Russia) the President of the Congress and Chairman of the Organizing Committee (including the members Ivan Matveevich Vinogradov, 1891–1983, Russia; Lavrentev; and Sergey Mergelyan, 1928–2008, Armenia–USA) in his opening speech welcomed and thanked the participants, especially Rolf Nevanlinna.

- At each Oslo 1936, Harvard 1950, Amsterdam 1954, Edinburgh 1958, and Stockholm 1962 Congress, two medals were awarded. The Indian tycoon Sir Dorabji Tata's (1859–1932) Trust intended to institute two new medals, similar to the Fields Medal. At the last moment, Indian authorities did not allow the money transfer, and the project was canceled. In any case, that year, due to an anonymous donor (whose name is still unknown), it was possible to award up to four Fields Medals. During the 1966 Congress in Moscow, the tradition of considering only young mathematicians was specified (and followed ever since) and put into writing: "candidates must be under forty".

The Fields Medal Committee consisted of the following: Georges de Rham (Chairman), Davenport, Max Deuring (1907–1984, Germany), William Srecko Feller (1906–1970, Croatia-USA), Lavrentev, Serre, Donald Clayton Spencer (1912–2001, USA), and René Thom. Georges de Rham in his speech announced "In view of the vast development of Mathematics during the last forty years, it appears that this number (of Medals) could judiciously be increased to four". In alphabetical order the four recipients of the medals are as follows: Michael Francis Atiyah (1929–2019, England–Lebanon), Paul Joseph Cohen, Alexander Grothendieck (1928–2014, Germany–France), and Stephen Smale (born 1930, USA). Michael Atiyah, Paul Cohen, and Stephen Smale (although he arrived at the ceremony late, just in time to listen to part of the laudation of his work) received the medals from the hands of the academician Keldysh; however, Grothendieck boycotted the ICM to protest Soviet military actions taking place in Eastern Europe, so on his behalf the medal was received by Léon Motchane (1900–1990, France), who founded the IHES in 1958. Then Henri Cartan spoke on Atiyah's achievements in K-theory, the index formula, and the Lefschetz formula. Thanks to Atiyah's work, topology and analysis have been put in close relation; Alonzo Church (1903–1995, USA) spoke on Cohen's solution to the continuum problem (which was Hilbert's first problem); Jean Dieudonné compared Grothendieck to Hilbert, and he condensed his talk by saying that Grothendieck was the principal craftsman in the renovation of algebraic geometry; and René Thom, after explaining why Stephen Smale's dissertation of 1956 was a seminal paper, spoke of Smale's great work on Poincaré's conjecture, which opened a whole chapter in differential topology.

There were 17 plenary addresses, 64 invited addresses, and 21000 proposals for communications received by the organizers. Two highlights of the Congress were as follows: Lennart Axel Edvard Carleson's (born 1928, Sweden) lecture, where he presented the results of his paper published in *Acta Mathematica* in 1966 with the solution to the long-standing problem posed by the Russian mathematician

Nikolai Luzin in 1913 regarding the pointwise convergence of Fourier series, and Kolmogorov's lecture on "Mathematical Education in Secondary Schools" (the attendance was so high that the lecture room had to be changed to a larger one). In the closing ceremony Georges de Rham praised the "cooperation between mathematicians of the Soviet Union and those of other countries, especially of Western Europe and the USA." He also announced the new EC of the IMU for the years 1967–1970: Henri Cartan as President, Lavrentev and Montgomery as Vice-Presidents, Frostman as Secretary, and Michael Atiyah, Chandrasekharan, György Hajós (1912–1972, Hungary), Edoardo Vesentini (1928–2020, Italy), and Kōsaku Yosida as members. The venue for the 1970 Congress in Nice was proposed by Jean Dieudonné in his capacity as Dean of the Faculty of Sciences of the Université de Nice. Finally, Ivan Petrovsky announced the ICM in Moscow closed.

21.1. Michael Francis Atiyah

He was born to the Lebanese writer Edward Atiyah (1903–1964) and his Scottish wife, Jean Levens, in Hampstead, London. Michael grew up in Sudan and Egypt. He attended a primary school in Khartoum, Sudan, during 1934–1941 and two secondary schools in Cairo and Alexandria, Egypt, during 1941–1945. Michael returned to England and studied at the Manchester Grammar School during 1945–1947. He then served with the Royal Electrical and Mechanical Engineers during 1947–1949. Atiyah studied at Trinity College, Cambridge, during 1949–1955. Michael received his doctorate in 1955 at the age of 26 for his dissertation on *Some Applications of Topological Methods in Algebraic Geometry* under the supervision of Douglas Hodge. He spent most of his academic career at the University of Oxford, Cambridge University, and the IAS, Princeton. Michael was Savilian Professor of Geometry and a professorial fellow of New College, Oxford, during 1963–1969; President of the LMS during 1974–1976; and President of the RSL during 1990–1995. He took part in the founding of the Isaac Newton (1642–1727, UK) Institute for Mathematical Sciences in Cambridge and was its first director during 1990–1996. He was Master of Trinity College, Cambridge, 1990–1997; Chancellor of the University of Leicester during 1995–2005; President of the RSE during 2005–2008; and an Honorary Professor at the University of Edinburgh from 1997 until his death. Michael married Lily Brown (1955–2018, Scotland) on 30 July 1955, and they had three sons. His main contributions are in the fields algebraic geometry, K-theory, index theory, gauge theory, the Dedekind eta function from a topological point of view, and the connections between quantum field theory, knots, and Donaldson (Simon Kirwan Donaldson, born 1957, England) theory. The seven volumes of Atiyah's collected papers include most of his work, except for his commutative algebra textbook. Michael supervised 26 doctorate students, including leading mathematicians Simon Donaldson and Nigel James Hitchin (born 1946, England). Among his many collaborators, the main three of whom he met at the IAS, Princeton, in 1955, are Raoul Bott (1923–2005, Hungary–USA) on Atiyah–Bott fixed-point theorem, Isadore Manuel Singer (1924–2021, USA) on the Atiyah–Singer index theorem, and Friedrich Hirzebruch on topological K-theory. Among several honors he was awarded the Fields Medal in 1966, the Copley Medal in 1988, and the Abel Prize in 2004. He was elected a foreign member of many academies, including the United States NAS,

Académie des Sciences, Paris, the Indian National Science Academy, the RAS, and the RSAS. Many universities have awarded Michael an honorary degree, including Bonn, St Andrews, Trinity College Dublin, Edinburgh, Cambridge, Rutgers, Brown, Oxford, Harvard, and the list continues. It is unfortunate that his eldest son died on 24 June 2002. Both Michael and Lily Atiyah were buried in Binning Memorial Wood, Tyninghame, Scotland. Michael's advice to all mathematicians is "If you attack a mathematical problem directly, very often you come to a dead end, nothing you do seems to work and you feel that if only you could peer round the corner there might be an easy solution. There is nothing like having somebody else beside you, because he can usually peer round the corner".

21.2. Paul Joseph Cohen

He was born to Abraham and Minnie Cohen (Jewish family that had immigrated to the United States from what is now Poland) in Long Branch, New Jersey, USA. From the age of nine he was brought up by his mother, since at that time his parents separated. He studied at Stuyvesant High School, New York City, and graduated there in 1950. During 1950–1953, he attended Brooklyn College in New York City, but he left the college without completing his bachelor's degree. He then attended the University of Chicago and obtained his masters and doctorate degrees in 1954 and 1958, respectively. His doctoral dissertation was entitled *Topics in the Theory of Uniqueness of Trigonometric Series*, written under the supervision of Antoni Zygmund (1900–1992, Poland-USA). In 1957, Cohen was appointed as an Instructor in Mathematics at the University of Rochester for a year; then he spent the academic year 1958–1959 at MIT, and during 1959–1961, he was a Fellow at the IAS, Princeton. Cohen was appointed as an Assistant Professor at Stanford University in 1961 and was promoted to the post of Associate Professor in 1962. In 1963, Cohen married Christina Karls (Sweden) and later had three sons. He was promoted to Full Professor at Stanford University in 1964. He became Marjorie Mhoon Fair Professor in Quantitative Science at Stanford in 1972. Although he officially retired in 2004, he continued teaching at Stanford until shortly before his death due to a rare lung disease at Stanford Hospital in Palo Alto. Cohen made significant contributions to mathematics: in 1959, he showed that any integrable function on a locally compact group is the convolution of two such functions, solving a problem posed by Walter Rudin (1921–2010, Austria–USA); in 1960, he made a breakthrough in solving the Littlewood conjecture (after John Edensor Littlewood, 1885–1977, UK) in classical Fourier analysis, and determined all the idempotent measures on a locally compact abelian group; in 1963, he used a mathematical technique called "forcing" to prove that the continuum hypothesis and the axiom of choice are independent from Zermelo–Fraenkel set theory; in 1966, Cohen published the monograph *Set theory and the Continuum Hypothesis*, which was based on a course he gave at Harvard in spring 1965; and in 1969, he published a highly original paper on p-adic cell decomposition. In 2006, just before his death, during the Gödel centennial conference in Vienna, Cohen gave a lecture describing his solution to the problem of the continuum hypothesis. Cohen was awarded the Bôcher Prize (1964), the Fields Medal (1966), and the National Medal of Science (1967). He also received an award from the President Lyndon Baines Johnson (1908–1973) in a ceremony in the White House on 13 February 1968. On 2 June 1995, Cohen received an honorary doctorate from the Faculty of Science and Technology at Uppsala University, Sweden. Cohen was a member of the AAAS, the United States NAS, and the APS. He used to play both the piano and violin and was an accomplished linguist, speaking Swedish, French, Spanish, German, and Yiddish. He and his wife hosted frequent dinner parties for students, colleagues, and friends.

21.3. Alexander Grothendieck

He was born in Berlin to anarchist parents Alexander (Sascha) Schapiro (1890–1942) and Johanna Grothendieck (1900–1957). His father moved to Paris to escape Nazism and his mother followed him soon after, leaving Alexander with Wilhelm Heydorn (1873–1958), a Lutheran pastor and teacher in Hamburg. In 1939, Alexander joined his parents in France. In 1940, Sascha was arrested under the law "undesirable dangerous foreigners", and he died in 1942. Alexander and his mother were also deported, but they escaped the Holocaust. Alexander separated from his mother, and he managed to attend the famous high school Collége Cévenol in Le Chambon-sur-Lignon. From 1940 to 1944, Chambon and neighboring villages provided shelter to some 5000 people, among them Jews fleeing persecution; Alexander was one of them, although he occasionally had to seek refuge in the woods during Nazi raids, surviving at times without food or water for several days. He obtained his baccalaureate at the College in 1945, and then enrolled at the University of Montpellier, where at first he did not perform well, failing such classes as astronomy; however, he rediscovered the Lebesgue measure. After graduating from Montpellier in 1948, he spent the years 1948–1949 at the ENS in Paris. There he attended Henri Cartan's seminar, which was on algebraic topology and sheaf theory. The other participants of the seminar were leading mathematicians including Claude Chevalley, Jean Delsarte, Jean Dieudonné, Roger Godement (1921–2016, France), Laurent Schwartz, and André Weil. In 1949, Alexander, on the advice of Henri Cartan and André Weil, moved to the University of Nancy, and under the supervisor of Jean Dieudonné and Laurent Schwartz he wrote his doctorate thesis *Produits tensoriels topologiques et espaces nucléaires* (Topological tensor products and nuclear spaces) and earned the degree in 1953. In 1953, he moved to the University of São Paulo in Brazil, at the beginning of 1955 he moved to the University of Kansas (Lawrence), and in 1957 he was invited to visit Harvard by Oscar Zariski, but the offer failed because he refused to sign a pledge promising not to work to overthrow the United States Government—a refusal that, he was warned, threatened to land him in prison. His mother died in 1957 from the tuberculosis that she contracted in camps for displaced persons. In 1958, he was appointed a Research Professor at the IHES, a new privately funded research institute, and remained there until 1970. Then he retired from scientific life after he found out that the IHES was partly funded by the military. In 1973, he joined as a Professor at the University of Montpellier and continued there until 1984. He then accepted a research position at the CNRS. Alexander formally retired from mathematics in 1988 and devoted himself to political and religious pursuits (first Buddhism and later, a more Catholic Christian vision). In 1991, he moved to the French village of Lasserre in the Pyrenees, where he lived in seclusion, still working on mathematics and his philosophical and religious thoughts until his death in 2014. Alexander's most productive period was from 1950 to 1970; his research created/extended the scope in several diverse fields such as modern algebraic geometry, commutative algebra, homological algebra, sheaf theory, cohomology, and category theory. Out of seventeen doctoral students he supervised, Pierre René Deligne (born 1944, Belgium) is most famous. In 1986, he wrote a 1000-page autobiographical manuscript, *Récoltes et semailles* (*Harvests and sowing*), which has been translated into several languages. In French the original manuscript was published in two volumes in January 2022, with additional texts by people of various professions who discuss certain aspects of the book. *The Grothendieck Festschrift*, published in 1990, was a three-volume collection of research papers to mark his sixtieth birthday in 1988. More than 20,000 pages of Alexander's mathematical and other writings are held at the University of Montpellier and remain unpublished. They have been digitized for preservation and are available in open access through the Institut Montpelliérain Alexander Grothendieck portal. Grothendieck had five children: a son with his landlady during his time in Nancy; three children, Johanna (1959), Alexander (1961), and Mathieu (1965), with his wife Mireille Dufour (about 1930–2008, born in France); and one child with Justine Skalba, with whom he lived in a commune in the early 1970s. In 1966, he received the Fields Medal for advances in algebraic geometry, homological algebra, and K-theory. In 1988, he declined the Crafoord Prize (after Alf Erik Holger Crafoord, 1908–1982, and his wife Anna-Greta Crafoord, 1914–1994, Sweden) with an open letter to the media. Grothendieck is considered by many to be one of the greatest mathematicians of the twentieth century.

In an obituary David Bryant Mumford (born 1937, England–USA) and John Torrence Tate Jr. (1925–2019, USA) wrote the following: Although mathematics became more and more abstract and general throughout the 20th century, it was Alexander Grothendieck who was the greatest master of this trend. His unique skill was to eliminate all unnecessary hypotheses and burrow into an area so deeply that its inner patterns on the most abstract level revealed themselves-and then, like a magician, show how the solution of old problems fell out in straightforward ways now that their real nature had been revealed.

21.4. Stephen Smale

He was born in Flint, Michigan, USA. He joined the University of Michigan in 1948. Smale was a marginal undergraduate student, getting mostly Bs, Cs, and even an F in nuclear physics in his sophomore and junior years. In spite of this performance, he was accepted as a graduate student of mathematics. Again, Smale performed poorly in his first years, earning a C average. At this point he received a letter from the department chair, Theophil Henry Hildebrandt, threatening to throw him out of the Michigan Ph.D. program if his grades did not improve. He began to take his studies more seriously and finally received his Ph.D. in 1957 for a thesis entitled *Regular Curves on Riemannian Manifolds*, written under the direction of Raoul Bott. He began his career as an instructor at the University of Chicago. In 1958, Smale astounded the mathematical world with a proof of a sphere eversion, that is, turning a sphere inside out without creating any crease. He made his reputation by proving the Poincaré conjecture (a simply connected closed 3-dimensional manifold is a 3-dimensional sphere) for all dimensions greater than or equal to 5; he later generalized the Poincaré conjecture in a 107-page paper that established the *h*-cobordism theorem. In 1960, Smale received a Sloan Research Fellowship and was appointed to the Berkeley mathematics faculty, moving to a professorship at Columbia the following year. In 1964, he returned to a professorship at Berkeley and continued until 1995. He became a Professor Emeritus at Berkeley in 1995 and took up a post as Professor at the City University of Hong Kong. From 2003 to 2012, Smale was a Professor at the Toyota Technological Institute at Chicago, a research institute closely affiliated with the University of Chicago. In 2009, he became a Distinguished University Professor at the City University of Hong Kong. His list of 48 Ph.D. students includes notable mathematicians Jacob Palis Jr. (born 1940, Brazil) and Morris William Hirsch (born 1933, USA). He is known for the generalized Poincaré conjecture, Handle decomposition, h-cobordism theorem, Homoclinic orbit, horseshoe map, Smale conjecture, Smale's 18 problems (in the spirit of the famous list of problems that Hilbert produced in 1900. It includes some of the original Hilbert problems, such as the Riemann hypothesis and the second half of Hilbert's sixteenth problem), Morse–Smale system, Morse–Smale diffeomorphism, Palais–Smale compactness condition (Richard Sheldon Palais, born 1931, USA), Blum–Shub–Smale machine (Lenore Carol Blum, born 1942, USA and Michael Ira Shub, born 1943, USA), Smale–Williams attractor (Robert Fones Williams, born 1928, USA), Morse–Palais lemma, Regular homotopy, Sard's theorem (Arthur Sard, 1909–1980, USA–Switzerland), sphere eversion, structural stability, Whitehead torsion (John Henry Constantine Whitehead 1904–1960, India–USA), and diffeomorphisms. He won the Fields Medal in 1966 for his work in low-dimensional topology, the same year he secured the Oswald Veblen Prize in Geometry; in 1988, Smale was the recipient of the Chauvenet Prize of the Mathematical Association of America (after William Chauvenet, 1820–1870, USA); in 1996 he was awarded the National Medal of Science by then President William Jefferson Clinton (born 1946); and in 2007, Smale was awarded the Wolf Prize in Mathematics. Smale has been awarded Honorary Degrees by the University of Warwick (1974), Queens University, Kingston, Ontario (1987), the University of Michigan (1996), Université Pierre et Marie Curie, Paris (1997), the City University of Hong Kong (1997), Rostov State University (1999), and the University of Genoa (2004). He has been made an Honorary Member of the Instituto de Matematica Pura e Aplicada, Rio de Janeiro (1990), Trinity Mathematical Society, Dublin (1991), Moscow Mathematical Society (1997), and the LMS (1998). Smale has always been politically active. He was involved in the Free Speech Movement with Mario Savio (1942–1996, USA) and participated in the protest against the Vietnam War. He even gave a speech on the steps of the Kremlin in 1966 in protest of U.S. policies in Vietnam. At one time he was subpoenaed by the House Un-American Activities Committee. He is ranked as one of the top five mineral collectors worldwide. Many of Smale's mineral specimens can be seen in the book *The Smale Collection: Beauty in Natural Crystals*.

22. Nice ICM 1970

This Congress was held in Nice, France, during 1–10 September 1970. The Congress was attended by 2811 participants from 60 countries. Olivier Guichard (1920–2004, France), Minister of National Education, declared the ICM in Nice open on Tuesday, 1 September 1970, at 9:30 am. Then, Henri Cartan, the President of the IMU, proposed electing Jean Leray (1906–1998, France), the Chairman of the Organizing Committee, as the President of the Congress and Paul Antoine Aristide Montel (1876–1975, France) as the Honorary President. Paul Montel and Jean Leray welcomed the members of Congress and thanked the people who had collaborated in the organization of the Congress. The Fields Medal Committee consisted of Henri Cartan (Chairman), Joseph Doob, Friedrich Hirzebruch, Lars Hörmander, Shokichi Iyanaga, Willard Milnor, Igor Rostislavovich Shafarevich, and Paul Turán (1910–1976, Hungary). Henri Cartan announced the committee's decision of four recipients of the medals in alphabetical order: Alan Baker (1939–2018, England), Heisuke Hironaka (born 1931. Japan), Sergei Petrovich Novikov (1938–2024, Russia), and John Griggs Thompson (born 1932, USA). The medals were presented by Olivier Guichard, who congratulated them. Unfortunately, Novikov was not able to be present at the ceremony to receive his medal (the Soviet authorities did not allow him to travel to the congress). Paul Turán reported on Baker's work on the theory of transcendental numbers and the applications to Diophantine equations and commented that "besides the worthy tendency to start a new theory in order to solve a problem it pays also to attack specific difficult problems directly". His work showed, at least in theory, that it is possible to determine all the solutions explicitly for a large class of equations. Grothendieck talked about Hironaka's work in algebraic geometry, particularly on the resolution of certain singularities and torus embeddings with implications in the theory of analytic functions, and complex and Kähler manifolds (after Erich Kähler, 1906–2000, Germany). Novikov became the first Soviet mathematician to be awarded the Fields Medal (he received the medal from Henri Cartan a year later on Vinogradov's 80th birthday and an IMU meeting in Moscow) on his work in geometric and algebraic topology. Michael Atiyah praised his work as having "great originality and very powerful technique both in its geometric and algebraic aspects". Richard Dagobert Brauer (1901–1977, Germany–USA) discussed Thompson's contribution to the classification of finite simple groups. There were 16 plenary talks, 242 invited expository talks, and 265 communications, which were printed in a booklet and distributed, i.e., there were no 10-minute talks. Among the expository lectures, Matiyasevich, a 23-year old mathematician from Russia, gave a negative solution of Hilbert's tenth problem (Matiyasevich's theorem). During the closing ceremony Jean Dieudonné for the future Congress suggested following the "Nice scheme", namely to have only 1-hour and 50-minute invited talks, plus written communications, but no 10-minute talks. However, two thirds of the Congress were in favor of abolishing short talks and returning to the previous tradition. Michael Atiyah, on behalf of the EC of the IMU, thanked all those who subsidized and organized the Congress. Then Henri Cartan announced the new EC of the IMU for the period 1971–1974: Chandrasekharan

(President), Adrian Albert and Lev Semyonovich Pontryagin (1908–1988, Russia) as Vice-Presidents, Otto Frostman as Secretary, and Michael Atiyah, Yukiyosi Kawada (1916–1993, Japan), Nicolaas Hendrik Kuiper (1920–1994, the Netherlands), Miron Nicolescu (1903–1975, Romania), and Edoardo Vesentini as members. Finally, Hans Arnold Heilbronn (1908–1975, Germany–Canada), on behalf of the Mathematical Society of Canada and on behalf of the University of British Columbia, invited the ICM to meet in 1974 in Vancouver, Canada. His offer was warmly accepted by the Congress. Henri Cartan then declared the ICM of 1970 closed.

22.1. *Alan Baker*

He was born in London, England, and educated at Stratford Grammar School, East London. From there he entered University College London, where he received a Bachelor of Science degree with First Class Honours in Mathematics in 1961. Then he moved to Trinity College at Cambridge to study for master and doctorate degrees with Davenport. During 1962–1965 he published eight research papers: Continued fractions of transcendental numbers (1962); On Mahler's classification of transcendental numbers (1964); Rational approximations to certain algebraic numbers (1964); On an analogue of Littlewood's Diophantine approximation problem (1964); Approximations to the logarithms of certain rational numbers (1964); Rational approximations to the cube root of 2 and other algebraic numbers (1964); Power series representing algebraic functions (1965); and On some Diophantine inequalities involving the exponential function (1965). In 1964, he became a Fellow of Trinity College for life. Alan Baker received his doctorate from the University of Cambridge for his thesis *Some Aspects of Diophantine Approximation* in 1965, written under the supervision of Harold Davenport. In 1966, he joined the faculty of Trinity College. He was a visiting scholar at the IAS, Princeton, in 1970. In 1974, he was a Visiting Professor at Stanford, the same year he was appointed Professor of Pure Mathematics at Cambridge University, a position he held until 2006 when he became an Emeritus Professor. Alan Baker was also a Visiting Professor at the University of Hong Kong in 1988, at the ETH Zurich in 1989, and at the Mathematical Sciences Research Institute (MSRI) in Berkeley, California, in 1993. Alan Baker made significant contributions in number theory, transcendence, linear forms in logarithms, Diophantine geometry, and Diophantine analysis. Alan Baker generalized the Gelfond–Schneider theorem (see Hilbert's seventh problem); he showed that if $\alpha_1, \cdots, \alpha_n$ are algebraic numbers (besides 0 or 1), and if $\beta_1, \cdots, \beta_n$ are irrational algebraic numbers such that the set $\{1, \beta_1, \cdots, \beta_n\}$ is linearly independent over the rational numbers, then the number $\alpha_1^{\beta_1}\alpha_2^{\beta_2}\cdots\alpha_n^{\beta_n}$ is transcendental. Among Alan Baker's famous books are *Transcendental Number Theory* (1975), *Transcendence Theory: Advances and Applications* (1977), *A Concise Introduction to the Theory of Numbers* (1984), (with Gisbert Wüstholz, born 1948, Germany), *Logarithmic Forms and Diophantine Geometry* (2007), and *A Comprehensive Course in Number Theory* (2012). In addition to the 1970 Fields Medal, Alan Baker received many honors, which include the Adams Prize (after John Couch Adams, 1819–1892, England) from the University of Cambridge (1972), election to the RSL (1973), an honorary doctorate from the Université Louis Pasteur Strasbourg (1998), an Honorary Fellow of University College London (1979), a Foreign Fellow of the Indian Academy of Science (1980), a Foreign Fellow of the NAS India (1993), a member of the Academia Europaea (1998), an Honorary Member of the Hungarian Academy of Sciences (2001), and a Fellow of the AMS (2012). In 1999 a conference was organized in Zurich to celebrate Alan Baker's 60th birthday. In appreciation Davenport once commented, "I had two very good students: Baker, to whom I would give a problem and he would return with a very good solution, and John Horton Conway (1937–2020, UK-USA), to whom I would give a problem and he would return with a very good solution to another problem".

22.2. Heisuke Hironaka

He was born in Yamaguchi, Japan. Hironaka's father ran a textile factory, and his mother was his father's third wife, as the first two died. Hironaka grew up in a family of fifteen children. He was the second eldest, having one older sister. Hironaka attended elementary school and then middle school, where he began to develop a liking for mathematics. Hironaka attended the boys' junior high school in Yanai; for this, he had to take a 30-minute train journey to school every day. He was inspired to study mathematics after listening to a lecture by a mathematics professor of Hiroshima University at his junior high school. In 1948, Hironaka applied to study mathematics at Hiroshima University, but was unsuccessful. In 1949, he applied to study physics at Kyoto University and was accepted. A main influence on Hironaka during his time at Kyoto was from Yasuo Akizuki (1902–1984, Japan), who was a pioneer of modern algebra in Japan. He was conferred both his Bachelor of Science in 1954 and his Master of Science in 1956 from Kyoto University. In 1956, Oscar Zariski visited Kyoto University; he advised Hironaka to go to Harvard University for further study. In 1957, he joined Harvard University for his doctorate, with Oscar Zariski as his thesis advisor. Hironaka became a friend of Grothendieck, who spent the academic year 1958–1959 at Harvard. He invited Hironaka to the IHES in 1959–1960, where he was only a visiting fellow. Hironaka was awarded a Ph.D. from Harvard in 1960 for his thesis *On the Theory of Birational Blowing-up*. He had already published three papers before submitting his thesis—On the arithmetic genera and the effective genera of algebraic curves (1957), A note on algebraic geometry over ground rings: The invariance of Hilbert characteristic functions under the specialization process (1958), and A generalized theorem of Krull-Seidenberg (Wolfgang Krull, 1899–1971, Germany and Abraham Seidenberg, 1916–1988, USA) on parameterized algebras of finite type (1960). Then, he joined as Associate Professor of Mathematics at Brandeis University from 1960 to 1963. Also, in 1960 he married Hironaka Wakako (born 1934, Japan), a Japanese writer and politician. She served four terms in the House of Councillors, the upper house of the National Diet, from 1986 until 2010. They had one son and one daughter. Next Hironaka was appointed to Columbia University, and then to Harvard in 1968. In 1975, Hironaka returned to Japan, where he was appointed a Professor at the Research Institute for Mathematical Sciences (RIMS) at Kyoto University. He became the Director of the Research Institute in Kyoto from 1983 to 1985; in 1991 he retired and became Professor Emeritus. In 1996, he became the President of Yamaguchi University and held this position until 2002. He then became Academic Director of the University of Creation, a private university in Takasaki, Gunma, Japan. His work includes the following: Hironaka's example, which shows that a deformation of Kähler manifolds need not be Kähler (1960);

proof that any algebraic variety can be replaced by (more precisely is birationally equivalent to) a similar variety that has no singularities (1964), for which he combined his commutative algebra experience from Kyoto, geometry of polynomials from Harvard, and globalization technique from the IHES, and his work generalized that of Zariski; and a course on the theory of several complex variables in 1977, and his lecture notes were written up and published in the book *Introduction to Analytic Spaces* (Japanese). Hironaka has been active in promoting mathematical education, particularly in Japan and South Korea. He has written or co-authored 26 books on mathematics and other topics. He has been awarded the Asahi Prize (1967) Japanese, Fields Medal (1970), Japan Academy Prize (1970), Guggenheim Fellowship (1971) after John Simon Guggenheim (1867–1941), Order of Culture (1975) Japanese, Person of Cultural Merit (1975) Japanese, Honorary Doctor of the Complutense University of Madrid (1981), Legion of Honour (2004) French, and Harvard Centennial Medal (2011). Hironaka has been elected to the Japan Academy, the AAAS, and academies in France, Russia, Korea, and Spain.

22.3. *Sergei Petrovich Novikov*

He was born in Gorky, Soviet Union (now Nizhny Novgorod, Russia). He grew up in a family of many talented mathematicians. In fact, besides his parents, his uncle Mstislav Vsevolodovich Keldysh was an outstanding mathematician and a leading Soviet scientist, working as the President of the USSR Academy of Sciences for many years. He had two elder brothers and two younger sisters. After completing his schooling, in 1955, Novikov entered the Faculty of Mathematics and Mechanics of Moscow State University and in 1960 received the Student Diploma on his dissertation entitled *Homotopy Properties of Thom Complexes,* written under the supervision of Mikhail Mikhailovich Postnikov (1927–2004, Russia), and then became a research student at the Steklov Institute of Mathematics in Moscow. Before graduation, in 1959, he published his important research paper *Cohomology of the Steenrod Algebra,* in the Journal *Doklady Akademii Nauk SSSR.* In 1962, he married Eleonora Tsoi (Novikova), and they had thre children. In 1963, Novikov was appointed to the staff of the Steklov Institute of Mathematics, where he continued until 1975. The following year, he was also appointed to the Department of Differential Geometry at Moscow University. In 1964, he received the Moscow Mathematical Society Award for young mathematicians and defended the thesis *Differentiable Sphere Bundles* to secure the equivalent to a Ph.D. degree in Physics and Mathematics. In 1965, he received a Doctor of Science degree in physics and mathematics for the thesis *Homotopy equivalent Smooth Manifolds,* also written under the supervision of Postnikov. The same year he joined the staff at the Department Mathematics and Mechanics of Moscow State University. In 1966, Novikov became a Corresponding Member of the Academy of Sciences of the Soviet Union. In 1971, he became Head of the Mathematics Division at the Lev Davidovich Landau (1908–1968, Russia) Institute for Theoretical Physics of the USSR Academy of Sciences and continued until 1993, and then became Principal Researcher at the same institute. In 1983, Novikov was also appointed the Head of the Department of Higher Geometry and Topology at Moscow State University. In 1984, he became the Head of the Group in Geometry and Topology of the Steklov Mathematical Institute of the

Academy of Sciences of the USSR. In 1985, Novikov became the President of the Moscow Mathematical Society, where he succeeded Kolmogorov, and remained in that role until 1996. Then, he moved to University of Maryland at College Park (USA), but retained close links with Russia, with research appointments at Moscow University, at the Landau Institute for Theoretical Physics, and as Head of the Geometry and Topology research groups at the Steklov Institute. In June 2000, June 2001, and November 2002, Novikov spent some time in Korea at the Institute For Advanced Study (Seoul, Korea), and in 2009 for several weeks he was at the Newton Institute for Mathematical Sciences, Cambridge, UK. He worked and enriched several different fields: geometry and topology (algebraic, homotopy, and differential topology, foliations, and topological phenomena in variational calculus); dynamical systems; mathematical and theoretical physics (the methods of algebraic, symplectic, and Riemannian geometry, topology and dynamical systems in general relativity, completely integrable systems and solitons, magnetoresistance in metals, field theory, quantum theory and spectral theory of operators on lattices and graphs). Novikov supervised 39 doctoral students and published more than 190 research articles. He was a member of the editorial boards of many leading scientific journals. In the literature Novikov is noted for the Adams–Novikov spectral sequence, Novikov conjecture, Novikov ring, Novikov–Shubin invariant (Mikhail Aleksandrovich Shubin, 1944–2020, Russia), Novikov–Veselov equation (Alexander Petrovich Veselov (born 1955, Russia), Novikov's compact leaf theorem, and the Wess–Zumino–Novikov–Witten model (Julius Erich Wess, 1934–2007, Styria–Germany; Bruno Zumino, 1923–2014, Italy–USA; Edward Witten, born 1951, USA). Novikov received many honors for his outstanding work: the Lenin Prize in 1967 (after Vladimir Lenin 1870–1924, Russia), became the first Soviet mathematician to be awarded the Fields Medal in 1970, the Lobachevsky Medal in 1981 (after Nikolai Ivanovich Lobachevsky, 1792–1856, Russia), the Wolf Prize in 2005, and the Lomonosov Gold Medal in 2020. Many societies honored Novikov with membership, such as the following: in 1981, he was elected a full member of the USSR Academy of Sciences (RAS since 1991), LMS (Honorary Member, 1987), Serbian Academy of Sciences and Arts (Honorary Member, 1988), Accademia dei Lincei (Foreign Member, 1991), Academia Europaea (Member, 1993), the United States NAS (Foreign Associate, 1994), Pontifical Academy of Sciences (member, 1996), European Academy of Sciences (fellow, 2003), and Montenegrin Academy of Sciences and Arts (Honorary Member, 2011). He was also awarded honorary doctorates from the University of Athens (1988), University of Tel Aviv (1990), and University of Loughborough (2016). He was a very influential mathematician.

22.4. John Griggs Thompson

He was born in Ottawa, Kansas, USA. After schooling Thompson received his Bachelor of Arts from Yale University in 1955. Then, he joined the University of Chicago to undertake research and completed his doctorate in 1959. His doctoral thesis was entitled *A Proof That a Finite Group with a Fixed-Point-Free Automorphism of Prime Order is Nilpotent*, which was written under the supervision of Mac Lane. From the title of his thesis, it is clear that he had proved the 60-year-old unsolved Frobenius conjecture that a finite group with an automorphism that does not fix any group element is necessarily nilpotent. This achievement was touted in *The New York Times*. He spent almost two years with the faculty at the University of Chicago; then in 1961–1962, he became an assistant at Harvard University. In 1962, Thompson was appointed Professor at the University of Chicago. In 1968, he accepted a fellowship at University College, Cambridge, in England. In 1970, he was appointed Rouse Ball Professor (after Walter William Rouse Ball, 1850–1925, England) of Pure Mathematics at Cambridge. In 1993, Thompson moved to the Mathematics Department of the University of Florida as a Graduate Research Professor. He is currently a Professor Emeritus of pure mathematics at the University of Cambridge and a Professor Emeritus of mathematics at the University of Florida. In 1963, jointly with Walter Feit (1930–2004, Austria–USA), he proved that all nonabelian finite simple groups are of even order. They published this result in *Solvability of Groups of Odd Order*, a 250-page paper that appeared in the*Pacific Journal of Mathematics* 13 (1963), 775–1029. This result stunned the world of mathematics, but it also led mathematicians to believe that a classification of finite simple groups might prove possible. Another major early step by Thompson towards the classification of finite simple groups was his classification of the finite simple groups in which every soluble subgroup has a soluble normalizer. In 1974, Thompson gave the classification of N-groups in six papers (in the *Bulletin of the AMS* and the *Pacific Journal of Mathematics*) totaling about 400 pages. He also needed his earlier results, which brought the total length up to more than 700 pages. The Thompson group Th is one of the 26 sporadic finite simple groups. Thompson also made major contributions to the inverse Galois problem. He found a criterion for a finite group to be a Galois group, which in particular implies that the monster simple group is a Galois group. Several results that are known with his name are the Feit–Thompson theorem, McKay–Thompson series (John Keith Stuart McKay, 1939–2022, Britain-Canada), Thompson factorization, Thompson order formula, Thompson subgroup, Thompson transitivity theorem, and Thompson uniqueness theorem. He has supervised 25 doctoral students and published more than 110 research papers. Thompson has received many awards for his outstanding contributions to mathematics: the Cole Prize in 1965 (after Frank Nelson Cole, 1861–1926, USA), Fields Medal in 1970, Senior Berwick Prize in 1982 (after William Edward Hodgson Berwick, 1888–1944, Britain), Sylvester Medal in 1985, Wolf Prize in 1992, Poincaré Medal in 1992, National Medal of Science in 2000, Abel Prize in 2008, and De Morgan Medal in 2013. The honorary doctorate degrees that Thompson has received are from Yale University in 1980, the University of Chicago in 1985, the University of Oxford in 1987, and Ohio State University in 2008. In 1971, he was elected to the United States NAS, and in 1979 he became a Fellow of the RSL.

23. Vancouver ICM 1974

This Congress was held in Vancouver, Canada, during 21–29 August 1974. This was the second time in Canada after exactly fifty years. The Congress was attended by 3121 participants from 60 countries (1271 from the USA). In the opening ceremony Chandrasekharan proposed that Harold Scott MacDonald Coxeter (1907–2003, England–Canda) be elected President of the Congress by acclamation. Coxeter then called Honourable Walter Stewart Owen (1904–1981), the Lieutenant Governor of British Columbia, who welcomed members of the Congress to Canada and to British Columbia. Professor Coxeter in his presidential address to Congress mentioned that "The present generation has been engulfed by a wave of anti-intellectualism, with the result that most universities are short of students. Young people find that the problem of looking for a job is not facilitated by a university education. The idea of art for art's sake is less prevalent than it used to be, and pure mathematics is abandoned in favour of applied mathematics, statistics, or computing". To emphasize the importance of mathematics, he recalled the famous quote of Hermann Minkowski (1864–1909, Poland–Germany), "The purpose of life is to behold the truth, to understand it well, and to expound it perfectly". The Fields Medal Committee consisted of Chandrasekharan (Chairman), John Frank Adams (1930–1989, UK), Kodaira, Pontryagin, Bernard Malgrange (1928–2024, France), Andrzej Mostowski (1913–1975, Poland–Ukraine–Canada), John Tate, and Zygmund. The Committee, as a surprise to everyone, elected only two names: Enrico Bombieri (born 1940, Italy) and David Bryant Mumford. The medals were presented by Honourable Walter Stewart Owen. Chandrasekharan reported on Bombieri's achievements in number theory, univalent functions, several complex variables, partial differential equations, and algebraic geometry, concluding that "Bombieri's versatility and strength have combined to create many original patterns of ideas". John Tate referred to Mumford's work as a "tremendously successful multi–pronged attack on problems of the existence and structure of varieties of moduli. Besides this he has made several important contributions to the theory of algebraic surfaces". There were 17 one-hour invited addresses, 157 half-hour invited addresses delivered within the sections, and 565 short ten-minute communications. Since there was a controversy in the section of invited lecturers, out of 42 Soviet mathematicians invited to the congress, only 22 attended. During the closing session Coxeter called on Chandrasekharan, the President of the IMU, to announce the new EC for a term of four years beginning 1 January 1975: Deane Montgomery (President), John William Scott Cassels (1922–2015, England) and Miron Nicolescu as Vice-Presidents, and Jacques-Louis Lions (1928–2001, France), Enrico Bombieri, Martin Kneser (1928–2004, Germany), Olli Erkki Lehto (1925–2020, Finland), Masayoshi Nagata, and Pontryagin as members. Chandrasekharan also said "The Congress has brought together mathematicians from many lands, united in a friendship which stems from a common devotion to mathematics, transcending the stresses of politics, and happily free from the strains of competitive sport". Then Rolf Nevanlinna, on behalf of the Finnish National Committee of Mathematics, invited the Congress to hold its next meeting in

Helsinki, which was accepted by acclamation. Coxeter then declared the Vancouver Congress closed.

23.1. Enrico Bombieri

He was born in Milan, Italy. Bombieri became interested in mathematics, particularly in number theory, when he was just thirteen years old. He came in contact with Giovanni Ricci (1904–1973, Italy), who made significant contributions in number theory, differential geometry, mathematical analysis, and the theory of series. Ricci encouraged Bombieri, so his foundation became sound in classical mathematics. He published his first mathematical paper, concerning the solution to a Diophantine equation, in 1957, while still in high school. In 1963, he received a Ph.D. degree in mathematics from the Universitá degli Studi di Milano under the supervision of Ricci, and then he studied at Trinity College, Cambridge, with Davenport. During this period he produced several significant results in number theory and complex analysis, including the growth of the remainder term in the elementary proof of the prime number theorem. Bombieri was an Assistant Professor (1963–1965) and then a Full Professor (1965–1966) at the Universitá di Cagliari, at the Universitá di Pisa in (1966–1974), and then at the Scuola Normale Superiore di Pisa in (1974–1977). From Pisa, he emigrated in 1977 to the USA, where he became a Professor at the School of Mathematics at the IAS, Princeton, and in 2011, Bombieri became Professor Emeritus. He also held positions at the University of Cagliari, the University of Pisa, and the Scuola Normale Superiore in Pisa. He has more than 140 publications and supervised six doctoral students. In 1966, he received the Caccioppoli Prize (after Renato Caccioppoli, 1904–1959, Italy) and in 1974 the Fields Medal for his major contributions to the study of prime numbers, univalent functions and the local Bieberbach conjecture, the theory of functions of several complex variables, and the theory of partial differential equations and minimal surfaces, in particular, the solution of Bernstein's problem in higher dimensions. He is also a recipient of several awards, including the Feltrinelli Prize in 1976 (after Antonio Feltrinelli, 1887–1942, Italy), the Balzan Prize in 1980, the Cavaliere di Gran Croce al Merito della Repubblica (the Knight Grand Cross of Merit of the Republic) Italy in 2002, the Pythagoras Prize in 2006, the AMS Doob Prize for his book *Heights in Diophantine Geometry* in 2008, the King Faisal Prize (established in 1976) in 2010, and the Crafoord Prize in 2020. He is a member, or foreign member, of several learned academies, including the Accademia Nazionale dei Lincei (elected 1976), the FAS (elected 1984), the United States NAS (elected 1996), the Academia Europaea, the French Académie des Sciences (Institut de France), the Accademia Nazionale (Rome), and the Royal Swedish Academy, and a Fellow of the AAAS. Bombieri, also accomplished in arts, explored for wild orchids and other plants as a hobby in the Alps when a young man. Frederick Justin Almgren (1933–1997, USA) and Montgomery described Bombieri abilities as follows: He has repeatedly demonstrated an ability to quickly master essentials of a complicated new field, to select important problems which are accessible, and to apply intense energy and insight to their solution, making liberal use of deep results of other mathematicians in widely differing areas. The breadth of his mathematical knowledge is clearly visible to those who know him and his work. He is also a fine writer of mathematics, and his lectures . . . are recognised for clarity which increases with the subtlety of the mathematical idea being explained.

23.2. David Bryant Mumford

He was born in Worth, Sussex, England, to an English father and American mother. His father started an experimental school in Tanzania and worked for the then newly created United Nations in 1945. Mumford enrolled at Phillips Exeter Academy, where in 1953 he received a Westinghouse Science Talent Search Prize for his relay-based computer project. Then he went to Harvard College and received a Bachelor of Arts degree in 1957 with Magna Cum Laude (with great praise); he was a Putnam Fellow in 1955 and 1956. Next Mumford became a Junior Fellow at Harvard University from 1958 to 1961. He completed his Ph.D. in 1961, with a thesis entitled *Existence of the Moduli Scheme for Curves of any Genus*, written under the supervisor of Oscar Zariski. In 1959, he married the poet Erika Jentsch Mumford (1935–1988, Switzerland–USA), with whom he has four children, and then married the artist Jenifer Gordon Mumford (1937–2018, USA). Mumford has written "I have been strongly supported throughout my career by the tireless love and understanding of two wonderful women". After graduating from Harvard, he was appointed to the staff there (1961–1962) and then to Assistant Professor (1962–1963). During 1962–1963, Mumford became a member of IAS, Princeton, and Visiting Professor at the University of Tokyo. He then came back to Harvard University as Associate Professor (1963–1967), and then he was appointed Professor (1967–1977). Next, Mumford became Eugene Higgins (1860–1948, USA) Professor. He was Chairman of the Mathematics Department at Harvard University from 1981 to 1984 and MacArthur Fellow (after John Roderick MacArthur, 1920–1984, USA) from 1987 to 1992. Currently, he is Emeritus Professor in the Mathematics Department at Harvard University and in the Division of Applied Mathematics at Brown University. Mumford was a Visiting Professor at the Tata Institute of Fundamental Research ((1967–1968) and (1978–1979)), Nuffield Professor at the University of Warwick (1970–1971), and Visiting Professor at the IHES (1976–1977). He has made significant contributions in algebraic geometry and then in research into vision and pattern theory. Mumford has more than 125 publications, has supervised 50 doctorate students, and has written several very influential monographs: *Geometric Invariant Theory* (1965, 1982, 1994); *Abelian Varieties* (1970, 1974); *Algebraic Geometry I: Complex Projective Varieties* (1976); *Tata Lectures on Theta* (Part I, 1982, Part II, 1983, Part III, 1991); *Filtering, Segmentation and Depth* (1993); and Neuronal Architectures for Pattern-theoretic Problems (1994). He has a long list of his results, which are often referenced in the literature: the Castelnuovo–Mumford regularity, Mumford's compactness theorem, Haboush's theorem, also known as the Mumford conjecture (William Joseph Haboush, born 1942, USA), the Hilbert–Mumford criterion, the stable mapping class group, the Mumford–Tate group, the Mumford measure, the Mumford vanishing theorem, the theta representation, the Manin–Mumford conjecture (Yuri Ivanovich Manin, 1937–2023, Russia–Germany), the Horrocks–Mumford bundle (Geoffrey Horrocks, 1932–2012, UK), the Deligne–Mumford moduli space of stable curves, the algebraic stack, the moduli scheme, Prym varieties, stable maps, and the Mumford–Shah energy functional (Jayant Shah, USA). He is the recipient of several awards and honors: Fields Medal (1974), elected to the United States NAS (1975), Honorary Fellow of the Tata Institute of Fundamental Research (1978), Honorary Doctorate of Science degree from the University of Warwick (1983), Foreign Member of the Accademia Nazionale dei Lincei (1991), Honorary Member of the LMS (1995), elected to the APS (1997), honorary doctorate degree from the Norwegian University of Science and Technology (2000), honorary doctorate degree from Rockefeller University (2001), Longuet-Higgins Prize (Hugh Christopher Longuet-Higgins, 1923–2004, UK) in 2005 and 2009, Wolf Prize in Mathematics (2008), Foreign Member of the RSL (2008), honorary doctorate from Brown University (2011), Banco Bilbao Vizcaya Argentaria (BBVA) Foundation Frontiers of Knowledge Award in the Basic Sciences category (2012), and Honoris Causa from the University of Hyderabad, India (2012).

24. Helsinki ICM 1978

This Congress was held in Helsinki, Finland, during 15–23 August 1978. The Congress was attended by 3038 registered participants from 83 countries (USA 612, France 281, Germany 261, Finland 223, Japan 192, UK 173, and Canada 138). During the opening ceremony Montgomery, the President of the IMU, opened the proceedings by proposing that Olli Lehto be elected President of the Congress by acclamation. Olli Lehto in his presidential address proposed Rolf Nevanlinna be elected Honorary President of this Congress, which was warmly accepted. After the welcome lectures of the President and Vice-President, Montgomery, the Chairman of the Fields Medal Committee, first mentioned the origin of the medals and then named the members of the Committee: Lennart Carleson, Martin Maximilian Emil Eichler (1912–1992, Germany–Switzerland), Ioan Mackenzie James (born 1928, England), Jürgen Kurt Moser (1928–1999, Germany–Switzerland), Yuri Vasilyevich Prokhorov (1929–2013, Russia), Béla Szökefalvi-Nagy (1913–1998, Romania–Hungary), and Jacques Tits (1930–2021, Belgium–France). He said the Committee had unanimously selected the following four individuals for the award: Pierre René Deligne, Charles Louis Fefferman (born 1949, USA), Gregori Aleksandrovitch Margulis (born 1946, Russia–USA), and Daniel Gray Quillen (1940–2011, USA). Rolf Nevanlinna, Honorary President of the Congress, presented the medals to Deligne, Fefferman, and Quillen. Unfortunately, Margulis was not granted an exit visa and was unable to attend the Congress (he was allowed to go to the West [Bonn, Germany] for the first time in 1979 for a three-month visit that was arranged by Hirzebruch. During that visit, Jacques Tits came to Bonn and at a small ceremony presented him the award.) Another related point of disputation was the jurisdiction over Fields Medals for Soviet mathematicians. After 1978 the Soviet Union put forward a demand that the USSR Academy of Sciences approve all Soviet candidates for the Fields Medal before it was awarded to them. However, the IMU insisted that the decisions regarding invited speakers and Fields medalists be kept under exclusive jurisdiction of the ICM committees appointed for that purpose by the IMU. After the opening ceremony Nicholas Michael Katz (born 1943, USA) explained that "Deligne's work centers around the remarkable relations, first envisioned by Weil, which exist between the cohomological structure of algebraic varieties over the complex numbers, and the diophantine structure of algebraic varieties over finite fields"; For the laudation of Fefferman, Lennart Carleson pointed out that "during the 1960s and 1970s, classical analysis was one of the most successful fields in all of mathematics. The reasons for this are the unification of methods from harmonic analysis, complex variables, and differential equations, and the discovery of the correct generalization to several variables. In many problems complications cannot be avoided, and intricate combinatorial arguments rather than polished theories are at the center. This general description also summarizes the work of Charles Fefferman. In an eminent way he masters these techniques"; Jacques Tits reported that Marguis' work " belonged to combinatorics, differential geometry, ergodic theory, the theory of dynamical systems, and the theory of discrete subgroups of real and p-adic Lie groups"; and in presenting the work of Quillen, Ioan James said "D.G.

Quillen's contributions to algebra are outstanding in their inventiveness, conceptual richness, and technical virtuosity. He is the prime architect of the higher algebraic K–theory, and is perhaps his finest achievement". There were 17 one-hour plenary addresses, 121 forty-five-minute addresses delivered within the sections, and about 500 ten-minute communications whose abstracts were printed in a booklet, and for the first time 40 posters were presented. Among the plenary lectures, André Weil talked on "History of Mathematics: Why and How", which was attended by more than 3000 participants. He mentioned that mathematics not only has a history, but it has a long one, which has been written about at least since Eudemus of Rhodes (about 370–300 BC, Greece). He also quoted Leibniz: Its use is not just that History may give everyone his due and that others may look forward to similar praise, but also that the art of discovery be promoted and its method known through illustrious examples. This passion for the history of the subject is a peculiarity that distinguishes mathematics from other sciences. At the closing ceremony, John Cassels, Vice-President of the IMU, announced the new EC for a term of four years beginning 1 January 1979: Lennart Carleson (President), Masayoshi Nagata and Yuri Prokhorov as Vice-Presidents, Jacques-Louis Lions as Secretary, and Enrico Bombieri, John Cassels, Martin Kneser, Olli Lehto, Czeslaw Olech (1931–2015, Poland), and Montgomery as members. For the ICM 1982 out of four competing countries Argentina, Germany, Israel, and Poland, Poland was chosen. Kazimierz Urbanik (1930–2005, Poland), on behalf of the Polish National Committee of Mathematics, invited the next ICM to Warsaw. He said, Poland, the home country of Stefan Banach (1892–1945), is eager to receive the world-wide mathematical community. His invitation was accepted by acclamation. Finally, Olli Lehto declared the 1978 ICM closed. Throughout the Congress an inspiring event was a book exhibition organized by Suomalainen Kirjakauppa (the largest bookshop chain in Finland).

24.1. Pierre René Deligne

He was born in Etterbeek, Brussels, Belgium. He was the youngest of his parents' three children. Even before he began his primary education during 1950–1956 at Schaerbeek (Belgium), Pierre was learning mathematics from his brother. When he was in primary school his brother taught him the formula for solving quadratic equations. During 1956–1962, Pierre had his secondary schooling at the Athénée Adolphe Max in Brussels. During this period his brother gave him some notes about solving cubic and quartic equations, including the famous complicated formula for cubics, which Pierre found very interesting; one of his teachers Jeff Nijs gave him a copy of Bourbaki's *Set Theory*, and he was delighted to have his "first real mathematical book"; a friend of his family gave Pierre a book on complex variables, which gave him "tremendous joy"; and Jeff Nijs introduced Pierre to Jacques Tits, with a request to take good care of Pierre. He attended Tits' courses and seminars at the university. After completing secondary schooling, Pierre joined the Université Libre de Bruxelles (ULB) as an undergraduate. In November 1964 Tits took Pierre to Paris to attend a Bourbaki seminar and introduce him to Grothendieck, who was visiting at the ENS in Paris. Pierre spent the academic year 1965–1966 at the ENS in Paris. He received his Licence en mathématiques (B.A.) in 1966. He continued to study for his doctorate at the ULB. During 1967–1968, he was a junior scientist at the

Fond National de la Recherche Scientifique in Brussels, at the same time being a guest at the IHES, where he worked with Grothendieck. In 1968, Pierre was awarded by the ULB his Doctorat en mathématiques for the thesis *Théoréme de Lefschetz et critères de dégénérescence de suites spectrales* (Lefschetz's theorem and criteria for degeneracy of spectral sequences), written under the supervision of Grothendieck. During 1968–1970 he was a visiting member at the IHES and during 1970–1984 a permanent member at the IHES. In 1972, he also received the equivalent of a Ph.D. from the University of Paris-Sud (France). In 1980, Pierre married Elena Vladimirovna Alexeeva, whom he met on one of his visits to Russia; they have two children. In 1984, Pierre joined as Professor at the IAS, Princeton, and became Emeritus in 2008. His work is best described by Peter Clive Sarnak (born 1953, South Africa–USA): There are very few mathematicians whose impact on modern mathematics comes close to that of Deligne. His research in algebraic geometry and arithmetic geometry have shaped these fields and led him to the solution of a number of long-standing problems, including the Weil Conjectures (which are the analogues of the notorious Riemann Hypothesis for varieties over finite fields) [A solution of the three Weil conjectures was given by Deligne in 1974] and the celebrated Ramanujan Conjecture in the theory of modular forms. Deligne's foundational contributions range from the above fields to representation theory of groups, differential equations and monodromy, topology . . . Many of the techniques and tools that he developed either in these papers or in response to questions posed to him (he is very approachable and generous) are at the bottom of much of the exciting research that is going in these fields today. Deligne's style is that of wanting to understand in simple and general terms things that are fundamental but appear to be very complex. His development of new insights and methods, as well as the solution of long-standing problems, follow naturally from this point of view. Of course, his striking success has a lot to do with his tremendous mathematical talent and especially his ability to think abstractly. He has published more than 100 research papers and supervised three doctoral students. Pierre has been showered with several prizes and honors, including the François Deruyts Prize (1974) awarded by the Belgium Royal Academy of Sciences; the Poincaré Medal (1974); a De Leeuw–Damry–Bourlart Prize (1975) from the Belgian National Science Foundation; the Fields Medal (1978); Membre associé étranger, Académie des Sciences, Paris (1978); Foreign Honorary Member, AAAS (1978); the Crafoord Prize (1988); Doctor honoris causa of the Vrije Universiteit Brussel (1989); Membre associé, Académie Royale de Belgique (1994); Doctor honoris causa of Ecole Normale Supérieure (1995); Honorary member of the Moscow Mathematical Society (1995); Honorary member of the LMS (2003); Foreign member, Accademia nazionale dei Lincei (2003); the Balzan Prize (1 million Swiss francs) in Mathematics (2004); a conference on the occasion of his sixty-first birthday took place at the IAS (2005); Foreign Associate of the United States NAS (2007); the Belgian post office issued a postage stamp in his honor (2007); the Wolf Prize (2008); Foreign Member of the RSAS (2009); member of the APS (2009); the Abel Prize (2013); and Foreign Member of the RAS (2016). "He doesn't own a car and bicycles everywhere, keeping his right pant leg perennially tucked into his sock. He has quite possibly never been seen in a suit, favouring instead well-worn sweaters in earth tones. In Princeton's flash rainstorms he has been known to strip down to the waist to minimise the damage, though he does not take this strategy to the logical extreme".

24.2. Charles Louis Fefferman

He was born in Washington, D.C., USA, to a Jewish family. Charles was a child prodigy: at the age of nine he read a fourth-grade mathematics textbook in a day or two, a fifth-grade textbook also in a day or two, and so on, and mastered calculus before the age of twelve. He entered Takoma Park Junior High School in 1962 but never went to high school for he headed to the University of Maryland, College Park, in 1963 when he was just fourteen years old. At the age of 15, when in his second year of study, he wrote his first mathematics paper *Cardinally maximal sets of nonequivalent order types*, which was published in the journal *Mathematical Logic Quarterly* in 1967. Another of his papers *A Radon-Nikodym theorem for finitely additive set functions* was also published in 1967 in the *Pacific Journal of Mathematics*. In 1966, at the age of 17, he graduated with a Bachelor of Science, with the highest distinction, majoring in mathematics and physics. Charles was awarded a 3-year National Science Foundation Fellowship to undertake research. Then, he moved to Princeton University and received his Ph.D. degree in 1969 for his thesis entitled *Inequalities for Strongly Singular Convolution Operators* , written under the supervision of Elias Menachem Stein (1931–2018, Belgium–USA). Based on his thesis work, Charles published a paper in the journal *Acta Mathematica* 124(1970), 9–36. He lectured at Princeton for the years 1969–1970 and then accomplish a full professorship at the University of Chicago at the age of 22, making him the youngest Full Professor ever appointed in the USA. Charles returned to Princeton in 1974, and at the age of 25, became a Full Professor, the youngest person to be promoted to the title. In 1975, he married Julie Anne Albert (USA), and they have two daughters. During 1999–2002 he headed the mathematics department at Princeton University, and Currently he is the Herbert E. Jones, Jr.' 43 University Professor of Mathematics. Charles has contributed several innovations that revised the study of multidimensional complex analysis by finding correct generalizations of classical low-dimensional results. He has also worked on partial differential equations and Fourier analysis, in particular convergence, multipliers, divergence, singular integrals, Hardy spaces, and harmonic analysis, and explored their application to a wide range of fields including fluid dynamics, spectral geometry, and mathematical physics. He has published more than 220 research papers and supervised 26 doctoral students and has made major contributions through his editorial work for several prestigious mathematical journals. He has visited several universities, including the California Institute of Technology (Caltech), Courant Institute of Mathematical Sciences, University of Paris, Mittag-Leffler Institute, Weizmann Institute, and University of Madrid. Charles has a younger brother Robert Fefferman, who received his bachelor's degree in mathematics from the University of Maryland in 1972 and his Ph.D. from Princeton University in 1975 for his thesis *A Theory of Entropy in Fourier Analysis*. On his work Charles has received several awards, including the Alan Tower Waterman (1892–1967, USA) Award in 1976 (the first person to received this award); Fields Medal in 1978; Stefan Bergman (1895–1977, Poland–USA) Prize in 1992; Bôcher Memorial Prize in

2008; Wolf Prize in 2017; and BBVA Foundation Frontiers of Knowledge Award in 2021.

24.3. Gregori Aleksandrovitch Margulis

He was born in Moscow, Russia, to a Russian family of Lithuanian Jewish descent. Gregori was educated at Moscow High School, graduating in 1962. The same year he won the silver medal at the International Mathematical Olympiad (IMO) and began his undergraduate studies at Moscow State University, and was awarded his first degree in 1967. Gregori continued at Moscow State University for his postgraduate studies, and in 1968 received the Young Mathematicians Prize from the Moscow Mathematical Society in 1968. In 1970, Gregori was awarded the degree of Candidate of Science (equivalent to Ph.D.) for the thesis *On Some Problems in the Theory of U-systems*, written under the supervision of Yakov Grigorevich Sinai (born 1935, Russia–USA). At the Institute for Problems in Information Transmission, he was a junior scientific worker during 1970–1974, senior scientific worker during 1974–1986, and in 1986 he became a leading scientific worker. Between 1988 and 1991 Gregori made several visits to the Max Planck Institute for Mathematics (MPIM) in Bonn, the IHES and Collége de France, Harvard University, and the IAS, Princeton. In 1991 he joined Yale University as a Chair, and currently he is Erastus Lyman De Forest (1834–1888, USA) Professor Emeritus of Mathematics. His early work with David Kazhdan (born 1946, Russia–Israel–USA) originated the Kazhdan–Margulis theorem, a basic result on discrete groups. His superrigidity theorem from 1975 clarified an area of classical conjectures about the characterization of arithmetic groups amongst lattices in Lie groups. His other work includes combining probabilistic ideas with p-adic analysis and algebraic geometric ideas to prove the Selberg–Piatetskii-Shapiro (Ilya Piatetski-Shapiro, 1929–2009, Russia–Israel) conjecture, which affirms that lattices in higher-rank Lie groups are arithmetic, a question whose origins date back to Poincaré, and proving the full conjecture of Alexander Oppenheim (1903–1997, Britain), which he proposed in 1929 concerning the representations of numbers by real quadratic forms in several variables. Gregori has also introduced methods from ergodic theory into Diophantine approximation. He has published more than 130 research papers and two books and produced 22 doctoral students. Gregori has received many awards for his work, including the Fields Medal in 1978, the Wolf Prize in Mathematics in 2005, and the Abel Prize in 2020. In 1995, he received the Humboldt Prize (after Friedrich Wilhelm Heinrich Alexander von Humboldt, 1769–1859, Germany); in 1996, he was honored by election as a member of the Tata Institute of Fundamental Research; in 1996, he was awarded the Lobachevsky International Prize of the RAS; in 2001, he was elected a member of the United States NAS; and in 2012, he became a Fellow of the AMS. His biography is available in 37 different languages. He is one of the most popular mathematicians around the globe.

24.4. Daniel Gray Quillen

He was born in Orange, New Jersey, USA, and had a younger brother. At the age of twelve, Quillen developed a passion for mathematics. He was successful in receiving a scholarship, which was enough for him to study at Newark Academy (a highly rated private secondary school), and a year before he should have completed his secondary schooling, he won a scholarship to study mathematics at Harvard University. He missed the last year of secondary school (however, because his performance was so outstanding, he was awarded his diploma) and entered Harvard University in September 1957. In 1959, Quillen took part in the 20th Individual and Team Putnam Competition and was named as a Putnam Fellow. He received his Bachelor of Arts degree in 1961 with Magna Cum Laude. His girlfriend Jean Plesset (whom he married in June 1961) wrote the following: ... he seemed to absorb his undergraduate mathematics courses like a sponge. He learned and understood all of every course he took. In fact, I noticed that he could reproduce by memory nearly every theorem and proof. He also had the talent of being able to identify what was important in a subject. Once when I got behind in a course, he managed to teach me all the important points in only three days. Not only did I get an A on the exam, but I also noticed a misprint in the examination paper! Quillen received his master's degree in 1962 and Ph.D. in 1964 for his thesis on partial differential equations entitled *Formal Properties of Over-Determined Systems of Linear Partial Differential Equations* under the supervision of Raoul Bott. Jean typed her husband's Ph.D. thesis. Quillen and Jean had two children before he completed his Ph.D. and four after. After receiving his doctorate, Quillen held appointments at MIT (1973–1988) and as the Waynflete Professor of Pure Mathematics at Magdalen College, Oxford, England (1984–2006). He also spent a number of years at several other universities. He visited France twice: first as a Sloan Fellow in Paris, during the academic year 1968–1969, where he was greatly influenced by Grothendieck, and then, during 1973–1974, as a Guggenheim Fellow. In 1969–1970, he was a visiting member of the IAS, Princeton, where he came under the influence of Michael Atiyah. Quillen retired at the end of 2006. He died from complications of Alzheimer's disease, which lasted for for more than 5 years, on 30 April 2011 in Gainesville, Florida. He was responsible for creating the subject of algebraic K-theory as it is pursued today and for demonstrating its power and elegance. He also made fundamental contributions to many other aspects of mathematics, including rational homotopy, model categories, formal groups, cyclic homology, and complex cobordism. He is remembered for Quillen's Q-construction, the Quillen–Suslin theorem (conjectured by Serre in 1955, Andrei Suslin, 1950–2018, Russia), the Bass–Quillen conjecture, the Quillen determinant line bundle, the Mathai–Quillen formalism (Varghese Mathai, India–Australia), Quillen's lemma, the Quillen metric, and Quillen's theorems A and B. Quillen published more than 50 research papers and supervised six doctoral students. His publications include *Homotopical Algebra* (1967) and, edited with Graeme Bryce Segal (born 1941, Australia–England) and Sheung Tsun Tsou, *The Interface of Mathematics and Particle Physics* (1990). He was awarded the Cole Prize in 1975 and Fields Medal in 1978.

25. IMU Abacus Medal (Previously Known as the Rolf Nevanlinna Prize)

Rolf Herman Nevanlinna was born (as Rolf Neovius for the first ten years) in Joensuu, a city in the eastern part of the Grand Duchy of Finland, at that time part of the Russian Empire. Many members of his family—his grandfather, father, uncle, and older brother—had talents for mathematics. Almost for the first 9 years his primary education was at home in Joensuu and then his family moved to Helsinki, where his father became a teacher at Helsinki High School. Rolf Neovius began attending the same school where his father taught mathematics and physics. In 1913, he graduated from the school, having performed very well, although he was not the best student in his year. However, at the same time he mastered the book *Introduction to Higher Analysis* by Ernst Lindelöf (a cousin of Nevanlinna's father), which inspired him to work on that topic for the whole of his life. Rolf Nevanlinna entered Helsinki University in 1913 and studied under the guidance of Ernst Lindelöf. In 1917, he received his Master of Philosophy in mathematics. On 2 June 1919, he defended his doctoral thesis *Über beschränkte Funktionen die in gegebenen Punkten vorgeschriebene Werte annehmen* (About limited functions that take prescribed values at given points), and on the same day married his cousin Mary Elisa Selin (1895–1992, Finland). They had four children. After receiving the degree he could only obtain a teaching position in a school, the position he kept until 1926. In 1920, he received an invitation from Edmund Landau to go to Göttingen but he did not accept immediately; rather he visited Germany in 1924. There, in addition to Edmund Landau, he met Hilbert, Courant, and Emmy Noether in Göttingen and Pavel Alexsandrov, Pavel Samuilovich Urysohn (1898–1934, Ukraine–France), and Carathéodory in Munich. Rolf Nevanlinna became a Lecturer at Helsinki University in 1922 and was appointed to Full Professor in 1926. He remained on the staff at the same University for the rest of his life, except for extensive travels he made to many different countries, and met several renowned mathematicians including Mittag-Leffler, Harald Bohr, Niels Henrik David Bohr (1885–1962, Denmark), Carleman, Harald Cramér (1893–1985, Sweden), Hadamard, Paul Montel, André Bloch (1893–1948, France), and Andreas Speiser (1885–1970, France). In 1930, Rolf Nevanlinna was offered Weyl's Chair at Göttingen, but he declined. In 1937, Rolf and Mary bought a summer home in Lohja (about 45 km west of Helsinki), which became a place where many visiting mathematicians spent time during the summers. He became rector of the University of Helsinki in the war years, from 1941 until 1944. During the war years he improved ballistic tables, for which he was awarded the Cross of Liberty, Second Class, and throughout his life he held this honor in special esteem. In 1946, he accepted a position at the University of Zurich and was also a member of the Academy of Finland until his retirement in 1963. However, Rolf Nevanlinna continued publishing his work right up to the time of his death in 1980 from cancer. In the mathematical world he is known for the so-called Nevanlinna theory, which appeared in the 100-page paper *Zur Theorie der meromorphen Funktionen* (On the theory of meromorphic functions) in the journal *Acta Mathematica* in 1925, and for his deep involvement in the development of the theory of harmonic measures. He published over 190 papers, several monographs/books, including *Le Théorème de Picard-Borel et la théorie des fonctions méromorphes* (*The Theorem of Picard-Borel and the theory of meromorphic functions*) in 1929, *Uniformisierung* (*Uniformization*) in 1953, *Absolute Analyse* (*Absolute analysis*) in 1959, and Einfhrung in die Funktionentheorie (*Introduction to function theory*) in 1965, and supervised 34 doctoral students. His first and most famous doctoral student was Lars Ahlfors, one of the first two Fields Medal recipients. Rolf Nevanlinna never needed much sleep. In the late 1930s he used to rise at 4, join his family at 10 until lunch time, then work again until 7, and spend the evening with his family. Throughout his life Rolf Nevanlinna played an active role in musical events. It was while he was setting up a chamber music society in 1945 that he met the author and translator Sinikka Kallio-Visapaa (1917–2002, Finland). After their first marriages had been dissolved, they married in 1958 and had a daughter. Rolf Nevanlinna received many honors for his contributions to mathematics: the International Wihuri Prize for Scientists and Artists (1958) and the Henrik Steffens Prize for Nordic culture (1967); Honorary member of the Deutsche Akademie (1938); the Finnish Mathematical Society (1955); the LMS (1959); the Swiss Mathematical Society (1962); the Society of Actuaries of Finland (1965); the Teachers of Mathematics and Physics (1965); the Göttingen Academy of Sciences (1967); the RSAS (1967); the Danish Academy of Sciences (1967); the German Academy of Scientists Leopoldina (1967); the Hungarian Academy of Sciences (1970); the Institut de France (1967); and the Finnish Academy of Science and Letters (1975). He was awarded honorary doctorate degrees by the universities of Heidelberg (1936), Bucharest (1942), Giessen (1952), Berlin (1955), Jyväskylä (1969), Glasgow (1969), Uppsala (1974), and Istanbul (1976). He was President of the IMU from 1959 to 1962.

In 1981, the IMU with the great efforts of Lennart Carleson (then the President of the IMU) decided to create a prize similar to the Fields Medal, with the goal that mathematics not lose contact with theoretical computer science. One year later, in April 1982, the IMU accepted the offer by the University of Helsinki to finance the prize. The prize was named the Rolf Nevanlinna Prize (in his honor) and was awarded at each ICM from 1982 to 2018 to a young mathematician dealing with all mathematical aspects of computer science, such as complexity theory, logic of programming languages, analysis of algorithms, cryptography, computer vision, pattern recognition, information processing, modeling of intelligence, scientific computing and numerical analysis, computational aspects of optimization and control theory, and computer algebra. The prize consists of a gold medal (14KT Gold Au 585) and a monetary prize, and the regulations are similar to those of the Fields Medal. On the obverse side, the medal presents the head of Nevanlinna and the inscription RH 83, which stands for Raimo Heino (1932–1995), the Finnish sculptor who designed the medal and the year 1983 when the first medal was minted. The reverse side shows the seventeenth-century seal of the University of Helsinki and the word Helsinki written in coded form. The name of the prize winner is engraved on the rim of the medal.

The front of the Rolf Nevanlinna Prize. The back of the Rolf Nevanlinna Prize.

Alexander Soifer (born 1948, Russia–USA), the President of the World Federation of National Mathematics Competitions, complained about the prize's honoring of Nevanlinna, as he was a supporter of Hitler and had acted as a representative for the Finnish Volunteer Battalion of the Waffen-SS during World War II. Soifer discussed Nevanlinna's wartime activities in a 2015 book and forwarded his personal and his organization's requests to the EC of the IMU to change the prize's name. In July 2018, the 18th General Assembly of the IMU decided to remove the name of Rolf Nevanlinna from the prize. It was later announced that the prize would be named the IMU Abacus Medal.

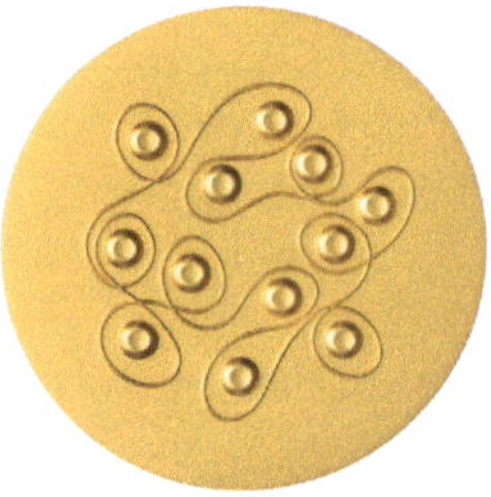

The front of the IMU Abacus Medal. The back of the IMU Abacus Medal.

26. Warsaw ICM 1982 Held in 1983

This Congress was due to be held in 1982, but because of the martial law introduced in Poland on 13 December 1981, it was rescheduled to 16–24 August 1983. In total, 2400 ordinary members from more than 60 countries registered for the Congress, but not all of them eventually turned up. In April 1982, the EC of the IMU, considering the scientific prospects for ICM 82 at that time, decided to postpone the Warsaw Congress by one year, which was confirmed in November 1982. At the same time the EC decided to hold the General Assembly of the IMU in Warsaw, as previously planned, in August 1982. The Fields Medal Committee consisted of Lennart Carleson (Chairman Ex Officio), Huzihiro Araki (1932–2022, Japan), Nikolai Nikolaevich Bogolyubov (1909–1992, Russia), Paul Malliavin (1925–2010, France), Mumford, Louis Nirenberg (1925–2020, Canada–USA), Andrzej Bobola Maria Schinzel (1937–2021, Poland), and Charles Terence Clegg Wall (born 1936, England), which reached its decision in the spring of 1982, and so Lennart Carleson announced at the General Assembly in August 1982 the names of the three winners: Alain Connes (born 1947, France), William Thurston, and Shing-Tung Yau (born 1949, China–USA). Similarly, for the newly established Rolf Nevanlinna Prize in mathematical aspects of information science, the Committee consisted of Jacques-Louis Lions (Chairman), Jacob Theodore Schwartz (1930–2009, USA), and Arto Kustaa Salomaa (born 1934, Finland), who announced the name of the winner Robert Endre Tarjan (born 1948, USA). For the Congress the medievalist historian Aleksander Gieysztor (1916–1999, Poland), the President of the Polish Academy of Sciences, agreed to be its patron. During the opening ceremony Lennart Carleson, the President of the IMU for the years 1979–1982, greeted the participants. He also announced that the President of the Organizing Committee, Czeslaw Olech, had been elected President of the Warsaw Congress. Wladyslaw Roman Orlicz (1903–1990, Poland) was elected Honorary President by acclamation. Czeslaw Olech in his presidential address opened the Congress and welcomed the participants and said "Warsaw is a known centre for mathematical research. It was here that the first specialised International Journal of mathematics in the world was founded. I am speaking of the Fundamenta Mathematicae. Here, for the last ten years, mathematicians from all over the world meet regularly at the Stefan Banach International Mathematical Centre, a common enterprise of the Academies of socialist countries. Let me express the hope that this Congress will contribute to all these international mathematical traditions to a considerable extent". Then Aleksander Gieysztor welcomed the participants and, in his lecture, added an intense review of the recent tragic history and the recovery of Poland and Polish mathematics, "The months of August and September encompass two important dates in the history of this country. Thirty nine years ago on the 1st of August the Warsaw Uprising began and September 1st 1939 was the first day of the Second World War. Both these months are times of national remembrance, of reflection upon the history of our country. During the Second World War the Polish scientific community was decimated. In particular, well over half of the actively working Polish mathematicians lost their lives. Many others found themselves in various countries all over the world. Universities, libraries and printing presses in Poland were largely destroyed. The educational system of the country was in ruins and scientific activity was disrupted. The fact that this Congress is being held in Warsaw in 1983, thirty-eight years after the war, gives evidence of the reconstruction of Polish science both in the organisational and the substantive sense. In particular, it is a proof of the renaissance and expansion of the Polish mathematical community. At present this community is many times larger than before the Second World War. The membership of the Polish Mathematical Society has increased at least fifteen-fold and there are active scientific groups in many universities and polytechnics. The Institute of Mathematics of the Polish Academy of Sciences has a very well supplied mathematical library, which serves the whole of Polish mathematics. This year we have celebrated the 10th anniversary of the activities of the Stefan Banach Mathematical Centre". Lennart Carleson then requested Honorary President Wladyslaw Orlicz to give the Fields Medals and the first Rolf Nevanlinna Prize to the winners. This was the first time that the names of the awardees were no surprise to the Congress. Huzihiro Araki opened his address on the work of Alain Connes as follows: "The theory of operator algebras, after being quietly nourished somewhat in isolation for thirty years or so, started a revolutionary development around late 1960s. Alain Connes came into this field just when the smoke of the first stage of the revolution was settling down. He immediately led the field to breathtaking achievements beyond the expectation of experts". The report on William Thurston's work by Charles Wall was read in Wall's absence: "Thurston has fantastic geometric insight and vision; his ideas have completely revolutionized the study of topology in two and three dimensions and brought about a new and fruitful interplay between analysis, topology, and geometry". Like Charles Wall, Nirenberg, who should have presented the work of Shing-Tung Yau, had not come to Warsaw himself but had sent the manuscript of his report: "Yau had done extremely deep work in global differential geometry and elliptic partial differential equations, including applications in three-dimensional topology and in general relativity theory. He is an analyst's geometer (or geometer's analyst) with remarkable technical power and insight. He has succeeded in solving problems on which progress had been stopped for years". For Robert Tarjan, Jacob Schwartz said "Tarjan has been a leader in both algorithm design and algorithm analysis, which lie in the intellectual heart of computer science". There were 12 one-hour plenary addresses, 1 sent the manuscript, and 123 forty-five minutes addresses delivered within the sections. During the General Assembly of the IMU in August 1982, the new EC for a term of four years beginning 1 January 1983 was elected as follows: Jürgen Moser as President, Ludvig Dmitrievich Faddeev (1934–2017, Russia) and Serre as Vice-Presidents, Olli Lehto as Secretary, and Sigeru Mizohata (1924–2002, Japan), George Daniel Mostow (1923–2017, USA), Mudumbai Seshachalu Narasimhan (1932–2021, India), Czeslaw Olech, and Jacob Palis Jr. as members. During the closing ceremony, Jack Kenneth Hale (1928–2009, USA), on behalf of the mathematical community of the USA, invited the 1986 Congress to be held at UC in Berkeley. It was received with acclamation. Japan had also showed an interest in holding the 1986 Congress, but because of the extreme hot summer of the Japanese main islands, Japan decided not to propose the invitation. Finally, Czeslaw Olech declared the ICM-82 in Warsaw to be closed. The Polish mathematicians were well pleased with the outcome of the Congress.

26.1. Alain Connes

He was born in Draguignan, a town near Cannes in the region of southeast France. His elder brother owns a software company and his younger brother is a medical doctor specialist for Crohn's disease. The family moved to Marseille when Alain was eight years old. Alain first attended high school at Lycée Saint-Charles in Marseille and then became a student of the classes préparatoires in Lycée Thiers (considered as one of the most demanding in France). Between 1966 and 1970 he studied at the ENS in Paris for his bachelor's degree. In 1971, he married Danye Chéreau (a teacher of Latin and Greek in high school). In 1973 he obtained a Ph.D. from Pierre and Marie Curie University, under the supervision of Jacques Dixmier (born 1924, France). The title of his thesis was *A Classification of Factors of Type III*. In an interview in 2021, Alain said "in the thesis he did two fundamental things. The first was to show that this time evolution was in fact independent of the state, which gives many invariants of von Neumann algebras, of factors. Factors were introduced by von Neumann to explore nontrivial factorizations of the Hilbert space in quantum mechanics. The second was the main thing, which was to reduce the Type III factors, which were the ones von Neumann had left out completely, to the Type II and automorphisms. In the thesis he also showed that there are factors which are hyperfinite but are not infinite tensor products. This result he announced in July 1972. It was not just an abstract result, but had many consequences that were surprising to people at the time". He held appointments at the National Centre for Scientific Research, Paris (1970–1974 and 1981–1984); Queen's University, Kingston, Ontario, Canada (1975); the University of Paris VI (1976–1980); the IAS, Princeton, 1978; the Léon Motchane Chair at the IHES since 1979; Emeritus Colléege de France Professor since 2017; the Collége de France, Paris (1984–2017); Vanderbilt University, Nashville, Tennessee, USA (2003–2011); and the Ohio State University (2012–2020), Columbus, USA. Alain's research interests focused on operator algebras and noncommutative geometry, which he applied to other areas of mathematics and theoretical physics, including number theory, differential geometry, and particle physics. Since the 1990s, he has been a proponent of the spectral Standard Model, which gives quantum behavior to positions in spacetime, sidestepping some of the problems with quantum gravity. He has more than 275 publications, several books, including *Noncommutative Geometry* in 1994, *Conversations on Mind, Matter, and Mathematics* in 1995, *Triangle of Thought* in 2001, *Noncommutative Geometry, Quantum Fields and Motives* in 2007, and *Le Théâtre quantique* (*The Quantum Theater*) in 2013, and he supervised 13 doctoral students. He served as editor for the *Journal of Functional Analysis*, *Inventiones Mathematicae*, *Communications in Mathematical Physics*, the *Journal of Operator Theory*, *Ergodic Theory and Dynamical Systems*, *Comptes Rendus de l'Académie des Sciences*, *Letters in Mathematical Physics*, *K-theory*, *Selecta Mathematica*, *Publications Mathématiques de l'IHES*, *Advances in Mathematics*, and the *Journal of Noncommutative Geometry*. He has received several prizes and awards: the Aimé Berthé Prize of the FAS in 1975, Peccot-Vimont Prize of the Collége de France in 1976, CNRS Silver Medal in 1977, Ampére Prize of the FAS in 1980, Fields Medal in 1982, Clay Research Award in 2000, Crafoord Prize in 2001, Peano Prize in 2001, and CNRS Gold Medal in 2004. He has earned several honorary doctorate degrees from Queens University, Kingston, Ontario, Canada (1979), the University of Rome Tor Vergata, Italy (1997), the University of Oslo, Norway (1999), the University of Southern Denmark, Denmark (2009), ULB, Belgium (2010), and Shanghai Fudan University, Shanghai, China (2017). Alain was elected member of several foreign academies and societies, including Foreign Associate Member of the Royal Danish Academy of Sciences (1980), Corresponding Member of the FAS (1980), Member of the FAS (1983), Norwegian Academy of Sciences (1993), Foreign Honorary Member of the AAAS (1990), Foreign Associate Member of the Norwegian Academy of Science (1993), Foreign Fellow of the Royal Society of Canada (1996), Foreign Associate Member of the United States NAS (1997), Foreign Associate Member of the RAS (2003), and Associate Member of the Royal Academy of Science of Belgium (2016). According to him mathematics is such an immense subject that there is room for everybody. Still, sociologically, when you are a beginner, it is very hard. He also said "Awards may have side effects. The utility of the awards is a delicate issue; In principle the Fields Medal is an encouragement for research. But, if it attracts too much publicity it can have negative effects".

26.2. William Paul Thurston

He was born in Washington, D.C., and died in Rochester, New York, USA. William Thurston suffered from congenital strabismus (a type of eye misalignment that can be present at birth or develop within the first six months of life) as a child, causing issues with depth perception. His mother worked with him as a toddler to reconstruct three-dimensional images from two-dimensional ones. William Thurston studied at New College, Sarasota, Florida. He received his bachelor's degree from New College in 1967 as part of its inaugural class. For his undergraduate thesis, he developed an intuitionist foundation for topology. Then, William Thurston moved to UC, Berkeley, to undertake research under the supervision of Morris Hirsch and Stephen Smale. He secured his doctorate in 1972 for a thesis entitled *Foliations of 3-Manifolds which are Circle Bundles*. This work showed the existence of compact leaves in foliations of 3-dimensional manifolds. After completing his Ph.D., William Thurston spent the academic year 1972–1973 at the IAS, Princeton, and then another year at MIT as an Assistant Professor. In 1974, he was appointed a Full Professor of Mathematics at Princeton University, where he remained until 1991, when he returned to UC, Berkeley, as Professor of Mathematics. In 1993, he was appointed Director of the MSRI at Berkeley. In 1996, while remaining at UC, Berkeley, he taught at UC, Davis (1996–2003) and then joined Cornell University (2003–2012) as a Professor of Mathematics and Computer Science. William Thurston died on 21 August 2012 in Rochester, New York, of a sinus mucosal melanoma that was diagnosed in 2011. His early work, in the early 1970s, was mainly in foliation theory. His more significant results include the following: The proof that every Haefliger structure (after André Haefliger, 1929–2023, Switzerland) on a manifold can be integrated to a foliation (this implies, in particular, that every manifold with zero Euler characteristic admits a foliation of codimension one). The construction of a continuous family of smooth, codimension-one foliations on the three-sphere whose

Godbillon–Vey invariant (after Claude Godbillon, 1937–1990, France, and Jacques Vey, 1943–1979, France) takes every real value. With John Mather, he gave a proof that the cohomology of the group of homeomorphisms of a manifold is the same whether the group is considered with its discrete topology or its compact-open topology. In 1979, he published a book *The Geometry and Topology of 3-Manifolds* and in 1997 a very influential book *Three-Dimensional Geometry and Topology*, for which he was awarded the first AMS Book Prize at the Joint Mathematics Meetings in Atlanta, Georgia. He was an early utilizer of computing in pure mathematics research. He inspired Jeffrey Renwick Weeks (born 1956, USA) to develop the SnapPea computing program. In mathematics William Thurston enriched several different topics, including automatic groups, Cannon–Thurston maps (James Weldon Cannon, born 1943, USA), the circle packing theorem, hyperbolic volume, hyperbolic Dehn surgery, the Thurston boundary, Milnor–Thurston kneading theory, Misiurewicz–Thurston points (Michal Misiurewicz, born 1948, Poland-USA), the Nielsen–Thurston classification (Jakob Nielsen, 1890–1959, Denmark), normal surfaces, orbifold notation, the Thurston norm, Thurston's double limit theorem, the Thurston elliptization conjecture, Thurston's geometrization conjecture, Thurston's height condition, and Thurston's orbifold theorem and Earthquake theorem. He supervised 36 doctoral students and published more than 155 papers. William Thurston has received many honors and awards: the Oswald Veblen Prize in Geometry (1976), Alan Tower Waterman Award (1979), Fields Medal (1982), Doob Prize (2005), and Steele Prize (2012). His famous quote is "Mathematics is not about numbers, equations, computations, or algorithms: it is about understanding".

26.3. Shing-Tung Yau

He was born in Swatow, Canton, Republic of China, the fifth of the eight children of his parents. After the revolution in late 1949, his father was concerned about the unstable political situation, so he brought the whole family to Hong Kong. Unfortunately, Yau's older sister died in 1962, an elder brother got a brain disease, and when Yau was fourteen years old, his father died. In Hong Kong he studied in Pui Ching Middle School and then moved to the Chinese University of Hong Kong from 1966 to 1969, but left before graduating. On the suggestion of one his teachers Stephen Salaff (1938–2012, USA–Canada), he enrolled in the Ph.D. program in mathematics at UC, Berkeley, in the fall of 1969. He received his Ph.D. the following year, in 1971, under the supervision of Shiing-Shen Chern. The title of his thesis was *On the Fundamental Group of Compact Manifolds of Non-Positive Curvature*. By this time he had published three papers: On the fundamental group of manifolds of non-positive curvature (1970), On the fundamental group of compact manifolds of non-positive curvature (1971), and Compact flat Riemannian manifolds (1971). He spent a year as a member of the IAS, Princeton, and then joined Stony Brook in 1972 as an Assistant Professor. In 1974, he moved to Stanford University as an Associate Professor. In 1976, he worked at UCLA as a visiting faculty and married physicist Yu-Yun Kuo, whom he knew from his time as a graduate student at Berkeley; they have two sons, Isaac Yau and Michael Yau. In 1979, he moved back to the IAS, Princeton, and became a Full Professor there in 1980. After four years, he moved to UC, San Diego, as a Chair Professor. In 1988, Yau was appointed Professor at Harvard University. In

April 2022, he retired from Harvard, where he was named William Caspar Graustein (1888–1941, USA) Professor of Mathematics Emeritus. In the same year, he moved to Tsinghua University in Beijing, China, as a Professor of Mathematics. Yau is the founder and director of several mathematical institutes, mostly in China. Yau has made major contributions to the development of modern differential geometry and geometric analysis. His most widely celebrated results include the following: analysis and geometry of the Plateau problem and minimal surfaces, Bernstein's problem for maximal surfaces, the Bogomolov–Miyaoka–Yau inequality (Fedor Alekseyevich Bogomolov, born 1946, Russia–USA, and Yoichi Miyaoka, Japan), the Donaldson–Uhlenbeck–Yau theorem (Karen Keskulla Uhlenbeck, born 1942, USA), the Frankel conjecture (Theodore Thomas Frankel, 1929–2017, USA), the geometry of positive scalar curvature, gradient estimates for partial differential equations, the Minkowski problem, the Monge–Ampére equation (Gaspard Monge, 1746–1818, France; Comte de Péluse, 1746–1818, France; and André-Marie Ampére 1775–1836, France), the Omori–Yau maximum principle (Hideki Omori, born 1954, Japan), the positive mass theorem, resolution of the Calabi conjecture and construction of Calabi–Yau manifolds (Eugenio Calabi, 1923–2023, Italy-USA), resolution of the Willmore conjecture in the non-embedded case (Thomas James Willmore, 1919–2005, UK), the SYZ conjecture and mirror symmetry (S: Andrew Eben Strominger, born 1955, USA, Y: Yau, Z: Eric Gallant Zaslow, USA), and the Thomas–Yau conjecture (Richard Paul Winsley Thomas, Britain). Yau has published more than 500 articles and several technical monographs, textbooks, and popular books such as *A history in sum: 150 years of mathematics at Harvard* (1825–1975), *From the Great Wall to the great collider: China and the quest to uncover the inner workings of the universe*, *The shape of a life: One mathematician's search for the universe's hidden geometry*, *The gravity of math: how geometry rules the universe*; *The Shape of Inner Space: String Theory and the Geometry of the Universe's Hidden Dimensions*; in addition he has supervised 75 doctoral students. He is the recipient of several prestigious honors and awards, including California Scientist of the Year in 1979, the John Joseph Carty (1861–1932, USA) Award in 1981, the Oswald Veblen Prize in Geometry in 1981, the Fields Medal in 1982, the Humboldt Research Award in 1991, the Crafoord Prize in 1994, the National Medal of Science in 1997, the Wolf Prize in 2010, and the Shaw Prize in 2023 (after Run Run Shaw, 1907–2014, China). He is also a member of several prestigious organizations, including the AMS (1971), AAAS (1982), New York Academy of Sciences (Fellow 1983), Society for Industrial and Applied Mathematics (1985), American Physical Society (1985), National Academy of Science (1993), RAS (Foreign Member, 2003), National Academy of Lincei (Foreign Member, 2005), and AMS (Fellow, 2013). Yao is either main editor or a member of the editorial board of several international journals: *Communications in Number Theory and Physics*, *Pure and Applied Mathematics Quarterly*, *Dynamics of Partial Differential Equations*, *Communications in Information and Systems*, *Journal of Mathematical Physics*, *Advances in Theoretical Mathematics and Physics*, *Asian Journal of Mathematics*, *Methods and Application of Analysis*, *Advances in Mathematics*, *Mathematical Research Letters*, *Communications in Analysis and Geometry*, *Communication in Mathematical Physics*, *Inventiones Mathematicae*, and *Journal of Differential Geometry*. According to Yau's autobiography, he became "stateless" in 1978 after the British Consulate revoked his Hong Kong residency due to his United States permanent residency status. Regarding his status when receiving his Fields Medal in 1982, Yau stated "I am proud to say that when I was awarded the Fields Medal in mathematics, I held no passport of any country and should certainly be considered Chinese". Yau remained "stateless" until 1990, when he obtained United States citizenship.

26.4. Robert Endre Tarjan

He was born in Pomona, California. His younger brother James Edward Tarjan (born 1952, USA) became a chess grandmaster. As a child, Robert read very many science fiction books and wanted to be an astronomer. He became interested in mathematics after reading Martin Gardner's (1914–2010, USA) Mathematical Games column in *Scientific American* and became passionate about mathematics in the eighth grade. While Robert was in high school, he worked with IBM punch card collators. In 1964, he worked for the first time with real computers while studying astronomy at the Summer Science Program. In 1969, Robert received a bachelor's degree in mathematics from Caltech. In 1971, he obtained his master's degree in computer science and in 1972 a Ph.D. in computer science (with a minor in mathematics) from Stanford University. At Stanford, he was supervised by Robert Floyd (1936–2001, USA) and Donald Ervin Knuth (born 1938, USA), and the title of his Ph.D. dissertation was *An Efficient Planarity Algorithm*. After receiving his Ph.D. he worked at several places: Assistant Professor of Computer Science, Cornell University (1972–1973); Miller Research Fellow, UC, Berkeley, California (1973–1975); Assistant Professor of Computer Science (1974–1977) and Associate Professor of Computer Science (1977–1980), Stanford University; Member of Technical Staff, AT&T Bell Laboratories, Murray Hill, New Jersey (1980–1989); Adjunct Professor of Computer Science, New York University (1981–1985); James Smith McDonnell (1899–1980, USA) Distinguished University Professor of Computer Science, Princeton University (from 1985); Co-Director, National Science Foundation Center for Discrete Mathematics and Theoretical Computer Science (1989–1994, 2001–); Fellow, NEC Research Institute, Princeton, New Jersey (1989–1997); Visiting Scientist, MIT (1996); Chief Scientist, InterTrust, and Senior Research Fellow, Science and Technology Advanced Research Laboratories Labs, InterTrust Technologies Corporation, Sunnyvale, California (1997–2001); Corporate Fellow, Compaq Computer Corporation, Houston, Texas (2002); Chief Scientist (2002–2003) and Senior Fellow (2003–2013), Hewlett Packard Corporation, Palo Alto, California; Visiting Researcher (2013–2014), Microsoft Research, Microsoft, Mountain View, California; and Chief Scientist (2014–), Intertrust Technologies, Sunnyvale, California. Robert with his collaborators has made outstanding contributions in data structures, graph algorithms, combinatorial optimization, computational complexity, computational geometry, and parallel algorithms. He has over 500 publications to his credit, and out of 27 doctoral students he has supervised 26 at Princeton and Stanford. His work has been cited more than 95,000 times. He has received several honors and awards, including the Guggenheim Fellowship, 1978–1979; the Rolf Nevanlinna Prize in Information Science in 1983 (first recipient); the United States NAS Award for Initiatives in Research in 1984; the Lanchester Prize (after Frederick William Lanchester, 1868–1946, England) of the Operations Research Society of America in 1984; Fellow, AAAS in 1985; the A. M. Turing Award (after Alan Mathison Turing, 1912–1954, England) of the Association for Computing Machinery (ACM) in 1986; Member, the United States NAS in 1987; Member, National Academy of Engineering in 1988; Fellow of the American Association for the Advancement of Science in 1990; Member of the APS in 1990; Foundation Fellow, Institute for Combinatorics and its Applications in 1991; Fellow of the ACM in 1994; Fellow of New York Academy of Sciences in 1994; the Paris Kanellakis Award (after Paris Christos Kanellakis, 1953–1995, Greece–USA) in Theory and Practice; the Blaise Pascal Medal (after Blaise Pascal, 1623–1662, France) in Mathematics and Computer Science, European Academy of Sciences in 2004; Fellow, Society for Industrial and Applied Mathematics in 2009; Edelman Award (after Franz Edelman, about 1909–1982, Germany–USA), Institute for Operations Research and the Management Sciences (INFORMS), member of winning Hewlett-Packard (HP) team in 2009; Caltech Distinguished Alumni Award in 2010; and doctorate in mathematics, University of Waterloo, in 2015. Robert jointly holds at least 36 US patents, the first he obtained in 1989 and the 36th in 2019. Robert now lives in Princeton and Silicon Valley with his wife Nayla Marie Rizk.

27. Berkeley ICM 1986

This Congress was held at UC, Berkeley, California, USA, during 3–11 August 1986. In total, 3586 ordinary members from at most 79 countries (2324 from USA and for the first time 47 from Peoples Republic of China and Taiwan) registered for the Congress. The President Jürgen Moser of the IMU welcomed the participants and proposed to elect the Chairman of the Steering Committee Andrew Gleason as President of the Congress, which was accepted by acclamation. Andrew Gleason in his presidential speech after welcoming the all audience said the following: Mathematics has always been useful. Many of the oldest written records of human civilisation are accounting documents, and in fact today accounting still is the largest application of mathematics. But we are rapidly moving into a period in which more and more applications of mathematics are being found. New mathematical questions are being asked by scientists, engineers, and managers—often questions of an entirely different sort from those previously considered. New mathematical answers are being found often involving ideas previously thought to be entirely abstract and utterly non-utilitarian. As mathematicians we can justly be proud that the concepts we have worked so hard to develop are helping people to understand the real world just as they have helped us to understand our platonic world. There is a lesson in this, I think, and it is that, as we enter this new era dominated by computers, we should not fall into the trap of utilitarianism, but remember that the greatest progress in mathematics is always made by trying to understand the fundamental structures that underlie the subject rather than attempting to solve purely utilitarian problems. Andrew Gleason then recognised Mary Ellen Rudin (1924–2013, USA), the Chairman of the United States National Committee for Mathematics, who said the following: Exactly fifty years ago at the Congress held in Oslo, Norway, the first Fields Medals were awarded. The two 1936 Medals went to Jesse Douglas, who is no longer living, and to Lars Ahlfors, who was then a young man not yet thirty years of age. In special celebration of the fiftieth anniversary of the Fields Medal and of Professor Ahlfors' fifty years of continued contributions to mathematics, I would like to nominate Professor Lars Ahlfors to be Honorary President of the Congress. Lars Ahlfors was elected by acclaim and came to the lectern and said the following: I accept this great honour with a good conscience because I consider myself a link between this International Congress and the one in 1936, fifty years ago, the occasion on which the Fields Medals were given for the first time. I understand that my only duty here will be the pleasure of handing out the Fields Medals and the Rolf Nevanlinna Prize. At that time the circumstances were quite different; the idea of the medals had been approved in Zurich in 1932, but there had been no publicity about it and when I arrived in Oslo I did not know that the Medal had become a reality, and if I had known it I would not have considered myself the right candidate. As a matter of fact, I had not been told anything officially until I entered the room where the opening ceremony would take place, but there I was shown a place somewhere in front, and I may have had my suspicions. Well, I had more than that. I had been warned beforehand by somebody who by mistake congratulated me a day before. But up to that point it had been a secret at least officially, even to myself. There was no tradition to go by and no protocol to follow. As was mentioned here, two medals were given, one to me and one to Jesse Douglas, who was then at MIT while I happened to be a visiting lecturer at Harvard. In that way it so happened that both medals went to Cambridge, Massachusetts. Unfortunately, Douglas could not accept his medal in person because according to the Congress record he was too tired. I do not know, but maybe he had good reason to be tired after a long and strenuous journey. I would not expect that to happen today. His medal was then accepted by Norbert Wiener as representative of MIT. Then, after the lecture of Calvin Cooper Moore (1936–2023, USA), Andrew Gleason introduced Richard Johnson (born 12 April 1928, USA), Acting Science Advisor to the President Ronald Wilson Reagan, the 40th President of the United States (1911–2004), who talked on behalf of the President:

"On behalf of the American people, I am pleased to welcome you to the United States. For only the second time in the twentieth century the century that history will remember best for the remarkable discoveries and tremendous advances made in science and technology—this country is privileged to host the best mathematicians from some seventy nations around the world. I would like to use this occasion to congratulate, in advance, the winners of the Fields Medals and the Rolf Nevanlinna Prize. You recipients know who you are, but the suspense is beginning to wear on the rest of us, who are eager for the announcement and the opportunity to give you the accolades and recognition you so richly deserve.

Here in the United States, and I'm sure in your countries as well, my colleagues in science and technology engage in a certain friendly rivalry between our various disciplines. For example, I might say: "Physics is the most important of the sciences because it seeks to uncover the secrets of the tiniest particles of matter which make up our universe". The biologist might reply, "What could be more significant to humanity than understanding the building blocks of life itself". Or the chemist: "Don't underestimate the value of chemistry". But we scientists are not a contentious bunch by nature, and I can think of at least two points on which American scientists would echo resounding accord: First, science and technology are essential to improving the quality of life for all mankind, and second, mathematics is essential to every field of science and technology.

Of course, for me, it is ample honour to stand before this August gathering as a representative of the United States government, but I derive great personal pride and pleasure from the opportunity this event provides me, as a representative of the American scientific community, to express the gratitude of my fellow scientists to the mathematicians of the world, whose tireless efforts and manifold contributions form the very foundation upon which our work is built. We owe a large measure of our success to you. As science and technology progress at a breakneck pace—with mathematics as the fundamental driving force—we will continue to look to you for guidance, direction, and assistance. But today, I would also like to urge you to take on a role beyond solely enhancing your own research capabilities and contributions.

Throughout the world, science and technology increasingly are acknowledged to be essential to a nation's economic strength, industrial productivity, national security, and overall quality of life. While science is never static, right now we are in the midst of an unprecedented era of revolution in virtually every field of science and technology—a revolution that we created, and one which we have a responsibility to sustain and, indeed, to lead. The most important point, and the principal source of my concern, is that we must also possess the ability to respond to the opportunities afforded by this rapidly progressing scientific environment. To do so will require a strong base of talent—men and women, like you, who will lead the world's science and technology talent enterprise into the unforeseeable reaches of the twenty-first century. The pressing question is whether or not we will have the science and technology talent base adequate to meet the challenges of the future. Looking at current statistical indicators, the alarming answer, in most countries, is no.

We in the United States recognise that we have a serious problem. Fewer and fewer young people are studying science, mathematics, engineering, and technology; fewer and fewer young people are pursuing advanced degrees in these disciplines; and fewer and fewer young people are choosing careers in the scientific and technological fields. If this trend is allowed to continue, this country, and others similarly afflicted, will be unequipped to maintain the level of scientific leadership on which our improving standard of living, and the more general quality of life, depends.

To my mind, the most important aspect of this Congress is its international nature. Like mathematics itself, it transcends the barriers of language and ideology, the boundaries of geography, and the adversarial climate of competition. You are convened here this week, in the spirit of cooperation, to share your latest discoveries and to learn about new developments, and to pursue your mutual interests and the solutions to common problems. Perhaps that is what compels me to share this growing problem of an inadequate talent base with you, and to turn to you for help in solving it.

All of us who are not mathematicians feel a keen sense of envy at the abilities you possess. The intrinsic beauty (especially as now seen in 3-D colour), the coherence, the elegance of mathematics makes it an entirely worthwhile pursuit in its own right. You have the rare talent to appreciate fully the depth and power of your subject. But, with ability and talent come obligations and responsibilities, especially to those not so blessed. What you do in your laboratories, at your computer terminals, and in your studies is remarkable—indeed, it has changed the course of the world. But you must do more. It is no longer enough to be practitioners of science. You must also become citizens of science—leaders of a uniquely gifted community, bound by the common goal of assuring that the progress you have made and the improvements you have wrought for humanity will continue. Especially, you must help to assure that there is an expanding, well-qualified generation of scientists, engineers, and technologists to succeed you.

What the young students of the world need most, in my view, is someone to imbue them with the excitement and enthusiasm that brought you here today, someone to communicate to them the importance of science and technology to society, to demonstrate to them that mathematics, physics, biology, chemistry, and their sister disciplines are challenging pursuits, worthy of their highest interest and attention. Many young teachers, I hasten to add, need to hear this as well. No one is better qualified to carry those messages than the individuals who have made eminently successful careers out of the quest for knowledge. In short, the best spokesmen for mathematics, physics, biology, and chemistry are mathematicians, physicists, biologists, and chemists.

Unfortunately, too many students, especially at the grammar school level, still regard science and mathematics as "too hard", too difficult. To them, these subjects look ponderous, abstract, and impenetrable, and many children dismiss them before they've had a chance to appreciate the fun and excitement inherent in the challenge of discovery. At that moment, a potential scientist or mathematician is lost—for now, more than ever before, the attitudes and academic foundations developed in the early school years determine the future course of a student's education and career. In the current scientific and technological climate, with a growing demand for an expanded talent base, we cannot afford to lose these students in grammar school—well before there is a need for a carefully weighed career choice.

Therefore, I believe it is incumbent upon you to become active participants in the community of science, to help others to grasp the broad importance of science and technology to the very fabric of our daily lives—to help them understand the momentous potential of science and technology to enhance the quality of life for all mankind. Certainly, you can point with pride to the eradication of diseases, to the agricultural revolution, to hurricane forecasts, to the transportation, automation, electronics, and information revolutions, as examples. We must, of course, recognize and limit the risks associated with modern uses of science and technology. But, further, we must convey to our young students not only factual information on the present extensive benefits, but also the great challenges, personal opportunities, and potential future benefits associated with the scientific and technological disciplines.

I urge you to get involved in developing the talent bases needed in the twenty-first century for expanding the contributions of science and technology to humanity. On a small scale, you can, of course, accomplish a great deal simply by going to your local schools and talking to the teachers and the children about the contributions that they have the power to make through science. On a larger scale, you can work through existing mechanisms, like your professional societies, and enlist the help of your colleagues in devising innovative solutions to this set of perplexing problems. That, after all, has been your mission within the discipline of mathematics; now I challenge you with this added responsibility to mankind.

Individuals of the highest calibre must be sought out, trained, nurtured, and encouraged by every means possible to carry on the tradition of excellence you represent. I can think of none better suited to the task than you, who, by your example, your actions, and your words can express the merit and rewards of a life in science.

In closing, I have a personal message from a man who is himself excited by science and technology and firm in his commitment to their invaluable role in international health and prosperity".

The famous quote of Rabindranath Tagore (1861–1941, India) from *Gitanjali* supplements President Reagan's suggestions to teachers: A teacher can never truly teach unless he is still learning himself. A lamp can never light another lamp unless it continues to burn its own flame. The teacher who has come to the end of his subject, who has no living traffic with his knowledge but merely repeats his lessons to his students, can only load their minds, he cannot quicken them.

The Fields Medal Committee consisted of Jürgen Moser (Chairman), Pierre Deligne, James Gilbert Glimm (born 1934, USA), Lars Hörmander, Kiyosi Ito, Willard Milnor, Sergei Novikov, and Conjeevaram Srirangachari Seshadri (1932–2020, India). Jürgen Moser announced the unanimous decision of the committee to award the prize to three people: Simon Kirwan Donaldson, Gerd Faltings (born 1954, Germany), and Michael Hartley Freedman (born 1951, USA). For the Rolf Nevanlinna Prize in mathematical aspects of information science, the committee consisted of Ludwig Faddeev (Chairman), Stephen Arthur Cook (born 1939, USA–Canada), and Shmuel Winograd (1936–2019, Israel–USA). Ludwig Faddeev announced the unanimous decision of the committee to award the prize to Leslie Gabriel Valiant (born 1949, Hungary–UK–USA). The medals were presented by the Honorary President of the Congress Lars Ahlfors. Donaldson's work was presented by Michael Atiyah: In 1982, when he was a second-year graduate student, Simon Donaldson proved a result that stunned the mathematical world. Together with the important work of Michael Freedman, Donaldson's result implied that there are "exotic 4-spaces, i.e., 4-dimensional differential manifolds which are topologically but not differentiably equivalent to the standard Euclidean 4-space R^4. What makes this result so surprising is that $n = 4$ is the only value for which such exotic n-spaces exist". Barry Charles Mazur (born 1937, USA) said of the work of Faltings: One of the great moments in mathematics was when Gerd Faltings revealed the circle of ideas which led him to the proof of the conjecture of Mordell (after Louis Joel Mordell, 1888–972, USA–UK). This conjecture ... had stood as a goad and an elusive temptation for over half a century. Freedman's work was presented by Willard Milnor: Michael Freedman has not only proved the Poincaré hypothesis for 4-dimensional topological manifolds, thus characterizing the space S^4, but has also given us classification theorems, easy to state and to use but difficult to prove, for much more general 4-manifolds. The simple nature of his results in the topological case must be contrasted with the extreme complications which are now known to occur in the study of differentiable and piecewise linear 4-manifolds. Valiant's work was praised by Volker Strassen (born 1936, Germany): Theoretical computer science is in the stage of formulating its central problems and devising the proof techniques for their solution. Valiant has been eminently involved in this process, not only by answering a number of recalcitrant open questions, but above all by developing important new concepts, which have led him to discover deep and beautiful connections between problems that had seemed to be totally unrelated.

The Organizing Committee invited 16 one-hour plenary speakers (2 could not come, 1 did not even send the manuscript, and for the other the manuscript was received and read); 148 were invited to deliver forty-five minutes addresses, but only 132 were present at the Congress, and for 11 of those missing lectures were read; and 731 ten-minute short communications were given and a large number of informal seminars were arranged by participating mathematicians. During the closing ceremony Jürgen Moser thanked Marshall Stone, who played a decisive role in re-establishing the IMU in 1950 after it ceased to exist in 1932. He also informed the decision of the General Assembly of the IMU, which met on 31 July and 1 August: the New EC of the IMU for 1987–1990 was Ludwig Faddeev as President, Walter Feit and Lars Hörmander as Vice-Presidents, Olli Lehto as Secretary, and John Henry

Coates (1945–2022, Australia–England), Hikosaburo Komatsu (1935–2022, Japan), László Lovász (born 1948, Hungary), Jacob Palis Jr., and Conjeevaram Seshadri as members, and Andrew Gleason as ex officio member. Then, Masayoshi Nagata invited the audience to the next Congress with the following words: On behalf of the Japanese Committee for Mathematics, I have the honour of inviting you to the next ICM in Kyoto (this time was fully prepared). Kyoto had been the capital of Japan for about one thousand years and can show you some of the old Japanese culture. Hoping that you will accept our invitation, I welcome all of you to the next ICM to be held in August 1990 in Kyoto. DMV also strongly proposed Munich; however, it was decided to favor the opening of the congresses to Asia, and thus Kyoto was chosen. Andrew Gleason then declared the Congress closed. An important feature of the Congress was an educational materials exhibition consisting of 40 booths representing 26 exhibiting firms was open throughout the Congress.

27.1. Simon Kirwan Donaldson

He was born in Cambridge, England. Simon was one of his parents' four children, having an older brother, an older sister, and a younger brother. Like his father both his brothers became engineers. Simon initiated his studies in a preparatory school in Cambridge and during 1970–1975 for secondary school education attended Sevenoaks School in Sevenoaks (about 75 miles from Cambridge). While in secondary school his father taught him some mathematical techniques, which inspired him to become a mathematician. At Sevenoaks School he won a scholarship to study mathematics and physics at Pembroke College, Cambridge, which he entered in 1976. Simon secured his Bachelor of Arts in 1979 and continued to study Part III of the tripos at Cambridge until 1980. In Cambridge, John Frank Adams was very impressed with his final examinations and wrote to him to congratulate him on his solutions. John Adams also recommended him to study for a doctorate at Oxford. In 1980, Simon began postgraduate work at Worcester College, Oxford, first under the supervision of Nigel Hitchin and then with Michael Atiyah. In 1982, Simon proved a result that stunned the mathematical world; this result in the form of a paper entitled *Self-dual connections and the topology of smooth 4-manifolds* was published in the *Bulletin of the AMS* in 1983. Simon was awarded his doctorate from Oxford in 1983 for the thesis *The Yang-Mills Equations on Kähler Manifolds* (Yang Chen-Ning, born 1922, China, and Robert Laurence Mills, 1927–1999, USA). After receiving his doctorate he joined All Souls College, Oxford, as a Junior Research Fellow. The academic year 1983–1984 Simon spent at the IAS, Princeton. During this visit he made a trip to the University of Maryland, where he met Nora. They married and have three children; Simon also has a step-daughter. Nora obtained her Ph.D. degree from the University of Maryland in 1988 for the thesis A non-parametric estimation of the tumour onset time in a serial screening experiment. After returning to Oxford he went back to All Souls College and worked until 1985 on a Post-Doctoral Research Fellowship. In 1985, Simon was appointed as Wallis Professor (after John Wallis, 1616–1703, England) of Mathematics at St Anne's College, Oxford. The year 1997–1998 he spent at Stanford University, and then moved to Imperial College, London, as a Professor of Pure Mathematics, where he continues. In addition in 2014, Simon joined the Simons Center for Geometry and Physics at Stony Brook as a permanent member. His work has been regarded as a seminal new synthesis between pure and applied mathematics, i.e., between advancements in mathematical theory and mathematics used to solve practical problems in science, engineering, and economics. In essence, Simon utilized mathematical concepts used by physicists to solve purely mathematical topological problems. Results that bear his name are as follows: Donaldson theory, the Donaldson theorem, Donaldson–Thomas theory (Richard Thomas), the Donaldson–Uhlenbeck–Yau theorem, K-stability, K-stability of Fano varieties, and the Yau–Tian–Donaldson conjecture (Tian Gang, born 1958, China). He has published more than 140 research papers and three books, *The geometry of four-manifolds* (1990), *Floer homology groups in Yang-Mills theory* (2002), and *Riemann surfaces* (2011), and supervised 52 doctoral students. Simon has received many honors for his work: the Junior Whitehead Prize from the LMS in 1985; FRS of London in 1986; Fields Medal in 1986; William Hopkins Prize from the Cambridge Philosophical Society in 1991 (after William Hopkins, 1793–1866, UK); Royal Medal from the Royal Society in 1992; Crafoord Prize in 1994; Polya Prize from the LMS in 1999; Elected to the United States NAS in 2000; King Faisal International Prize in 2006; Frederic Esser Nemmers Prize in 2008; Shaw Prize in 2009; Foreign member of the RSAS in 2010; knighted in 2012; Fellow of the AMS in 2012; Breakthrough Prize in Mathematics in 2015; Oswald Veblen Prize in 2019; and Wolf Prize (2020). In 2014, Simon was awarded Docteur Honoris Causa by the Université Joseph Fourier, Grenoble, France, and in 2017 Doctor Honoris Causa by the Universidad Complutense de Madrid, Spain.

27.2. Gerd Faltings

He was born in Gelsenkirchen-Buer, West Germany, to well-educated parents. After primary school he attended the Max-Planck-Gymnasium, a high school in Gelsenkirchen, and received his diploma in 1972. During his last years in high school, he participated twice successfully in the *Bundeswettbewerb Mathematik* (Federal Mathematics Competition), so he became a member of the *Studienstiftung des deutschen Volkes* (Academic Foundation of the German People), a foundation dedicated to the support of talented students. From 1972 to 1978, Faltings studied mathematics and physics at the Westphalian Wilhelm University of Münster (in 2023 the university was renamed as the Universitt Münster). In 1978, he finished with a diploma (in local cohomology) and a Ph.D., both about topics in commutative algebra. The title of his thesis was *Über Macaulayfizierung* (About Macaulayfication), which he wrote under the supervision of Hans-Joachim Nastold (1929–2004, Germany). Following the award of his doctorate, Faltings went to the USA, where he spent a year performing postdoctoral work as a Research Fellow at Harvard University in 1978–1979. Returning to Münster, he became assistant to Nastold, and in 1981 obtained a habilitation (a formal qualification needed to become a university Professor) in mathematics. From 1982 to 1984, he was Professor at the University of Wuppertal. During 1985–1994, he was Full Professor at Princeton University. In addition, in the fall of 1988 and in the academic year 1992–1993 he was a visiting scholar at the IAS, Princeton. In 1994, he returned to Germany and from 1994 to 2022, he was a director of the MPIM in Bonn, and currently he is a Retired Scientific Member there. His work in algebraic geometry led to important results in number theory, including for any given exponent $n > 2$, there are only finitely many counterexamples to Fermat's Last Theorem: the equation $a^n + b^n = c^n$ has no positive integer solutions for $a, b,$ and c for $n > 2$ (after Pierre de Fermat, 1601–1665, France). He proved the Tate, Shafarevich, and Mordell conjectures over number fields. His main interests are arithmetic geometry (Diophantine equations and Shimura varieties), p-adic cohomology (relating crystalline to étale in p-adic Hodge theory), and vector bundles on curves (Verlinde formula, loop groups, and theta divisors). He is known for Faltings's theorem, Falting's height, and Faltings's product theorem. He has published more than 85 highly influential research papers and supervised 17 doctoral students. Faltings' publications include *Rational Points* (1984); with Ching-Li Chai (born 1956, Taiwan) *Degeneration of Abelian Varieties* (1990); and *Lectures on the Arithmetic Riemann-Roch Theorem* (1992). In December 1984 he married Angelika (she died in 2011); his two daughters were born in 1985 and 1988. He has received several honors and awards: the Dannie Heineman (1872–1962, Belgium–USA) Prize from the Academy in Göttingen in 1983; Fields Medal in 1986; Guggenheim Fellowship in 1988; Leibniz Prize in 1996; Karl Georg Christian von Staudt (1798–1867, Germany) Prize in 2008; Heinz Gumin (1928–2008, Germany) Prize in 2010; King Faisal International Prize in 2014; Shaw Prize in 2015; and Cantor Medal in 2017. He was also elected Foreign Member of the Royal Society in 2016 and United States NAS International Member in 2018. He received an honorary doctorate degree from the University of Münster in 2012.

27.3. Michael Hartley Freedman

He was born in Los Angeles, California, USA, to the famous Benedict Freedman (1919–2012, USA) and Nancy Mars Freedman (1920–2010, USA). His father was an aeronautical engineer, musician, writer, and mathematician. His mother Nancy performed as an actress and also trained as a dancer and writer. His parents cowrote a series of well-known novels. Michael has two sisters: Johanna, who has a Ph.D. in psychology from Stanford and is a Professor at UC, Irvine, Medical School, and Deborah, who is an opera singer and teaches voice, sometimes at UC, Berkeley. In the beginning, Michael was interested in painting and mathematics; however, in 1968 when he entered UC, Berkeley, he decided to study mathematics, but dropped out after two semesters. The same year, he was admitted to Princeton University's Graduate School and continued his studies. Michael was awarded a doctorate by Princeton in 1973 for his doctoral dissertation entitled *Codimension-Two Surgery*, written under the supervisor of William Browder (born 1934, USA). After graduating, Michael returned to Berkeley, where he was a Lecturer in the Department of Mathematics until 1975. In 1976, he was appointed Assistant Professor in the department of mathematics at UC, San Diego. Michael was promoted to Associate Professor at UC, San Diego, in 1979. He spent the year 1980/81 at the IAS, Princeton, and then returned to UC, San Diego, where in 1982 he was promoted to Professor. He was also appointed the Charles Lee Powell Chair of Mathematics at UC, San Diego, in 1985. In 1998, he left the academic world and accepted a position with the Theory Group at Microsoft Research, a division of Microsoft Corporation. Later he became the Director of Microsoft Station Q (Quantum) at UC, Santa Barbara, where his team was involved in the development of the topological quantum computer.

He has published more than 135 research papers, several of which include quantum computation, such as the following: Quantum computation and the localization of modular functors (2001); Projective plane and planar quantum codes (2001); Poly-locality in quantum computing (2002); Simulation of topological field theories by quantum computers (2002); Topological quantum computation (2003); Approximate Counting and Quantum Computation (2005); Topological quantum computation (2006); Topological quantum computing with only one mobile quasiparticle (2006); Interacting anyone in topological quantum liquids: The golden chain (2008); Measurement-Only Topological Quantum Computation (2008); and Topological Phase in a Quantum Gravity Model (2008). Michael has also published four books: *Surgery on Codimension 2 Submanifolds* (1977); *Classification of Four-Dimensional Spaces* (1982); *Selected Applications of Geometry to Low-Dimensional Topology* (1989) with Feng Luo; and *Topology of 4-Manifolds* (1990) with Frank Stringfellow Quinn, born 1946, USA. He supervised 16 doctoral students at UC, San Diego. Michael was married twice, having one son with his first wife and three with his second wife, Leslie. Freedman has received many honors for his work: Sloan Award 1980; California Scientist of the Year in 1984; MacArthur Foundation Fellow in 1984–1989; elected to the United States NAS in 1984; elected to the AAAS in 1985; Fields Medal in 1986; Oswald Veblen Prize in Geometry 1986; National Medal of Science 1987; Humboldt Award 1998; and Guggenheim Fellowship Award 1994. According to him "Mathematics is not so much a collection of different subjects as a way of thinking. As such, it may be applied to any branch of knowledge. I want to applaud the efforts now being made by mathematicians to publish ideas on education, energy, economics, defence, and world peace. Experience inside mathematics shows that it isn't necessary to be an old hand in an area to make a contribution".

27.4. Leslie Gabriel Valiant

He was born in Budapest, Hungary, to a chemical engineer father and a translator mother. He was brought up in England, studying at Tynemouth High School (in 1969 renamed as Norham High School) North Shields, Tyne and Wear. He completed his school education at Latymer Upper School, London. Then, he was educated at King's College, Cambridge, receiving his Bachelor of Arts degree in mathematics in 1970. Next, Valiant moved to Imperial College, London, to study computer science, and after receiving a Diploma of Imperial College, he enrolled at the University of Warwick, where he undertook research for a doctorate in computer science with Michael Stewart Paterson (born 1942, Britain) as his advisor. He received his Ph.D. degree in 1974 for his thesis *Decision Procedures for Families of Deterministic Pushdown Automata*. After the completion of his thesis research in 1973, he spent the year 1973–1974 at Carnegie Mellon University in Pittsburgh, Pennsylvania, as a Visiting Assistant Professor. After the award of his Ph.D. during 1974–1976, Valiant taught at the University of Leeds as a Lecturer, and then during 1977–1982 at the University of Edinburgh as a Lecturer and later as a Reader. Valiant started teaching at Harvard University in 1982 as Gordon McKay Professor and in 2001 became Thomas Jefferson Coolidge Professor of Computer Science and Applied Mathematics at the Harvard School of Engineering and Applied Sciences. Valiant has performed astonishing work in theoretical computer science, producing several results of great beauty and originality. He formulated the Probably Approximately Correct (PAC) model of learning, which introduced the field of Computational Learning Theory and became a theoretical basis for the development of machine learning. Through this and other work, he brought about the realization that machine learning is the central concept in artificial intelligence. His earlier work in Automata Theory includes an algorithm for context-free parsing, which is still the asymptotically fastest known one. In the field of Complexity Theory, he has formulated the notion of #P-completeness (Sharp-P completeness) to explain why certain enumeration and reliability problems are intractable. In his 2013 book *Probably Approximately Correct: Nature's Algorithms for Learning and Prospering in a Complex World* he argues that evolutionary biology does not explain the rate at which evolution occurs; he writes "The evidence for Darwin's general schema for evolution being essentially correct is convincing to the great majority of biologists. This author has been to enough natural history museums to be convinced himself. All this, however, does not mean the current theory of evolution is adequately explanatory. At present the theory of evolution can offer no account of the rate at which evolution progresses to develop complex mechanisms or to maintain them in changing environments". Valiant created the bulk synchronous model as an organizing principle for large parallel computing systems. In addition, he devised the widely used method of routing information in large computer systems by randomization in space. He also introduced the concept of Holographic Algorithms inspired by the Quantum Computation Model. In 2024 he published a monograph *The Importance of Being Educable,* which suggests a computational model for cognitive capability that separates humans from other existing species on Earth, and thereby sets a goal for AI systems. His ideas have united computer science, probability and statistics, combinatorics, and even aspects of statistical physics. He has more than 100 research publications and has supervised 16 doctoral students. He has received several awards and honors, including the Rolf Nevanlinna Prize in 1986; FRS of London in 1991; Fellow of the Association for the Advancement of Artificial Intelligence in 1992; Knuth Prize in 1997; member of the United States NAS in 2001; European Association for Theoretical Computer Science Distinguished Achievements Award in 2008; and Turing Award in 2010. In 1977, he married Gayle Lynne Dyckhoff; they have two sons, Gregory John Valiant and Paul Andrew Valiant. Like their father both are also theoretical computer scientists.

28. Kyoto ICM 1990

This Congress was held in Kyoto, Japan, during 21–29 August 1990. The Congress was attended by 3954 full members from 76 countries (2409 from Japan). Ludwig Faddeev, the President of the IMU, opened the Congress with the remark that this is the first Congress in the history of the IMU to take place outside of Europe and North America [in Asia]. He also said that the numbers of participants in this Congress were the highest in the history of the ICM; however, he missed the numbers of the Moscow ICM 1966. He nominated Hikosaburo Komatsu to be the President of the Congress, which was approved unanimously. In his presidential address Hikosaburo Komatsu first welcomed the participants and then introduced the EC of the Congress: Kunihiko Kodaira (the first Japanese Fields medalist) as President; Kiyosi Ito and Heisuke Hironaka (the second Japanese Fields medalist) as Vice-Presidents; Hikosaburo Komatsu as Chairman; Huzihiro Araki as Secretary; Hirosi Toda (born 1928, Japan) as Treasurer; and Shigeru Iitaka (born 1942, Japan), Sigeru Mizohata, and Masayoshi Nagata as members. About Japan and its culture, Hikosaburo Komatsu said "I have often wondered why mathematicians do have Congresses and what Congresses mean to them. My answer is that Congresses are to mathematicians what Bon and New Year Festivities are to Japanese, in which they abandon their daily life completely. Japanese are believed to work continuously without vacations, but that is not true. Even in the Edo Period there were two one-week long holidays. One is the New Year Festivities and the other is the Bon Festivities which take place a week earlier than this time of the year. On these holidays people are relieved from labour and go back to their native home. People are not allowed to cook on the first days of the Festivities, so that they have a busy time preparing all meals before the holidays start. New Year Festivities are associated with the future. We renew everything we can and start again, Bon Festivities are for the past, We receive ancestors' ghosts, make conversations with them, and then send them back. In cities like Kyoto people decorate their entrance halls with their treasures and keep the doors open. The whole city becomes a big museum. In the countryside people gather in the village square and dance. There is no distinction between performers and spectators; all dance. That is the way Japanese refresh themselves, inherit their traditions and unite. Bon and New Year Festivities also give young people the opportunity to meet together to make a new family. I would like to ask all speakers at the Congress to make their lectures accessible to a wide audience, and not just to the specialists, at least in the first part. This is certainly not the time to work in a daily manner". Then, Akio Hattori (1929–2013, Japan), President of the Mathematical Society of Japan, welcomed the audience and proposed that Kiyosi Ito be elected Honorary President of this Congress. After a few more welcoming lectures, the recipients of the Fields Medals and the Rolf Nevanlinna Prize were announced by the respective Chairmen of the committees, which were appointed by the IMU in April, 1988. The Fields Medal Committee consisted of Ludwig Faddeev (Chairman Ex Officio), Michael Atiyah, Jean-Michel Bismut (born 1948, France), Enrico Bombieri, Charles Fefferman, Kenkichi Iwasawa (1917–1998, Japan), Peter David Lax (born 1926, Hungary–USA), and Igor Shafarevich. The Rolf Nevanlinna Prize Committee consisted of László Lovász (Chairman), Alexandre Joel

Chorin (born 1938, USA), Michael Oser Rabin (born 1931, Israel–USA), and Volker Strassen. Fields Medals were awarded to Vladimir Gershonovich Drinfeld (born 1954, Ukraine), Vaughan Frederick Randal Jones (1952–2020, New Zealand), Shigefumi Mori (born 1951, Japan), and Edward Witten. The Rolf Nevanlinna was awarded to Aleksandr Aleksandrovich Razborov (born 1963, USSR–USA). All the medals were presented by Kosuke Hori (1934–2023, Japan), then Minister of Education, Science, and Culture.

For the winners the commendation came after the opening ceremony; Yuri Manin's report for Drinfeld was read by Michio Jimbo (born 1951, Japan): Manin concentrated upon the two subjects that were Drinfeld's main preoccupation in the previous decade: Langlands' program (a series of conjectures, theorems, and insights aimed at an understanding of the Galois groups of dimension one) and quantum groups. In both domains, Drinfeld's work constituted a decisive breakthrough and had prompted a wealth of research. Joan Sylvia Lyttle Birman (born 1927, USA) spoke about the work of Vaughan Jones: In 1984, he discovered an astonishing relationship between von Neumann algebras and geometric topology. He found a new polynomial invariant for knots and links in 3-space. As time went on, it became clear that his discovery had to do in a bewildering variety of ways with widely separated areas of mathematics and physics. She also praised his informal style of working and his "openness and generosity ... in the best tradition and spirit of mathematics". Heisuke Hironaka, in speaking about the work of Shigefumi Mori, pointed out that the most profound and exciting development in algebraic geometry during the last decade or so was the Minimal Model program or Mori's program, in connection with the classification problems of algebraic varieties of dimension three. Mori's theorems on algebraic threefolds were stunning and beautiful in their totally new features, unimaginable by those who had been working in the traditional world of algebraic or complex analytic surfaces. For Edward Witten, Ludwig Faddeev read Atiyah's address, adding his own comments: Atiyah called attention to the remarkable renaissance in the interaction between mathematics and physics. The mathematical community had benefited from this interaction in two ways. First, mathematicians had been spurred into learning some of the relevant physics and collaborating with colleagues in theoretical physics. Second, and more surprisingly, many of the ideas emanating from physics had led to significant new insights into purely mathematical problems, and remarkable discoveries had been made in consequence. "In all this large and exciting field, Edward Witten stands out clearly as the most influential and dominating figure. Although he is definitely a physicist, his command of mathematics is rivalled by few mathematicians. Time and again he has surprised the mathematical community by a brilliant application of physical insight leading to new and deep mathematical theorems". László Lovász cited the work of Razborov as "groundbreaking work on lower bound for circuit complexity". His work was received with great interest and discussed enthusiastically at seminars all around the world. In an area where any step forward seemed almost hopeless (but which was at the same time a central area of theoretical computer science), his results meant that deep methods could be developed and obtaining strong lower bounds for algorithms was not impossible.

There were 15 one-hour plenary addresses, which included for the first time since 1932 a lecture by a woman—Karen Keskulla Uhlenbeck; 138 forty-five minutes lectures of invited speakers; and 620 short communications. During the closing ceremony Ludwig Faddeev referred to the scientific program of the congress; he said "I was glad to observe how prominently mathematical physics was represented in its connections with other domains of mathematics". He stated that the Emperor Hirohito and Empress Nagako of Japan had invited the winners of the Fields Medals and the Rolf Nevanlinna Prize to visit them in Tokyo. The Honorary President of the Congress, Kiyosi Ito, as well as Heisuke Hironaka and I were also present. The interest expressed by the Imperial Family in the work of our Congress is a great honour to us all. The congress was also informed of the election of the new EC for the period 1991–1994: Jacques-Louis Lions (President), John Coates and David Mumford as Vice-Presidents, Jacob Palis Jr. as Secretary, and James Greig Arthur (born 1944, Canada), Albrecht Dold (1928–2011, Germany), Hikosaburo Komatsu, László Lovász, Eduard Zehnder (born 1940, Switzerland), and Ludwig Faddeev as members. For the 1994 Congress it was assumed that Munich would be the site; however, because of the choice of Kyoto over Munich, the German plans were not reissued. Thus to continue the series of congresses, Srishti Dhar Chatterji (1935–2017, India–Switzerland) invited the participants to the next ICM in Zurich for a third time, which was unanimously accepted. Hikosaburo Komatsu, President of the Congress, then closed the meeting and addressed the Congress with the following exquisite words: "I felt that we are at another turning point in the history of mathematics. The previous one was marked at the Second Congress in 1900 when Hilbert gave his famous lecture, since then we have obtained an enormous number of general results by axiomatisation and abstract formulation, often at the hands of mathematical giants. This time it is a transition from abstract simplification to more concrete synthesis. We are now in a fortunate time when we can solve many problems which remained open for many years in spite of all the efforts of past generations of mathematicians. We no longer have a single genius but many people work together developing new strong streams. It was only many brooks last time at the Congress in Berkeley. They meet together and now we see a big river or a sea or even an ocean".

28.1. Vladimir Gershonovich Drinfeld

He was born in Kharkov (now Kharkiv, Ukraine, formerly a part of the USSR), in a Jewish family. His father Gershon Ikhelevich Drinfeld (1908–2000, Ukraine) was a mathematics Professor at Kyiv University and Kharkiv University, and his mother Frida Iosifovna Lutskaya-Litvak (1921–2011, Ukraine) was a Professor of Latin. At an very early age, Vladimir's father started teaching him mathematics. During 1965–1969, he attended School 27 in Kharkiv. In 1969, Vladimir wrote an interesting paper entitled "A cyclic inequality" (Russian), which was published in *Matematicheskie Zametki* in 1971; its English version was published the same year in the *Mathematical Notes* of the Academy of Sciences of the USSR. At the age of 15, Drinfeld represented the Soviet Union at the IMO in Bucharest, Romania, and won a gold medal with a full score of 40 points. Then he entered at the Mathematical Department of Lomonosov Moscow State University, obtaining an undergraduate degree in 1974, postgraduate degree in 1977, Candidate of Sciences degree in 1978, and Doctor of Sciences degree in 1988 under the supervision of Yuri Manin. Before obtaining his doctorate degree, Vladimir had thirteen papers in print and had proved remarkable results concerning the Langlands program (after Robert Phelan Langlands, born 1936, Canada–USA) for function fields, especially a proof of the global Langlands conjecture for $GL(2)$ over a global function field. However, mainly because of anti-Semitism and not being birthed in Moscow, he could not get a job in Moscow. From 1978 to 1980 he worked as an Assistant Professor at Bashkir State University in Ufa. In Ufa he met his future wife, with whom he has a son. In 1981, Vladimir returned to Kharkiv and lived with his parents. There he worked at the B I Verkin Physical Engineering Institute for Low Temperature Physics and Engineering (part of the National Ukrainian Academy of Sciences) until 1998. Then, with his family, he moved to the USA and has been working at the University of Chicago since January 1999. Currently he is Harry Pratt Judson (1849–1927, USA) Distinguished Service Professor. In mathematics he is known for the Drinfeld center, Drinfeld double, Drinfeld level structure, Drinfeld module, Drinfeld upper half plane, Drinfeld twist, Drinfeld–Sokolov reduction (Vladimir V. Sokolov, Russia), Drinfeld–Sokolov–Wilson equation (George Wilson, England), ADHM construction (after Michael Atiyah, Vladimir Drinfeld, Nigel Hitchin, and Yuri Manin) of instantons, Manin–Drinfeld theorem, Yetter–Drinfeld category (David Nelson Yetter, USA), chiral algebra, chiral homology, quantum groups, the geometric Langlands correspondence, the Grothendieck–Teichmüller group, Lie-* algebra, opers, quantum affine algebra, quantized enveloping algebra, quasi-bialgebra, quasi-triangular quasi-Hopf algebra, and the Ruziewicz problem (Stanislaw Ruziewicz, 1889–1941, Poland). Since 2018, he has been working on prismatic cohomology. This is a new cohomology theory for p-adic formal schemes introduced by Bhargav Bhatt (born 1983, India–USA) and Peter Scholze (born 1987, Germany). He has more than 65 research publications and has supervised 12 doctoral students. He was awarded the Fields Medal (1990), Wolf Prize (2018), and Shaw Prize (2023). In 2016, he was elected to the United States NAS.

28.2. Vaughan Frederick Randal Jones

He was born in Gisborne, New Zealand. Vaughan completed his primary education at St. Peter's School in Cambridge (New Zealand), and then from 1966 to 1969, Auckland Grammar School, where he made enduring friendships and developed his lifelong interest in math and science. He subsequently enrolled at the University of Auckland in 1970 and received a Bachelor of Science degree in 1972 and Master of Science degree with First Class Honours in mathematics in 1973. Then, Vaughan Jones was awarded a Swiss Government Scholarship, which enabled him to undertake research in Switzerland. He attended the University of Geneva, initially for physics but later transferring to mathematics. It was while he was pursuing his Ph.D. that he met Martha Myers (USA), whom he married in 1979; together they have three children. The same year, Vaughan was awarded his Ph.D. in mathematics, defending his thesis entitled *Actions of Finite Groups on the Hyperfinite II_1 Factor*, under the supervision of André Haefliger. He received his favorite watch along with the first prize of his professional career, the Prix Vacheron Constantin. In 1980, he moved to the USA, where he joined as an Earle Raymond

Hedrick (1876–1943, USA) Assistant Professor of Mathematics (1980–1981), and then became an Associate Professor at the University Pennsylvania (1981–1984). In 1984, he moved to the Mathematical Science Research Institute, Berkeley, California. In 1985, he was appointed as a Professor of Mathematics at UC at Berkeley. In 2011, he joined Vanderbilt University, where he became the Stevenson Distinguished Professor of Mathematics. He was also a Distinguished Alumni Professor at the University of Auckland and Professor Emeritus at UC, Berkeley. During 1994–2020, he became the founding Director and Chairman of the New Zealand Mathematics Research Institute. In his study of von Neumann algebras (algebras of bounded operators acting on a Hilbert space), Jones came across polynomials that are invariant for knots and links—simple closed curves in three-dimensional space. His discovery of a knot polynomial, which became known as the Jones polynomial, led to further development of fields ranging from particle physics to molecular biology, with practical applications in the understanding of the knotting of DNA. His name also appears in the Aharonov–Jones–Landau algorithm (Dorit Aharonov, born 1970, Israel; Zeph Landau, USA), statistical mechanics, and conformal quantum field theory. One can appreciate the depth of his knowledge from the following publications: Actions of finite groups on the hyperfinite type II_1 Factor (1980), *Coxeter graphs and towers of algebras* (1989), *Subfactors and Knots* (1991), and *Introduction to Subfactors* (1997). He published 118 research articles and supervised 32 doctoral students. He created a strong sense of community among his students, holding weekly beer and pizza dinners on Fridays after his subfactor seminar and organizing math retreats that included windsurfing, kitesurfing, and skiing. He received several honors and awards, including the following: Fields Medal in 1990, FRS of London in 1990, awarded the Rutherford Medal by the Royal Society of New Zealand in 1991 (Ernest Rutherford, 1871–1937, New Zealand), Doctor of Science by the University of Auckland in 1991, Honorary Fellow of the Royal Society of New Zealand in 1991, Australian Academy of Science as a Corresponding Fellow in 1992, elected to the United States NAS in 1999, Norwegian Royal Society of Letters and Sciences in 2001, and Fellow of the AMS (2009). Vaughan died on 6 September 2020 at age 67 from health complications resulting from a severe ear infection. He was a generous man and an inspiring teacher.

28.3. Shigefumi Mori

He was born in Nagoya, Aichi, Japan. After completing his schooling at Tokai Junior and Senior High School in Nagoya, Mori attended Kyoto University, receiving his Bachelor of Science in 1973, Master of Science in 1975, and D.Sc. in 1978. He wrote his D.Sc. thesis *The Endomorphism Rings of Some Abelian Varieties* under the supervision of Masayoshi Nagata. During 1975–1980, he also worked as an assistant at the Faculty of Science, Kyoto University. Then, he joined Nagoya University and worked as a Lecturer at the Faculty of Science (1980–1982), Associate Professor (1982–1987), and Professor (1988–1990). Despite the positions Mori held in Japan during the years from 1977 to 1988, he spent much time in the USA. He was a Visiting Professor at Harvard during 1977–1980, the IAS, Princeton 1981–1982, Columbia University 1985–1987, and the University of Utah for periods during July and August 1987 (and again during 1991–92). In 1990, Mori returned to Kyoto University and joined as a Professor at the RIMS during 1990–2016; he was also Director of the RIMS during 2011–2014. In 2016, he joined Kyoto University Institute for Advanced Study (KUIAS) as a Director-General and Distinguished Professor. In 1978, Mori proved the Robin Cope Hartshorne (born 1938, USA) conjecture, which was posed in 1970, which claimed that projective spaces are the only smooth complete algebraic varieties with ample tangent bundles. Mori mainly worked in algebraic geometry, particularly in relation to the classification of three-folds and on the minimal model program. In 1998, Mori published a very successful monograph *Birational Geometry of Algebraic Varieties*, which he coauthored with Jáos Kollár (born 1956, Hungary–USA). Birational geometry is a sparsely studied branch of algebraic geometry with deep connections with many other parts of mathematics, such as differential geometry, arithmetic geometry, group theory, mirror symmetry, mathematical physics, etc. He has been awarded several honors and awards: the Iyanaga Prize of Mathematical Society of Japan in 1983, Chunichi Culture Prize of Japan in 1984, Autumn Prize of Mathematical Society of Japan in 1988, Inoue Academic Award of Japan in 1989, Cole Prize in 1990, Japan Academy Prize in 1990, Fields Medal in 1990, Person of Cultural Merit in 1990, Foreign Honorary Member of the AAAS in 1992, Member of the Japan Academy in 1998, honorary doctorate from the University of Turin in 2002, Fujihara Award of Japan in 2004, President of the IMU (2015–2018), Foreign Member of the RAS in 2016, Foreign Associate of United States NAS in 2017, honorary doctorate from University of Warwick in 2017, Kunihiko Kodaira Prize in 2019, Kyoto Prefecture Culture Prize for Outstanding Contribution in 2020, Order of Culture in 2021, and Foreign Member of the Academy of Sciences of Turin in 2023.

28.4. Edward Witten

He was born in Baltimore, Maryland, USA, to a Jewish family, as the eldest of four children. His father Louis Witten (born 1921, age 103 years, USA) was a theoretical physicist specializing in gravitation and general relativity. Edward attended the Park School of Baltimore up to grade twelve and in 1968 moved to Brandeis University (Waltham, Massachusetts), receiving his Bachelor of Arts degree with a major in history and minor in linguistics in 1971. In the late 1960s, he had inclinations toward journalism and politics. He published some articles in both *The New Republic* and *The Nation*, and in 1972 he worked for six months for the (unsuccessful) presidential campaign of George McGovern (1922–2012, USA). Edward attended the University of Michigan as an economics graduate student for only one semester, and then in 1973 enrolled in applied mathematics at Princeton University, receiving his Master of Science in 1974. He then shifted departments and secured a Ph.D. in physics in 1976 for the dissertation *Some problems in the short distance analysis of gauge theories*, under the supervision of David Jonathan Gross (born 1941, USA). After completing his doctorate, Edward went to Harvard University, where he was Postdoctoral Fellow during the session 1976–1977; then he was a Junior Fellow at the Harvard Society of Fellows during 1977–1980. In September 1980 Witten joined Princeton University as a Professor of Physics, where he continued until 1987 when he was appointed as a Professor in the School of Natural Sciences at the IAS, Princeton, and currently he is Emeritus Professor there. Edward has significantly contributed to string theory, topological quantum field theory, general relativity, and various areas of mathematics, and is considered the practical founder of M-theory. His ability to interpret physical ideas in mathematical form is quite unique. His name appears in several results, including Seiberg–Witten theory (Nathan Seiberg, born 1956. Israel), the Seiberg–Witten map, Seiberg–Witten invariants, the Wess–Zumino–Witten model, the Weinberg–Witten theorem (Steven Weinberg, 1933–2021, USA), the Gromov–Witten invariant (Mikhael Leonidovich Gromov, born 1943, Russia), the Horava–Witten domain wall (Petr Horava, born 1963, Prostejov), the Vafa–Witten theorem (Cumrun Vafa, born 1960, Iran-USA), the Witten index, the Britto–Cachazo–Feng–Witten recursion (Ruth Alexandra Britto-Pacumio, USA; Freddy Alexander Cachazo, Venezuela–Canada; and Bo Fang, China), Cachazo–Svrcek–Witten rules (Peter Svrcek, USA), the Witten conjecture, the Witten zeta function, the Hanany–Witten transition (Amihay Hanany, UK), and the Witten–Veneziano mechanism (Gabriele Veneziano, born 1942, Italy). Edward has a wealth of over 690 important publications that are in physics and he has supervised 13 doctoral students at Princeton University. His publications include *Superstring Theory* in 1987 with Michael Boris Green (born 1946, UK) and John Henry Schwarz (born 1941, USA) and *Current Algebra and Anomalies* in 1985 with Sam Bard Treiman (1925–1999, USA), Roman Wladimir Jackiw (1939–2023, Poland–USA), and Bruno Zumino. Edward has been married to Chiara Rosanna Nappi (born 1951, Italy), a Professor of physics at Princeton University, since 1979; they have three children. He has received an amazingly long list of awards: the MacArthur Fellowship in 1982, Albert Einstein (1879–1955, Germany–USA) Medal in 1985, International Centre for Theoretical Physics (ICTP) (since 1997, Abdus Salam ICTP) Dirac Medal in 1985, Alan Tower Waterman Award in 1986, Fields Medal in 1990 (the first physicist to receive the Fields Medal), James Madison (1842–1926, USA) Medal in 1993, Golden Plate Award of the American Academy of Achievement in 1997, Dannie Heineman Prize in 1998, Oskar Benjamin Klein (1894–1977, Sweden) Medal in 1998, Nemmers Prize in 2000, National Medal of Science in 2002, Pythagoras Award in 2005, Harvey Prize in 2005 (after Leo Harvey, 1887–1973, Israel), Henri Poincaré Prize in 2006, Crafoord Prize in 2008, Lorentz Medal in 2010, Isaac Newton Medal in 2010, Breakthrough Prize in Fundamental Physics in 2012, Kyoto Prize in 2014, and Albert Einstein Award in 2016. He has been awarded honorary doctorate degrees from Brandeis University (1988), Hebrew University of Jerusalem (1993), Columbia University (1996), University of Southern California (2004), Johns Hopkins University (2005), Harvard University (2005), and the University of Pennsylvania (2022). He has been elected a Fellow of numerous academies and societies, such as the AAAS (1984), American Physical Society (1984), United States NAS (1988), APS (1994), RSL (1998), Academy of Sciences of Paris (2000), Pontifical Academy of Sciences (2006), and the AMS in 2012. He also appeared in the list of *Time* magazine's 100 most influential people of 2004.

28.5. Aleksandr Aleksandrovich Razborov

He was born in Belovo, Russia. Aleksandr undertook his undergraduate studies at Moscow State University, in the Department of Mechanics and Mathematics, and received his degree in 1985. The same year he became a graduate student at the Steklov Mathematical Institute and in 1987 defended his Ph.D. thesis *On Systems of*

Equations in Free Groups under the supervision of Sergei Ivanovich Adian (1931–2020, USSR–USA), and was hired by the Institute. In 1991, he defended his doctoral thesis *Lower Bounds in the Boolean Complexity*. During 1991–2000 he worked at the Steklov Mathematical Institute as a Leading Researcher, and from 2000 to 2008 as a Principal Researcher, and continues to work there.In 2008, Aleksandr joined the Department of Computer Science, University of Chicago, as Andrew MacLeish (1838–1928, Scotland–USA) Distinguished Service Professor. At the IAS he has been a member ((1993–1994) and (2000–2003))) and Visiting Professor (2003–2008). He was also Visiting Researcher, Department of Computer Science, Princeton University, during 1999–2000. From 2008, he has also been a Resident Adjoint Professor at Toyota Technological Institute in Chicago. Razborov's main interest is in combinatorial group theory, circuit complexity, proof complexity, communication complexity, complexity theory, quantum computations, extremal combinatorics, and discrete mathematics. In 1994, with Steven Rudich (born 1961, USA) he introduced the notion of natural proof (a certain kind of proof establishing that one complexity class differs from another one). He has published more than 200 research publications and given over 50 plenary and invited talks. In 1980, he received a gold medal at the 1979 IMO; in 1990, the Rolf Nevanlinna Prize; in 2007, the Gödel Prize of the European Association for Theoretical Computer Science and the Special Interest Group on Algorithms and Computation Theory of the ACM; and in 2013, the David Peter Robbins (1942–2003, USA) Prize of the AMS. In 1993, he was elected to the Academia Europea; in 2000, he became a Corresponding Member of the RAS; and in 2020, he became a member of the AAAS. He serves as an editorial board member of several international journals and member of several program committees.

29. Zurich ICM 1994

This Congress was held in Zurich, Switzerland, during 3–11 August, 1994. The Congress was attended by 2476 full members from 92 countries. The President of the IMU Jacques-Louis Lions in his opening speech said the following: Already now mathematics, in addition to its intrinsic importance, is one of the keys for the development of other sciences and of industry. Everything indicates that this already fundamental role will increase during the next century. This implies responsibilities for us and for our governments to: (1) continue, and even increase the support to mathematical research of the highest quality, (2) further develop collaborations and exchanges with other disciplines and with industry, (3) help as much as possible the Mathematical Instruction and the Mathematical Research in countries suffering of difficult economic situations, and to (4) explain as clearly as possible what we are doing to a not too specialized public. He also announced that the President of the Organizing Committee of the ICM, Henri Claude Carnal (born 1939 Switzerland), would be appointed as the President of the Congress by acclamation. Henri Carnal in his presidential speech welcomed all the participants to Zurich and then reminded them of the lasting quality of mathematical ideas and universality of mathematical activity. He proposed the name of Beno Eckmann (1917–2008, Switzerland), who had been Secretary of the IMU from 1956 to 1961, for election by acclamation as the Honorary President of the Congress. Beno Eckmann greeted the Congress in three of the official languages of Switzerland (German, French, and Italian), excusing himself for not having done so in the fourth, Romansch. In his speech Beno Eckmann referred to the Hermann Weyl quote "Mathematics, besides language and music, is one of the primary manifestations of the free creative power of the human mind and it is the universal organ for world-understanding through theoretical construction. It has to remain an essential element of the knowledge and abilities we have to teach, of the culture we have to transmit to the next generations". He also said "Whether mathematicians like it or not, the computer is here to stay". Next, Minister Ruth Dreifuss (born 1940, Switzerland), then Head of the Federal Department of Home Affairs, in her address talked about pure and applied mathematics and their role in society. Then the names of the awardees of the Fields Medals and the Rolf Nevanlinna Prize were announced by the respective Chairmen of the committees. The Fields Medal Committee consisted of David Bryant Mumford (Chairman), Luis Angel Caffarelli (born 1948, Argentina–USA), Masaki Kashiwara (born 1947, Japan), Barry Mazur, Alexander Schrijver (born 1948, the Netherlands), Dennis Parnell Sullivan (born 1941, USA), Jacques Tits, and Sathamangalam Ranga Iyengar Srinivasa Varadhan (born 1940, India–USA). The Rolf Nevanlinna Prize Committee consisted of Jacques-Louis Lions (Chairman), Hendrik Willem Lenstra Jr. (born 1949, the Netherlands), Yuri Vladimirovich Matiyasevich, Robert Endre Tarjan, and Masaya Yamaguti (1925–1998, Japan). Fields Medals were awarded to Jean Louis, baron Bourgain (1954–2018, Belgium), Pierre-Louis Lions (born 1956, France), Jean-Christophe Yoccoz (1957–2016, France), and Efim Isaakovich Zelmanov (born 1955, Russia–USA). The Rolf Nevanlinna Prize was awarded to Avi Wigderson (born 1956, Israel). The medalists came forward and received their medals and prizes from the Honorary President Beno Eckmann.

For the laureates laudations came after the opening ceremony. Luis Caffarelli presented the work of Jean Bourgain, "Bourgain's work touches on several central topics of mathematical analysis: the geometry of Banach spaces, convexity in high dimensions, harmonic analysis, ergodic theory, and finally, nonlinear partial differential equations from mathematical physics. In all of these areas, he made spectacular inroads into questions where progress had been blocked for a long time. This he did by simultaneously bringing into play different areas of mathematics: number theory, combinatorics, probability, and showing their relevance to the problem in a previously unforeseen fashion". Srinivasa Varadhan described the work of Pierre-Louis Lions, "Lions' has made unique contributions covering a variety of areas, from probability theory to partial differential equations. The choice of his problems has always been motivated by hard problems in physics, engineering and economics. His work is important because he has developed techniques that, with variations, can be applied to classes of such problems". Adrien Douady (1935–2006, France) presented the work of Jean-Christophe Yoccoz (translation from French), "Yoccoz is a pure product, and of the best vintage, of the French system. He explained 12 of his contributions to the theory of dynamical systems. Walter Feit explained that Efim Isaakovich Zelmanov has received a Fields Medal for the solution of the restricted Burnside problem" (after William Burnside, 1852–1927, England). For this he used his earlier fundamental contributions to Jordan algebras. Yuri Matiyasevich mentioned that Avi Wigderson's work "has made a lot of wonderful contributions to diverse areas of the mathematical foundations of computer science" and highlighted his "impressive results connected with the so called zero-knowledge interactive proofs".

There were 16 one-hour plenary addresses, which included two women, Baroness Ingrid Daubechies (born 1954, Belgium–USA) and Marina Evseevna Ratner (1938–2017, Russia–USA); 145 forty-five-minute lectures from invited speakers; and about 900 short communications. Additionally, there were five lectures by invitation of the ICMI and another five by invitation of the International Commission on the History of Mathematics. The last plenary lecture was by Andrew John Wiles (born 1953, England) on *Modular forms, elliptic curves, and Fermat's Last Theorem*, in which he presented his proof of Fermat's Last Theorem and remarked that "one step in the argument was not complete". Immediately after Wiles' lecture, the closing ceremony took place. The Congress was also informed of the election of the new EC for the period 1994–1998: David Bryant Mumford (President), Vladimir Igorevich Arnold and Albrecht Dold as Vice-Presidents, Jacob Palis Jr. as Secretary, and James Greig Arthur, Simon Kirwan Donaldson, Björn Engquist (born 1945, Sweden), Shigefumi Mori, Kalyanapuram Rangachari Parthasarathy (1936–2023, India), and Jacques-Louis Lions as members. During the closing ceremony, Jacques-Louis Lions, President of the IMU, announced that the General Assembly had unanimously approved that the next ICM 1998 would take place in Berlin. Then, Friedrich Hirzebruch invited the audience to the next ICM; he recalled the third ICM in Heidelberg; he hoped that the formerly divided city of Berlin would be a symbol for improved worldwide cooperation; and he said that many Berlin mathematicians were eager to make the Congress a success. Henri Carnal then declared the Congress closed.

29.1. Jean Louis, Baron Bourgain

He was born in Ostend, Belgium. His father René Bourgain (1926–2011, Belgium) was a Professor of physiology and his mother was a paediatrician; he also had seven-year-younger sister, Claire Bourgain. Jean attended primary and high school in Ostend and graduated in 1971. The same year he enrolled in a mathematics degree at the ULB. Ingrid Daubechies enrolled at the ULB at the same time as Jean but she wanted to major in physics. Jean began his study of the 'Licentiaat' in 1973 and was awarded the degree (equivalent to a Master of Science) in 1975. In his thesis, which was written under the supervision of Freddy Delbaen (born 1946, Belgium–Switzerland), Jean gave a purely geometric proof of the fact that every weakly compact convex set in a Banach space is the closed convex hull of its strongly exposed points. This work was published in the *Proceedings of the AMS* in September 1975. Again in 1975, he won a Belgium Research Fellowship to study for his doctorate at the ULB. In 1977, again under the supervision of Freddy Delbaen, Jean was awarded his Ph.D. degree from the ULB. By 1978 he had eleven papers in print, all submitted while he was still undertaking research for his Ph.D.; further, during the same period he attended several conferences and gained a reputation as an exceptional mathematician. His habilitation was awarded in 1979 "for work on the structural theory of Banach Spaces and the relation between their local and infinite dimensional properties". After finishing his fellowship in 1981, Jean joined the ULB as a Professor and continued there until 1985. The same year he joined the University of Illinois Urbana-Champaign for ten years, and then from 1984 to 2018 he was Professor at the IHES, Bures-sur-Yvette in France, and at the IAS, Princeton. From 2012 to 2014, he was also a visiting scholar at UC, Berkeley. He made several significant contributions in mathematical analysis and its application to partial differential equations, mathematical physics, combinatorics, number theory, ergodic theory, and theoretical computer science. He published over 500 research publications and five very influential (mostly co-authored) monographs: *New Classes of L_p-Spaces* (1981), *Banach Spaces with a Unique Unconditional Basis, up to Permutation* (1985), *Global Solutions of Nonlinear Schrödinger Equations* (1999), *Green's Function Estimates for Lattice Schrödinger Operators and Applications* (2004), and *Mathematical Aspects of Nonlinear Dispersive Equations* (2009). He received several honors and awards: the Empain Prize by the Belgium National Science Foundation in 1983, Salem Prize in 1983 (after Raphaël Salem, 1898–1963, Greece–France), Lady Davis (after Henriette Marie Meyer, 1872–1963, and her husband Mortimer Barnett Davis, 1866–1928, Canada) Professor of Mathematics at the Hebrew University in Jerusalem in 1988, Ostrowski Prize in 1991, Fairchild Distinguished Professor (after Sherman Mills Fairchild, 1896–1971, USA) at Caltech in 1991, Fields Medal in 1994, elected to the Academy of Sciences in Paris in 2000, elected to the Polish Academy of Sciences in 2000, elected to the Academia Europaea in 2008, elected a Foreign Member of the RSAS in 2009, Shaw Prize in 2010, elected to the United States NAS in 2011, Crafoord Prize in 2012, elected to the Royal Flemish Academy of Arts and Sciences in 2013, Baron by King Philippe of Belgium (2015), Breakthrough Prize in Mathematics in 2017, and Steele Prize in 2018. Jean was a member of several editorial boards of journals, including the *Annals of Mathematics*, the *Journal de l'Institut de Mathématiques de Jussieu*, the *Publications Mathématiques de l'IHES*, the *International Mathematical Research Notices*, the *Journal of Geometrical and Functional Analysis*, the *Journal d'Analyse de Jérusalem*, the *Journal of Discrete and Continuous Dynamical Systems*, the *Journal of Functional Analysis*, the *Duke Mathematical Journal*, the *Journal of the European Mathematical Society* (EMS), and *Comptes Rendus of the Academy of Sciences* in Paris. Jean married the mathematician Mei-Chu Chang ,who was awarded a Ph.D. in 1982 from UC, Berkeley, for the thesis Some results on stable rank 2 vector bundles and reflexive sheaves on $\mathbf{P}^3$. They have one child, Eric Bourgain-Chang, who is also a mathematician. In October 2014 Bourgain was diagnosed with pancreas cancer. It was a miracle that he survived and worked for four and a half years after he was diagnosed. The creator of this miracle was his younger sister, Professor of Medicine, Claire.

29.2. Pierre-Louis Lions

He was born in Grasse, Alpes-Maritimes, France, the only child of Jacques-Louis Lions and Andrée Olivier. Pierre-Louis had his secondary education at Lycée Pasteur (outskirts of Paris) and then moved to the ENS from 1975 to 1979. He received his doctorate from the Pierre and Marie Curie University—Paris VI in 1979. The title of his thesis was *Sur quelques classes d'équations aux dérivees partielles non linéaires et leur résolution numérique* (On some classes of nonlinear partial differential equations and their numerical resolution), written under the supervision of Haïm Brézis (1944–2024, France). During (1979–1981), Pierre-Louis was a researcher at the CNRS. Then in 1981, he became Professor at the University of Paris Dauphine University. While still holding this post he was attached to the CNRS as Director of Research in 1995. He has also held the position of Professor of Applied Mathematics at the École Polytechnique from 1992. In 2002, Pierre-Louis was also appointed Professor at the Collége de France as the chair of Partial and Partial Derivative Equations. Since 2014, he has also been a Visiting Professor at the University of Chicago, USA. Pierre-Louis is known for a number of contributions to the fields of partial differential equations and the calculus of variations. With Haïm Brézis he gave new results about maximal monotone operators in Hilbert space. With Bertrand Mercier (born 1949, France) he proposed a "forward–backward splitting algorithm" for finding a zero of the sum of two maximal monotone operators. He was the first mathematician to give a solution to Boltzmann's equation (after Ludwig Eduard Boltzmann 1844–1906, Austria) with proof. With Michael Grain Crandall (born 1940, USA), he introduced the concept of viscosity solutions for nonlinear partial differential equations, which has a wide range of applications. With Jean-Michel Lasry (born 1947, France), he introduced and developed the theory of medium-field games and its applications, in particular to economics and finance. He has published more than 300 research papers, supervised 20 doctoral students (some of which have received prestigious medals and awards), and been an editorial board member of almost 25 journals; in addition he has written several books: *Generalized solutions of Hamilton-Jacobi equations* (1982), *Mathematical topics in fluid mechanics. Vol. 1. Incompressible models* (1996), *Mathematical topics in fluid mechanics. Vol. 2. Compressible models* (1998), *On Euler equations and statistical physics* (1998), and *The mathematical theory of thermodynamic limits: Thomas-Fermi type models*

(1998). Pierre-Louis has been honored by several medals and awards: Doistau-Blutet Foundation Prize in 1986, IBM Prize in 1987, Prize of the Philip Morris tobacco and cigarette company in 1991, Ampére Prize in 1992, Fields Medal in 1994, and elected member of the Paris Academy, Naples Academy, and European Academy. He is also Commandeur of the Légion d'Honneur (France's highest civilian and military honor). Pierre-Louis has been awarded honorary doctorates from Heriot-Watt University in Edinburgh, Scotland; Narvik University College; and City University of Hong Kong. In 1979, he married Lila Laurenti, with whom he has one son.

29.3. Jean-Christophe Yoccoz

He was born in Paris, France, in a family of renowned intellectuals and scientists. His father as well as maternal grandfather were distinguished mathematicians, and his mother was a famous theoretical physicist. Both of his parents were Professors at the Pierre and Marie Curie University (Paris VI). It was with his family that he developed an early interest in mathematics and quickly showed exceptional talents in this area. Yoccoz attended the Lycée Louis-le-Grand (secondary school); by then he was already a silver medalist at the 1973 IMO and a gold medalist in 1974. In 1975, he was placed first in the entrance examination for the ENS and completed an agrégation in mathematics in 1977 in joint first position. Yoccoz completed his National Service in Cooperation at the Instituto de Matemática Pura e Aplicada (IMPA) in Rio de Janeiro, Brazil, in 1981–1983. He obtained his doctorate in 1985 at the École Polytechnique for the thesis *Centralisateurs et conjugaison différentiable des difféomorphismes du cercle* (Centralizers and differentiable conjugation of circle diffeomorphisms), which was written under the supervision of Michael Robert Herman (1942–2000, France–USA). In his thesis, he improved theorems of his supervisor by giving simpler proofs but also obtaining the same results under weaker hypotheses. After completing his doctorate, he joined the Jussieu Mathematics Center—Paris Rive Gauche as a researcher. In 1987, he took up a position at the University of Paris-Sud, and in 1997 became a Professor at the Collége de France, where he remained until his premature death in 2016. His work on dynamical systems, particularly on ergodic theory and the study of holomorphic applications, is revolutionary in the field. He is famous for the Yoccoz puzzle (a combinatorial technique that proved useful to the study of Julia sets). He published more than 55 research papers and supervised 14 doctoral students. He received many prestigious recognitions throughout his career: Salem Prize in 1988, Fields Medal in 1994, member of Bourbaki Group, member of the FAS, member of the Brazilian Academy of Sciences, Chevalier in the French Legion of Honor in 1995, and Grand Cross of the Brazilian National Order of Scientific Merit in 1998.

29.4. Efim Isaakovich Zelmanov

He was born in Khabarovsk, USSR, to a Jewish family. After completing his schooling Efim entered Novosibirsk State University in 1972, when he was 17 years old. He obtained his master's degree in 1977, and then he was appointed to the staff at the same university. He taught there while continuing with his own research. In 1980, he received his Ph.D. from the same university, defending his thesis entitled

Jordan Division Algebras, written under the supervision of Leonid Arkadievich Bokut (born 1937, USSR) and Anatoly Illarionovich Shirshov (1921–1981, USSR). His thesis changed the whole of the subject of Jordan algebras by extending results from the classical theory of finite dimensional Jordan algebras to infinite dimensional Jordan algebras. The same year he was appointed as a Junior Researcher at the Institute of Mathematics of the USSR Academy of Sciences at Novosibirsk. In 1985, he was awarded a doctorate (habilitation) at Leningrad (now St. Petersburg) State University. Then, Efim was promoted to Senior Researcher and in 1986 to Leading Researcher at the Institute of Mathematics of the USSR Academy of Sciences. In 1987, he left the Soviet Union and worked as a Professor: during 1990–1994 at the University of Wisconsin-Madison; during 1994–1995 at the University of Chicago; during 1995–2002 at Yale University; during 2002–2022 at UC, San Diego, as a Rita Atkinson Endowed Chair Professor (he occupied the same office as had earlier been occupied by Fields Medalists Shing-Tung Yau and Michael Hartley Freedman); and from 2022 Chair Professor, Southern University of Science and Technology. Efim's contribution to mathematics goes far beyond his remarkable research and teaching achievements, especially on combinatorial problems in nonassociative algebra and group theory, including his solution of the restricted Burnside problem. He has published more than 90 research papers and supervised 13 doctoral students. He is either an editor or member of the editorial board of several major mathematics journals, including the *Annals of Mathematics*, the *Journal of Algebra*, and the *Journal of the AMS*. He wasawarded the Fields Medal in 1994, Collége de France Medal in 1992, and Andre Aizenstadt Prize in 1996. Efim is a member of the United States NAS (2001), at the age of 47, the youngest member of the mathematics section of the academy; Fellow of the AAAS (1996); Foreign Member of the Spanish Royal Academy of Sciences; Foreign Member of the Korean Academy of Science and Technology; and Fellow of the AMS (2012). Efim was awarded honorary doctorates from the University of Hagen Germany (1997), the University of Alberta Canada (2011), Taras Shevchenko National University of Kyiv, Ukraine (2012), Universidad Internacional Menéndez Pelayo in Santander, Spain (2015), and the University of Lincoln, UK (2016).

29.5. Avi Wigderson

He was born in Haifa, Israel, to Jewish parents who eventually escaped to Israel from Nazi Germany while almost all members of their family died in the Holocaust. Avi has two younger brothers. After completing his primary schooling, he attended Hebrew Reali High School in Haifa for his secondary education. After graduation he spent three years completing the required military service. In 1977, for his undergraduate studies, Avi enrolled at Technion, the Israel Institute of Technology, taking mainly mathematics and computer science courses. In 1980, he was awarded a Bachelor of Science 'Summa Cum Laude' (with highest honors) in computer science from Technion. At Technion he met his wife Edna Rothenstein, a mathematics student. They married in their final year as undergraduates at Technion, and they have three children. Avi went on to graduate study at Princeton University, and in 1981 he was awarded the degree of Master of Science in Engineering in computer science, and in the following year a Master of Arts degree in computer science. In 1983, he received his Ph.D in computer science. He defended his doctoral dissertation entitled *Studies in computational complexity*, under the supervision of Richard Jay Lipton (born 1946, USA). During (1983–1984) Avi conducted postdoctoral work as a Visiting Assistant Professor in the Department of Computer Science at UC, Berkeley, and from 1985 to 1986 as a Fellow at the MSRI in Berkeley. In 1986, he was appointed as a Senior Lecturer in the Department of Computer Science at the Hebrew University; in 1987 he was promoted to Associate Professor. While continuing to hold this position, during 1990–1992 Avi was a Visiting Associate Professor in the Department of Computer Science at Princeton University. While in the USA, he was promoted to Professor at the Computer Science Institute of the Hebrew University. In 1992, he returned to the Hebrew University and in 1993 he was made Chairman of the Computer Science Institute. In August 1995 he became a Visiting Professor in the Department of Computer Science, Princeton University, and a member of the School of Mathematics at the IAS, Princeton. In 1999, he took a position at the IAS, Princeton, and in 2003 he gave up his Hebrew University position to take up full-time residence at the IAS, Princeton, as Herbert H. Maass Professor at the School of Mathematics. Avi has made significant contributions in various fields of mathematics and computer science, including complexity theory, parallel computation, combinatorics and graph theory, Combinatorial Optimization Algorithms, Randomness and Cryptography, and Distributed and Neural Networks. He developed the Zig Zag product together with Omer Reingold (Israel) and Salil Vadhan (USA), which links complexity theory, graph theory, and group theory. With Silvio Micali (born 1954, Italy) and Oded Goldreich (born 1957, Israel), he demonstrated that zero-knowledge proofs can be utilized in proving a public result on secret data in secret. He has written more than 370 research publications in computer science and about 400 in mathematics, and has also produced 14 doctoral students. He has also written a very influential book entitled *Mathematics and Computation: A Theory Revolutionizing Technology and Science* (2019). Avi has received several awards and honors: Rolf Nevanlinna Prize in 1944, Levi Leonard Conant (1857–1916, USA) Prize in 2008, Gödel Prize in 2009, elected as a member of the AAAS in 2011, elected as an ACM Fellow for "contributions to theoretical computer science and mathematics" in 2018, Knuth Prize in 2019, Abel Prize in 2021, and Turing Award 2024. In 2023, Technion awarded him a honorary doctorate degree. He is a member of several editorial boards of leading journals, including *Journal of the ACM, Journal of the AMS, Society for Industrial and Applied Mathematics (SIAM) Journal on Discrete Mathematics, Information and Computation*, and *Complexity Theory*.

30. Berlin ICM 1998

This Congress was held in Berlin, Germany, during 18–27 August, 1998. The Congress was attended by 3346 participants from 98 countries (65% from Europe). During the opening ceremony the President of the IMU David Bryant Mumford welcomed the participants and, in his speech said "Mathematics is usually explained and justified to the world at large by giving examples of important inventions that could not have been made without its help. This is embodied in the myth that we mathematicians concern ourselves with eternal truths, which we hand on to physicists, who pass them on to chemists and engineers, etc. who finally pass them on to mankind as a whole. There are definitely important examples of ideas passing along this chain (in fact in both directions!) but I also think it is a rather narrow view to isolate mathematics on such a pedestal. There is a more socially grounded view, which says that mathematics and mathematicians are deeply embedded in human culture and are tied to the Arts in particular where the love of abstraction also flourishes". He also said "Although the links are sometimes hidden, mathematics is tightly woven with all of art and science". He proposed that Martin Grötschel (born 1948, Germany) be elected by acclamation as President of the 1998 ICM, who greeted the participants. Then Karl-Heinz Hoffmann (born 1939, Germany), the President of the DMV, gave a speech. He referred to the quote of Robert Musil (1880–1942, Hungary-Switerzeland), "Mathematics (as a science) is the bravery of pure reason, one of the few we have today. ... It can be said that we live entirely on the results. ... This whole being that runs ... and stands around us not only depends on mathematics for its comprehensibility, but has effectively been created by her, rests in its ... existence upon her". He also said "Mathematics has not only given birth to her extremely successful daughter, computer science, but mathematical methods are also used in their own rights and thus have become the backbone of modern technology". As the President of the DMV, he asked to elect by acclamation Friedrich Hirzebruch as Honorary President of the ICM'98. Friedrich Hirzebruch in his lecture described the changes in Germany in the 94-year lapse between the two German congresses. The 1904 Heidelberg Congress had been an exhibition of the wealth and power of the German Empire. Next, the greeting message of (Former President of Germany) Roman Herzog (1934–2017, Germany) was read; he expressed the meaning of the Berlin 1998 Congress: "Berlin symbolizes the division of Germany, for the city itself was divided by a wall, but it also symbolizes the reunification of Germany as a democratic state with scientific freedom". He also conveyed "The connection between physics and mathematics has always been of fundamental importance. In their origins hardly distinguishable from one another, these two disciplines have once again become especially closely linked. New mathematical theories emerge from ideas in physics, and the communication of physical results is impossible without mathematics". Then after few more lectures the names of the laureates of the Fields Medals and the Rolf Nevanlinna Prize were announced by the respective Chairmen of the committees. The Fields Medal Committee consisted of Yuri Ivanovich Manin (Chairman), John Macleod Ball (born 1948, England), John Coates, Johannes Jisse Duistermaat (1942–2010, the Netherlands), Michael Hartley Freedman, Jürg Martin Fröhlich (born 1946, Switzerland), Robert Duncan MacPherson (born 1944, USA), Kyoji Saito (born 1944, Japan), and Stephen Smale. The Rolf Nevanlinna Prize Committee consisted of David Bryant Mumford (Chairman), Björn Engquist, Frank Thomson Leighton (born 1956, USA), and Aleksandr Aleksandrovich Razborov. Fields Medals were awarded to Richard Ewen Borcherds (born 1959, South Africa–UK–USA), William Timothy Gowers (born 1963, England), Maxim Lvovich Kontsevich (born 1964, Russia–France), and Curtis Tracy McMullen (born 1958, USA). The Rolf Nevanlinna Prize was awarded to Peter Williston Shor (born 1959, USA). The Fields Medals were presented by the Honorary President Friedrich Hirzebruch. The Rolf Nevanlinna Prize was presented by Olli Lehto. During the ceremony Friedrich Hirzebruch also offered a silver plaque to Andrew John Wiles (he was then beyond the traditional age limit of 40 years) as a special tribute from the IMU "on the occasion of his sensational achievement", Fermat's Last Theorem.

The last item of the opening ceremony was the commendation for the laureates. Peter Goddard (born 1945, England) presented the work of Richard Borcherds: contributions to algebra, the theory of authomorphic forms, and mathematical physics, including the introduction of vertex algebras and Borcherds' Lie algebras, the proof of the Conway–Norton (after Simon Phillips Norton, 1952–2019, England) moonshine conjecture, and the discovery of a new class of automorphic infinite products. Béla Bollobás (born 1943, Hungary–Britain) described the work of William Gowers: contributions to functional analysis and combinatorics and developing a new vision of infinite-dimensional geometry, including the solution of two of Banach's problems and the discovery of the so-called Gowers' dichotomy: every infinite-dimensional Banach space contains either a subspace with many symmetries (technically, with an unconditional basis) or a subspace every operator on which is Fredholm of index zero. Clifford Henry Taubes (born 1954, USA) presented the work of Maxim Kontsevich: contributions to algebraic geometry, topology, and mathematical physics, including the proof of Witten's conjecture of intersection numbers in moduli spaces of stable curves, construction of the universal Vassiliev invariant of knots (after Victor Anatolyevich Vassiliev or Vasilyev, born 1956, Russia), and formal quantization of Poisson manifolds (after Siméon Denis Poisson, 1781–1840, France). Steve Smale presented the work of Curtis McMullen: contributions to the theory of holomorphic dynamics and geometrization of three-manifolds, including proofs of Bers' conjecture (after Lipman Bers, 1914–1993, Latvia–USA) on the density of cusp points in the boundary of the Teichmller space, and Kra's theta function conjecture (after Irwin Kra, born 1937, USA). Ronald Lewis Graham (1935–2020, USA) talked about the work of Peter Shor: a strong geometrical flavor, typically coupled with deep ideas from probability, complexity theory or combinatorics, and always woven together with brilliance and insight of the first magnitude. These have been the principal driving forces behind the development of quantum computing.

There were 21 one-hour plenary addresses, which included one woman, Dusa NcDuff (born 1945, UK); 169 forty-five-minute lectures of invited speakers; 1098 short fifteen-minute contributions and 236 poster presentations; and 235 ad hoc talks of fifteen minutes. The special evening lecture by Andrew Wiles on "Twenty Years of

Number Theory" on 19 August attracted an audience of about 2,300. In his lecture he observed the follwoing: One change in number theory over the last twenty years is that it has become an applied subject (Perhaps one should say it has gone back to being an applied subject as it was more than two thousand years ago). During the closing ceremony David Mumford, after thanking various committees, announced the selection of new EC for the period 1998–2002: Jacob Palis Jr. (President), Simon Kirwan Donaldson and Shigefumi Mori as Vice-Presidents, Phillip Augustus Griffiths (born 1938, USA) as Secretary, and Vladimir Igorevich Arnold, Jean-Michel Bismut, Björn Engquist, Martin Grötschel, Madabusi Santanam Raghunathan (born 1941, India), and David Mumford as members. David Mumford also noted the decision that the ICM 2002 would be held in Beijing, China. Then, the President of the Chinese Mathematical Society Kung Chin Chang thanked the Executive Committee and invited all participants to Beijing in 2002. Finally, Martin Grötschel declared the Congress to be closed. An important feature of the Congress was the extensive use of electronic communication and information in the organization of the congress: letters were emailed, the possibility of electronic registration was offered and used by two thirds of the participants, a server with up-to-date information was set up, and 95 percent of the invited and contributed presentations were submitted electronically. The plenary and invited lectures were made available on the Internet before the Congress started. The opening ceremony was transmitted worldwide on the Internet.

30.1. Richard Ewen Borcherds

He was born in Cape Town, South Africa, but the family moved to Aldermaston in the UK when he was six months old. Later his father became a Lecturer of Physics at Birmingham University, where his particular interests were the use of computers in physics and the involvement of scientists in politics. Richard attended King Edward's School in Birmingham. He was a keen chess player and by the age of fourteen he was Midlands under 21 Chess Champion. Then, Richard attended Trinity College, Cambridge, as an undergraduate student, and after the award of his Bachelor of Arts degree he advanced to undertake research supervised by John Conway. Richard was appointed as a Research Fellow at Trinity College, Cambridge, in 1983 and held this post until 1987. He was awarded a Ph.D. degree in 1985 for his thesis *The Leech Lattice and Other Lattices*. He consecutively published three significant papers: in 1984 *A Monster Lie Algebra*, in 1985 *The Leech Lattice*, and in 1986 *Vertex Algebras, Kac-Moody Algebras, and the Monster*. During the academic year 1987–1988, Richard was Morrey Assistant Professor at UC, Berkeley. In 1988, he returned to Cambridge and joined the Royal Society University as a Research Fellow and continued until 1992, and then spent the following year as a Lecturer at Cambridge. In 1993, he was appointed as Professor of Mathematics at UC, Berkeley. In 1996, Richard returned to Cambridge and spent three years there as a Royal Society Professor at the Department of Pure Mathematics and Mathematical Statistics. In 1999, he again joined the Department of Mathematics at UC, Berkeley, as a Professor and continues to hold this position. He is known for his work in lattices, group theory, infinite-dimensional algebras, and quantum field theory. His proof of the monstrous moonshine conjecture using ideas from string theory in 1989 is considered as indispensable (he writes that the inspiration necessary to prove the conjecture came while traveling in India). He has published more than 30 research papers and supervised 11 doctoral students. Richard has been awarded several honors and awards: the EMS Prize in 1992 (one of the first recipients), Whitehead Prize in 1992, FRS of London in 1994, Fields Medal 1998, Fellow of the AMS in 2012, and the United States NAS in 2014. Richard is married to the topologist Fr. Ursula Gritsch and has two daughters.

30.2. William Timothy Gowers

He was born in Marlborough, Wiltshire, England. His father William Patrick Gowers (1936–2014, England) was a composer, mainly known for his film scores. He has two sisters, the writer Rebecca Gowers and the violinist Katharine Gowers. Timothy attended King's College School, Cambridge, and was a choirboy in the King's College choir. From there he attended Eton College as a King's Scholar, where he was taught by an excellent mathematics teacher Norman Arthur Routledge (1928–2013, UK). In 1981, Timothy won a gold medal at the IMO with a perfect score. After completing school he matriculated at Trinity College. In 1989, his first paper *Symmetric block bases in finite-dimensional normed spaces* was published. In 1990, Timothy was awarded his doctorate degree for his thesis *Symmetric Structures in Banach Spaces* at Trinity College, Cambridge, written under the supervision of Béla Bollobás. In 1989, Timothy was appointed as a Research Fellow at Trinity College, where he continued until 1993. In 1991, he was appointed as a Lecturer at University College, London, and spent four years there. He was promoted to Reader in 1994. In 1995, Timothy was appointed as a Lecturer at the University of Cambridge. In 1998, he was named Rouse Ball Professor of Mathematics at Cambridge. During 2000–2002, he was Visiting Professor at Princeton University. In 2020, he was appointed Professeur titulaire de la chaire Combinatoire at the Collége de France, a historic institution dedicated to popularizing science. Currently he is holding teaching and research positions at Cambridge and at University College, London. He has made several foundational contributions in the fields of functional analysis, combinatorics, and quasirandom groups. Specifically, in 1992, he showed that not every infinite-dimensional Banach space has an infinite-dimensional subspace that admits an unconditional Schauder basis (after Juliusz Pawel Schauder, 1899–1943, Poland); in 1997, Timothy proved that the Szemerédi regularity lemma (after Endre Szemerédi, born 1940, Hungary–USA) necessarily comes with tower-type bounds; in 2003, he established a regularity lemma for hypergraphs; and in 2005, he introduced the notion of a quasirandom group. Timothy has also written several works popularizing mathematics, including *Mathematics: A Very Short Introduction* (2002), which describes modern mathematical research for the general reader. He has written more than 60 research papers and supervised 13 doctoral students. Timothy has been awarded several honors and awards: the Whitehead Prize in 1995, British Mathematical Colloquium (BMC) Morning Speaker in 1995, EMS Prize in 1996, Fields Medal in 1998, FRS of London in 1999, BMC Plenary Speaker in 2003, Mathematical Association of America (MAA) Hedrick Lecturer in 2006, member of the APS in 2010, Young Researchers in Mathematics in 2010, Euler Book Prize in 2011, Knight Bachelor in 2012, Listed in *Nature*'s 10 people who mattered in 2012, honorary doctorate on the University of St Andrews' 600th Anniversary celebrations in 2013, De Morgan

Medal in 2016, Sylvester Medal in 2016, and AMS Colloquium Lecturers 2016. In 1988, Timothy married Emily Thomas, a classicist and Cambridge academic: they divorced in 2007. Together they had three children. In 2008, he got married for a second time, to Julie Barrau, a University Lecturer in British Medieval History at the University of Cambridge. They have two children together.

30.3. Maxim Lvovich Kontsevich

He was born in Khimki, near Moscow, USSR (now Russia), to a talented family. His father Lev Rafailovich Kontsevich (born 1930, USSR) is a orientalist and Candidate of Sciences, who created the Kontsevich system. Maxim attended secondary school in Moscow and became engrossed in mathematics and physics at an early age. At the age of sixteen he was placed second in the National Mathematical Olympiad Competition, and because of this achievement he was offered a place at Moscow State University. There Maxim was taught by distinguished professors, in particular Israel Moiseevich Gelfand (1913–2009, Russia–USA). In 1983, he published two papers *The Growth of the Lie Algebra Generated by Two Generic Vector Fields on the Line* (with Alexandre Aleksandrovich Kirilloff (Kirillov), born 1936, Russia), and *Algebras of Intermediate Growth* (with Kirillov and Alexander Ivanovich Molev, born 1961, Russia–Australia). In 1985, he left the university without a degree to become a researcher at the Institute for Information Transmission Problems in Moscow and continued there until 1990. While at the Institute he further published three papers *The Virasoro Algebra*, *Teichmller Spaces*, and *Jackson Networks on Countable Graphs* in 1988. The same year he visited the Centre de Physique Théorique, Marseille-Luminy (France). Maxim's work was well recognized at the MPIM in Bonn; in recognition he was invited to the Institute for three months in 1990. A few days before his time there, he attended a five-day annual international meeting, the Mathematische Arbeitstagung, where he sketched a proof of the Witten conjecture to the amazement of Michael Atiyah and other mathematicians, and his invitation to the Institute was subsequently extended to three years. In 1991, for a short period he visited Harvard University, and during 1992–1993 the IAS, Princeton. In 1992, he also received his doctor rerum naturalium (Doctor of Natural Sciences) at the University of Bonn under the supervision of Don Bernard Zagier (born 1951, Germany–USA). The title of his thesis was *Intersection Theory on the Moduli Space of Curves and the Matrix Airy Function*, in which he outlined a proof of Witten's conjecture. In 1993, he was appointed as a Professor of Mathematics at UC, Berkeley, which he left in 1995 to join the IHES as a Permanent Professor. Since November 1997, Maxim has been a Chair holder at Rutgers University, one month per year. He is also a distinguished Professor at the University of Miami. He has made several significant advances in algebraic geometry, topology, and mathematical physics, including knot theory, quantization, and mirror symmetry. He has published 75 research articles and supervised nine doctoral students. Maxim is the recipient of several awards and honors: the Otto Hahn Medal in 1992; EMS Prize in 1992; Henri Poincaré Prize in 1997; Prize of the International Congress of Mathematical Physics, Brisbane in 1997; Fields Medal in 1998; Crafoord Prize in 2008; Shaw Prize in 2012; Fundamental Physics Prize in 2012; Breakthrough Prize in Mathematics in 2014; and the United States NAS (Foreign Associate) in 2015. He is a member of several editorial boards of prestigious journals, including *Compositio Mathematica* from 1994; *International Mathematical Research Notices* from 1994; *Publications Mathematiques IHES* from 1996; *Selecta Mathematica* (New Series) from 1996; *Letters in Mathematical Physics* from 1999; *Journal of Noncommutative Geometry* from 2007; and *Communications in Number Theory and Physics* from 2007.

30.4. Curtis Tracy McMullen

He was born in Berkeley, California, USA. In 1976 Curtis entered Williams College, Williamstown, Western Massachusetts, and in 1980 graduated as a Valedictorian (with Highest Honours in mathematics and an additional concentration in physics). During his undergraduate years Curtis went to Stanford for a year and took a real analysis course from Benjamin Weiss (born 1941, USA–Israel), who was a Visiting Professor from Jerusalem. He was awarded a Herchel Smith (1925–2001, England–USA) Fellowship to study at the University of Cambridge in England and he spent the academic year 1980–1981 at Emmanuel College, Cambridge. In 1981, he returned to the USA to begin research at Harvard University. He obtained his Ph.D. in 1985 for the thesis *Families of Rational Maps and Iterative Root-Finding Algorithms*, written under the supervision of Dennis Sullivan, who was at that time a Professor at City University in New York and the IHES at France, so he had to spend a semester in France. His first paper *The Hausdorff Dimension of General Sierpinski Carpets* was published in 1984, before he submitted his thesis. During each of the summers from 1980 to 1985 he undertook combinatorial research and computer programming at the IBM Thomas John Watson (1874–1956, USA) Research Center, Yorktown Heights, New York. His work there involved VLSI design problems: graph theory, logic synthesis, Boolean minimization, and sparse matrix processing. He spent the academic year 1985–1986 at MIT as Clarence Lemuel Elisha Moore (1876–1931, USA) Instructor in Mathematics and the year 1986–1987 at the IAS, Princeton, as a member. In 1987, he was appointed as an Assistant Professor at Princeton University. In 1990 Curtis was promoted to Full Professor at Princeton but, in the same year, he accepted a full professorship at UC, Berkeley. In 1998, he was appointed to a professorship at Harvard University, in 2001 he was named Maria Moors Cabot Professor at Harvard, and from 2017 to 2020 he was the Chair of the Mathematics Department. He has been a frequent visitor at the MSRI, IHES, and MPIM in Bonn. He has made stunning contributions in the fields Complex Dynamics, Hyperbolic Geometry, and Teichmüller Theory. He has published more than 85 research papers, supervised 19 doctoral students, and written two very influential monographs: *Complex Dynamics and Renormalization* in 1994 and *Renormalization and 3-Manifolds Which Fiber over the Circle* in 1996. Besides several lectures on his research at prestigious institutions, he has also given excellent lectures to the general public. He has been awarded several honors and awards: the Sloan Doctoral Dissertation Fellowship from 1984 to 1985, Presidential Young Investigator from 1988 to 1993, Salem Prize in 1991, Fields Medal in 1998, elected to the AAAS in 1998, Honorary Doctor of Science degree by Williams College in 1999, Guggenheim Fellowship in 2004, elected to the United States NAS in 2007, and Humboldt Research Award in 2011.

30.5. Peter Williston Shor

He was born in New York City to S. W. Williston Shor and Joan Bopp Shor (1924–2016, USA). He grew up in Washington, D.C., and Mill Valley, California. He graduated from Tamalpais High School in 1977 and was placed third in the 1977 USA Mathematical Olympiad. The same year he won a silver medal at the IMO in Yugoslavia. Then he moved to Caltech and completed his Bachelor of Science in 1981. Peter Shor secured his Ph.D. in Applied Mathematics from MIT in 1985. The title of his thesis was *Random Planar Matching and Bin Packing*, written under the supervisor of Frank Leighton. After receiving his Ph.D. degree, Peter Shor spent a year at the MSRI in Berkeley. Then, in 1986, he joined AT&T as a member of its research staff and continued there until 2003. Next, in 2004, Peter Shor joined the MIT faculty in applied mathematics as Full Professor. Currently, he is the Henry Adams Morss (USA) and Henry Adams Morss, Jr. (USA) Professor of Applied Mathematics in the Department of Mathematics at MIT. He is also affiliated with the Computer Science and Artificial Intelligence Laboratory (CSAIL). His main fields of interest have been algorithms, computational geometry, combinatorics, probability theory, and quantum computing and quantum information theory. He is acclaimed for Shor's algorithm, the Shor code, the CSS code (after Robert Calderbank, born 1954; Peter Shor; and Andrew Martin Steane, born 1965, UK), the SMAWK algorithm (after Peter Shor; Shlomo Moran, born 1947, Israel; Alok Aggarwal, India; Robert Wilber, USA; and Maria Margaret Klawe, born 1951, Canada–USA), the Stabilizer code, and the quantum threshold theorem. Peter Shor has more than 110 publications and has supervised 11 doctoral students all at MIT. He has been showered with several honors and awards: Putnam Fellow in 1978, Rolf Nevanlinna Prize in 1998, Dickson Prize in Science from Carnegie-Mellon in 1998, MacArthur Fellowship in 1999, Gödel Prize in 1999, King Faisal International Prize in 2002, member of the National Academy of Science in 2002, INFORMS Computing Society Prize in 2007, Distinguished Alumni Award from Caltech in 2007, Fellow of the AAAS in 2011, Dirac Medal in 2017, BBVA Foundation Frontiers of Knowledge Award in Basic Sciences in 2017, Micius Quantum Prize in 2018, IEEE (Institute of Electrical and Electronics Engineers) Eric Eden Sumner (1923–1993, Australia–USA) Award in 2018, ACM Fellow in 2019, member of the National Academy of Engineering in 2020, Lise Meitner (1878–1968, Austria–USA) Distinguished Lecture and Medal in 2022, Fellow of the AMS in 2022, and Breakthrough Prize in Fundamental Physics in 2023.

30.6. Andrew John Wiles

He was born in Cambridge, England. His father Maurice Frank Wiles (1923–2005, England) was a theologian and his mother Patricia Margaret (Mowll) Wiles (1927–2005, England) had studied mathematics and physics; they married in 1950 and had three children, Patrick David Wiles (born 1951, England), Andrew Wiles, and Alison Ruth Wiles (born 1955, England). During 1955–1959, the family moved to Nigeria, so Andrew Wiles had primary schooling in Nigeria. In 1959, the family returned to Cambridge, and Andrew Wiles spent his 1959–1960 school year at King's College School, Cambridge. At this school he was taught mathematics by Mary Briggs (1918–2009, Australia–England), whose other students include Timothy Gowers and Rouse Ball. Andrew Wiles' interest in Fermat's Last Theorem began while he was studying at King's College School. From 1966 to 1970 he studied at The Leys School in Cambridge; here he was taught mathematics by a number theorist who gave him a copy of the famous book *An Introduction to the Theory of Numbers* written by Hardy and Edward Maitland Wright (1906–2005, England). He also got hold of Davenport's book *The Higher Arithmetic*. These two books encouraged him to go deeper in number theory. In 1971, Wiles entered Merton College, Oxford, and in 1974 received his bachelor's degree in mathematics. Then, he joined Clare College, Cambridge, and in 1979 he received his doctorate under the supervision of John Coates for his thesis *Reciprocity Laws and the Conjecture of Birch and Swinnerton-Dyer* (after Bryan John Birch, born 1931, England, and Henry Peter Francis Swinnerton-Dyer, 1927–2018, England). From 1977 to 1980 Wiles was a Junior Research Fellow at Clare College, Cambridge, and also a Benjamin Peirce (1809–1880, USA) Assistant Professor at Harvard University. At Harvard he worked with Barry Mazur on modular forms. Their collaboration led to a jointly authored paper, which resulted the resolution of the Kenkichi Iwasawa conjecture. In 1981, for a short period, he was a Visiting Professor at the Sonderforschungsbereich Theoretische Mathematik (Collaborative Research Center Theoretical Mathematics) in Bonn, and then he took a position at the IAS, Princeton, where he became a Professor in 1982. He spent the spring of 1982 at the University of Paris, Orsay, France, as a visiting Professor. In 1985–1986, Andrew Wiles was a Guggenheim Fellow at the IHES and at the ENS. In 1988, he went to Oxford University, where he spent two years as a Royal Society Research Professor, and then he returned to Princeton. In 1994, he was named Eugene Higgins Professor of mathematics and in 2009 James Smith McDonnell Distinguished University Professor of Mathematics. He retired in 2012 and returned to Oxford as Royal Society Professor. In May 2018, he was appointed Regius Professor of Mathematics at Oxford, the first in the university's history. He made history in proving the Coates–Wiles theorem, settling the main conjecture of Iwasawa theory, and in 1993, the Taniyama–Shimura conjecture for semistable elliptic curves, thereby proving Fermat's Last Theorem (boyhood dream). For proving this theorem, he worked for seven years in isolation. His paper "Modular Elliptic Curves and Fermat's Last Theorem" was published in the *Annals of Mathematics* 141:3 (1995), 443–551, accompanied by a necessary additional article, "Ring-Theoretic Properties of Certain Hecke Algebras", coauthored with Richard Lawrence Taylor (born 1962, England). Andrew Wiles has supervised 23 doctoral students including Richard Taylor. Over the years he has received numerous honors and awards: the LMS Whitehead Prize in 1988, FRS of London in 1989, Speaker at International Congress in 1994, Rolf Schock Prize in 1995, Ostrowski Prize in 1995, Fermat Prize in 1995, Wolf Prize in 1995/6, BMC plenary speaker in 1996, the United States NAS Award in Mathematics in 1996, AMS Colloquium Lecturer in 1996, Royal Society Royal Medal winner in 1996, Foreign Associate of the United States NAS in 1996, AMS Cole Prize for number theory in 1997, MacArthur Fellowship in 1997, Wolfskehl Prize in 1997, IMU Silver Plaque in 1998 (Don Bernard Zagier referred to the plaque as a "quantized Fields Medal"), King Faisal International Prize in Science in 1998, Clay Award in 1999, Knight Commander of the Order of the British Empire by the Queen in 2000, LMS Honorary Member in 2001, Pythagoras Award in 2004, Shaw Prize in 2005, Abel Prize in 2016, Copley Medal in 2017, and De Morgan Medal in 2019. In 1988, Andrew Wiles married Nada Canaan, who has a Ph.D. in molecular biology from Princeton; they have three daughters.

31. Beijing ICM 2002

This Congress was held in Beijing, China, during 20–28 August 2002. The Congress was attended by 4270 participants from 104 countries (52 percent from developing countries, including 1973 from China). In the opening ceremony the President of the IMU Jacob Palis Jr. welcomed the participants and said this Congress was the first in the new millennium; taking place in a developing country; time the top governmental official of the host country China's President Jiang Zemin (1926–2022) came to the ICM opening ceremonies; and time the IMU General Assembly has elected a woman to its EC and also a Chinese person. This Congress was also the first in which several participants made the trip to China. Then Vice Premier of China Li Lanqing (born 1932) in his speech said "Our social progress depends on scientific innovation, and mathematics is fundamental to science. Mathematics expressed the theory of relativity and the quantum mechanics in the early 20th century; since then mathematicians has played a vital role in inventing computers, designing space and energy programs, and investigating the structure of DNA molecules. Mathematics is the language of the universe. Mathematical methods are used extensively in economics, medicine, agriculture, architecture, arts and all other fields of modern knowledge". Next, elected Honorary President Shiing-Shen Chern of the Congress welcomed the gathering and said "In recent studies different fields were not only found to have contacts, but were merging. We might even foresee a unification of mathematics, including both pure and applied, and even the possibility of the emergence of a new Gauss". Then there was a formal speech from Zhou Guangzhao (born 1929), the President of the China Association for Science and Technology. This was followed by the speech of Wen-Tsun Wu (1919–2017), the President of the Congress; he quoted Karl Marx's (1818–1883, Germany) words: "Each science could be considered to be perfect only if it permits the successful application of mathematics". Liu Qi (born 1942), then Mayor of Beijing, in his speech said "The intellectual fruits achieved in the field by mathematicians exert far-reaching influences on the progress of science and technology of human society and on the development of social culture and people's way of life". After one more formal lecture from Zhi-Ming Ma (born 1948), the Chairman of the Organizing Committee and President of the Chinese Mathematical Society, there was the medal and prize awarding ceremony. The Fields Medal Committee consisted of Yakov Grigorevich Sinai (Chairman), James Greig Arthur, Spencer Janney Bloch (born 1944, USA), Jean Louis, Baron Bourgain, Helmut Hermann W. Hofer (born 1956, Germany–USA), Yasutaka Ihara (born 1938, Japan), Herbert Blaine Lawson, Jr. (born 1942, USA), Sergei Petrovich Novikov, George C. Papanicolaou (born 1943, Greece–USA), and Efim Isaakovich Zelmanov. Fields Medals were awarded to only two people, Laurent Lafforgue (born 1966, France) and Vladimir Alexandrovich Voevodsky (1966–2017, Russia–USA). The Rolf Nevanlinna Prize Committee consisted of Michael Oser Rabin (Chairman), Andrey Aleksandrovich Agrachev (born 1952, Russia), Ingrid Daubechies, Wolfgang Hackbusch (born 1948, Germany), and Alexander Schrijver. The Rolf Nevanlinna Prize was awarded to Madhu Sudan (born 1966, India–USA).

The Fields Medals were presented by Jiang Zemin. The Rolf Nevanlinna Prize was presented by the Secretary of the IMU Phillip Augustus Griffiths.

The opening ceremony ended with the laudations of the works of the awardees. Gérard Laumon (born 1952, France) spoke on the work of Laurent Lafforgue: He is recognized for making a major advance in the Langlands program (after Robert Phelan Langlands, born 1936, Canada), thereby providing new connections between number theory and analysis. Christophe Soulé (born 1951, France) on the work of Vladimir Voevodsky: He is recognized for developing new cohomology theories for algebraic varieties, thereby providing new insights into number theory and algebraic geometry. Shafi Goldwasser (born 1959, USA) spoke on the work of Madhu Sudan: He is recognized for contribution to probabilistically checkable proofs, to non-approximability of optimization problems, and to error-correcting codes. Jacob Palis Jr. said "The achievements of Fields Medalists and Rolf Nevanlinna Prize winner show great depth and originality. The choice of problems, their methods, and their results are quite different from one another, and this diversity exemplifies the vitality of the whole of the mathematical sciences. The world mathematical community applauds their outstanding work". Two new mathematical prizes were announced. One was the Gauss Prize for applications of mathematics, to be jointly awarded every four years by the IMU and the DMV. The first award would be presented at the 2006 International Congress. The other was the Abel Prize, created by the Norwegian Government on the occasion of the bicentenary of Niels Henrik Abel, to be awarded annually by the NASL. This prize was meant to recognize contributions of extraordinary depth and influence to the mathematical sciences. The first award was scheduled for 2003.

During the closing ceremony Jacob Palis Jr. affirmatively answered the following questions: Is it worthwhile to have such a comprehensive Congress, covering an impressive array of areas of mathematics, with 20 one-hour plenary talks (which included three women: Sun-Yung Alice Chang, born 1948, China–USA; Shafi Goldwasser; and Dame Frances Clare Kirwan, born 1959, Britain), 174 forty-five minutes lectures by invited speakers; and many (almost 1200) short communications (including posters)? Were the lectures well presented in trying to reach a large mathematical audience, avoiding technical details, and in offering an overview of the themes discussed and the prospect for research in the future? Is the Congress still attractive to a significant number of mathematicians from all over the world? Has it been organized in a way that led to the presence of a magical atmosphere combining friendship and inspiration for creativity in mathematics? He especially thanked the Local Organizing Committee (almost 300 volunteers) and announced the selection of the new EC of the IMU for the period 2003–2006: John Macleod Ball (President), Jean-Michel Bismut and Masaki Kashiwara as Vice-Presidents, Phillip Augustus Griffiths as Secretary, and Andrei Andreevich Bolibrukh, Martin Grötschel, Zhi-Ming Ma (for the first time a Chinese mathematician), Ragni Piene (born 1947, Norway) (for the first time a woman), Madabusi Santanam Raghunathan, and Jacob Palis Jr. as members. The newly elected President of the IMU John Ball in his speech said "I would like to reserve some special words for the Honorary President Shiing-Shen Chern of the Congress. Despite his great age he was instrumental in ensuring the strong backing of the Chinese government for the Congress, and in his speech at the

Opening Ceremony, and at other occasions during the Congress, he demonstrated the wisdom, warmth and dignity which are his hallmark. Chern had hoped to attend the Closing Ceremony, but could not do so. But I am sure that his colleagues will convey to him our appreciation, not only for his contributions to this Congress, but also for his remarkable influence on our subject". John Ball also mentioned "we meet again in Spain in 2006," (India and Italy had sought the nomination). Then, Carles Casacuberta (born 1961, Spain) in his short speech invited all participants to the next ICM to be held in Madrid in 2006. Next, Ludwig Faddeev in his speech called himself "a veteran of the ICM" (he stated attending in 1962). He also said "The main idea of the ICM is to confirm the unity and universality of mathematics". Finally, after a very short speech from Abderrahman Boukricha (born 1971, Tunisia), Zhi-Ming Ma declared the 2002 ICM to be closed.

There were several important features of the Congress: The opening ceremony was also attended by a large group of children wearing T-shirts with the slogan "I want to be a mathematician". A total of forty-six satellite conferences were held all over Asia, including in Shanghai, Tianjin, Hanoi, Kyoto, Lhasa, Macau, and Taipei; one was even held in Moscow. There were three public lectures to popularize mathematics and its applications by John Nash, Mary Louise Poovey (born 1950, USA), and Wen-Tsun Wu. A public satellite lecture by Stephen Hawking entitled "Brave New World" was followed by more than 2200 people. Edward Witten at the end of his last one-hour plenary lecture made the following remarks. "All of us here at ICM 2002 love mathematics and science for their beauty and because we love to understand things. Mathematics and science are also important in society for many reasons. They are the basis for the technology that is so important in the modern world. Mathematics and science also require and help to develop the sort of independent, critical thinking without which the emergence of the modern world would scarcely have been possible. As the largest country and the most rapidly developing country in the world, China can play a very important role in the development of mathematics and science. Thus, it is fitting that ICM 2002 was held here. All of us foreign guests at ICM 2002 are grateful to our Chinese hosts for arranging this wonderful conference and for giving us the opportunity to visit this wonderful country, to see so many of the historic monuments, and to witness some of the rapid development and progress occurring in this country, which even for those who have read about it before is extremely eye-opening to see. Many of us leave with a feeling of regret that our visits are coming to a close and a hope that we have a chance to come back soon and to witness further progress in this country. I am sure you will all want to join me in wishing our Chinese hosts and all guests from around the world all health, prosperity, and success in science and a future of peace, democracy, and freedom".

31.1. Laurent Lafforgue

He was born in Antony, Hauts-de-Seine, France. Laurent has two brothers, Thomas Lafforgue (France) and Vincent Lafforgue (born 1974, France), both mathematicians. In 1972, Laurent attended the primary school Jules Ferry in Antony, and in 1977 moved to the Lycée Descartes. He received his Baccalauréat degree with distinction in 1984, and received the First Prize in mathematics in the Concours

Général (General Competition). He won two silver medals at the IMO in 1984 and 1985. After spending the two years 1984–1986 at the Lycée Louis-le-Grand in Paris preparing for his university studies, Laurent entered the ENS in Paris in 1986. He was awarded his Agrégation de Mathématiques in 1988. In 1990, he became chargé de recherche (research officer) at the CNRS and worked in the Arithmetic and Algebraic Geometry team at the Université Paris-Sud at Orsay. During 1991–1992, Laurent assumed necessary military service, and then returned to Université Paris-Sud at Orsay, where he received his doctorate degree in 1994 for his thesis *D-stukas de Drinfeld*, written under the supervision of Gérard Laumon. For his masterpiece work in his thesis, he was awarded the Peccot Prize from the Collége de France. Laurent continued to work at the CNRS, and in 1998 he earned a bronze medal. In 2000, he was promoted to directeur de recherche of the CNRS. Then, he was named as Professor at the IHES in Bures-sur-Yvette, France, where he continued until 2021, when he moved to Huawei Technologies France. One of his major contributions is establishing Langlands' Correspondences for a much wider class of cases than previously known. For this work, Andrew John Wiles announced "The crucial contribution by Laurent Lafforgue to solve this question is the construction of compactifications of certain varieties of modules. The proof, which is monumental, is the result of more than six years of concentrated efforts". This proved Laurent "A mathematician of remarkable strength and perseverance". In 2003, his major text *Chirurgie des grassmanniennes* (*Surgery on Grassmannians*) was published by the AMS. At the same time a new direction in his life began, namely, his passionate involvement in the problem of education. Dissatisfied with the education system in France (perhaps the same in most parts of the world), he believed mathematics should be taught in schools: "Let us take the example of the four operations: addition, subtraction, multiplication and division. Their teaching has been considerably retarded and neglected in recent decades, to where the majority of middle school children do not know the multiplication tables and many high school students are unable to add two fractions. These operations have been neglected because of the emergence of calculators, and the belief that an operation carried out by a machine can be the same thing as an operation carried out by a human spirit. It is the same thing as to result—supposing that one has calculated correctly and not made an error of fingering, and with the reservation that there are, just the same, many occasions where the calculator doesn't replace a mental calculation; I recently received a letter from a grandfather whose granddaughter had been fired after several hours as a salesgirl in a market because she was unable to make change. But above all, a calculator which one has programmed to perform certain operations knows only those operations for which it has been programmed. Whereas those same operations acquired and mastered by a student becomes nourishment for his spirit, empowers him, is digested by him, is made his own, enlarges and awakens his mathematical faculties and power. A familiarity with numbers, and similarly as to geometric objects, that permits the life that has been given him to enter, little by little, into the world of mathematics". Laurent was the recipient of the Clay Research Award in 2000, Jacques Herbrand Prize in 2001, and Fields Medal in 2002, and is an Académie des Sciences de Paris member. He received an honorary doctor degree from the University of Notre Dame in 2011. He is a devout Catholic and never married.

31.2. Vladimir Alexandrovich Voevodsky

He was born in Moscow, Russia. His father Aleksander Voevodsky (USSR) was Director of the Laboratory of High Energy Leptons at the Institute for Nuclear Research at the RAS, and his mother Tatyana (USSR) was a Chemistry Professor at Moscow University. Vladimir was kicked out of high school three times once for disagreeing with his teacher's assertion that the author Fyodor Mikhailovich Dostoevsky (1821–1881, USSR) was pro-communist. In 1983, he enrolled at Moscow State University but was expelled in 1989 without a diploma for refusing to attend classes that he called "academic failure". In 1989, his first research paper *Equilateral Triangulations of Riemann Surfaces, and Curves Over Algebraic Number Fields* was published jointly with George B. Shabat (USSR). Then, in 1990 and 1991, he published three independent and four joint papers with Mikhail Mikhailovich Kapranov (born 1962, USSR). In 1990, his friends Alexander Alekseevich Beilinson (born 1957, USSR–USA) and Mikhail Kapranov arranged for him to be accepted at Harvard University for graduate study. The same year Vladimir met Nadia Shalaby, his lifelong partner, at Harvard. They married in 1995 and had two children. Although the marriage ended in divorce in 2008, Vladimir and Nadia remained close friends all his life. He received his Ph.D. in mathematics from Harvard University in 1992 for his thesis *Homology of Schemes and Covariant Motives*, written under the supervision of David Kazhdan. It is worth noting that this Ph.D. was the only academic degree Vladimir ever received (without even applying to Harvard). After obtaining his Ph.D. he spent a year at the IAS, Princeton, and then returned to Harvard first as a Junior Fellow and then as a visiting scholar until 1996. Next, he spent a year 1996–1997 at the Max-Planck Institute in Germany, and then in 1997 joined the faculty at Northwestern University. In 1998, he accepted a position as a long-term member at the IAS, Princeton, and in 2002 he became a Professor (permanent member) of the IAS, Princeton, and remained there for the rest of his life. To give a flavour of applications of his work, in January 2005, he gave lectures at the University of Miami entitled Categories, Population Genetics and a Little of Quantum Physics. On 30 September 2017, Vladimir died at his home in Princeton from a sudden aneurysm and was discovered by friends. On 8 October, the IAS, Princeton held a Memorial Service for him, on 27 December, a funeral service was held for him in Moscow, and on 28 December a Memorial Mathematical Conference was held at the Steklov Mathematical Institute of the RAS. After one year during 11–14 September 2018 a memorial conference was held at the IAS, Princeton, and another during 10–14 September 2018 at the Euler International Mathematical Institute in St. Petersburg, Russia. In addition to developing a homotopy theory for algebraic varieties and formulating motivic cohomology, which earned Vladimir a Fields Medal in 2002, he is also known for the proof of the Milnor conjecture and motivic Bloch–Kato conjectures (after Willard Milnor and Kazuya Kato, born 1952, Japan) and for the univalent foundations of mathematics and homotopy type theory. Some of his work was in the area of developing "proof assistants", which entailed harnessing the computer to help mathematicians through the dauntingly intricate steps by which abstruse proofs are developed. He published 55 very influential research articles. He had a Sloan Fellowship during 1996–1998, NSF grant during 1995–1998, and Clay Prize Fellowship in 1999. He was also a member of the European Academy of Sciences since 2003. In 2016, Vladimir was awarded an honorary doctorate by the University of Gothenburg, Sweden. In pure mathematics, he possessed powers of imagination, visualization, and reasoning that could be applied at levels of abstraction almost impossibly remote from the minds and lives of most people.

31.3. Madhu Sudan

He was born in Madras (Chennai), India. Madhu Sudan received his bachelor's degree from the Indian Institute of Technology (IIT) in New Delhi in 1987 and his Ph.D. from UC, Berkeley, in 1992, defending his thesis *Efficient Checking of Polynomials and Proofs and the Hardness of Approximation Problems*, written under the supervision of Umesh Virkumar Vazirani (born 1957, India–USA). During 1992–1997, Madhu Sudan was a research staff member at the IBM Watson Research Center in Yorktown Heights, New York. From 1997 to 2002, he was Associate Professor at MIT in the Department of Electrical Engineering and Computer Science (EECS), and in 2003 became Professor. During 2005–2011, he became Fujitsu Chair Professor, MIT, EECS, and also Danny Lewin Outstanding Professor, MIT, EECS. He was also Associate Director, MIT Computer Science and Artificial Intelligence Laboratory (CSAIL) from 2007 to 2009 and Principal Researcher, Microsoft Research, from 2009 to 2015, and at the same time Adjunct Professor, MIT, EECS, from 2011 to 2015. In 1915 he joined the Center For Research on Computation and Society (CRCS) at Harvard John Alfred Paulson (born 1955, USA) School of Engineering and Applied Sciences as a Gordon McKay (1821–1903, USA) Professor. Madhu Sudan has made important contributions to several areas of theoretical computer science, including probabilistically checkable proofs, non-approximability of optimization problems, list-decoding algorithms, and error-correcting code. His interests also include property testing, which is the study of sublinear time to estimate the properties of massive data, and communication amid uncertainty, a mathematical study of the role of context in communication. He has more than 250 publications and has supervised 22 doctoral students. Madhu Sudan has received several honors and awards, including the Sakrison Memorial Award in 1993, ACM's Distinguished Doctoral Dissertation Award in 1993, Sloan Research Fellowship in 1998, NSF Career Award in 1999, Gödel Prize in 2001, Rolf Nevanlinna Prize in 2002, Distinguished Alumnus Award, IIT in New Delhi 2004, Guggenheim Fellow during 2005–2006, Fellow of ACM in 2009, Fellow of IEEE 2010, AAAS Member in 2010, Fellow of the AMS in 2013, Infosys Foundation Prize in the Mathematical Sciences in 2014, elected to the United States NAS in 2017, and IEEE Richard Wesley Hamming (1915–1998, USA) Medal in 2022. He is the Founding Editor of the journal *Foundations and Trends in Theoretical Computer Science* and has also been an editorial board member of several prestigious journals, including *SIAM Journal on Discrete Mathematics*, *Information and Computation*, *SIAM Journal on Computing*, *Journal of the ACM*, *IEEE Transactions on Information Theory*, and *Theory of Computing*.

32. Carl Friedrich Gauss (1777–1855, Germany) and Gauss Prize

He is considered as one of the greatest mathematicians of all time. He stood with his contemporaries Immanuel Kant (1724–1804, Germany), Johann Wolfgang von Goethe (1749–1832, Germany), Ludwig van Beethoven (1770–1827, Germany), and Georg Wilhelm Friedrich Hegel (1770–1831, Germany). He was born in the city of Brunswick in northern Germany. He was a child prodigy; later in life he joked that he could operate with numbers even before he could talk. Gauss corrected an error in his father's payroll accounts at the age of three. His elementary school teacher asked the class to add up the numbers from 1 to 100, expecting to keep them busy for a long time. Young Gauss found the formula $1 + 2 + \cdots + n = n(n+1)/2$ and instantly wrote down the correct answer. His father was a gardener and bricklayer without either the means or the inclination to help develop the talents of his son. Fortunately, Gauss' remarkable abilities in mental computation attracted the interest of several influential men in the community and eventually brought him to the attention of the Duke of Brunswick. The Duke was impressed with the boy and supported his further education, first at the Caroline College in Brunswick (1792–1795) and later at the University of Göttingen (1795–1798).

At the Caroline College, Gauss explored the work of Newton, Euler, and Lagrange. At the age of fourteen or fifteen, he discovered the *prime number theorem*, which was finally proved in 1896 by Hadamard and Vallée-Poussin, after great efforts by many mathematicians. He also invented the method of least squares for minimizing the errors inherent in observational data, which has broad applications in linear regression, signal processing, statistics, and curve fitting. Further, he conceived the Gaussian law of distribution (bell-shaped normal distribution) in the theory of probability. At university, when he was just eighteen, he discovered the law of quadratic reciprocity in number theory (which he called "the gem of arithmetic", and at least six separate proofs are found in his works) independently of Euler and made a wonderful geometric discovery. The ancient Greeks had known about ruler-and-compass constructions for regular polygons of $3, 4, 5$ and 15 sides, and for all others obtainable from these by bisecting angles. But this was all, and there the matter rested for 2000 years, until Gauss solved the problem completely. He proved that a regular polygon with n sides is constructible if and only if n is the product of a power of 2 and distinct prime numbers of the form $p_k = 2^{2^k} + 1$. In particular, when $k = 0, 1, 2, 3$, we see that each of the corresponding numbers $p_k = 3, 5, 17, 257$ are prime, so regular polygons with these numbers of sides are constructible. According to one story, Gauss approached his colleague Abraham Gotthelf Kästner (1719–1800, Germany) with this discovery; however, he told Gauss that the discovery was useless since approximate constructions were "well known". Further, he said that the construction was impossible, so Gauss' proof had to be flawed. Finally, he said that Gauss' method was something that he (Kästner) already knew about, so Gauss' discovery was unimportant. Despite Kästner's discouraging remarks, Gauss was so proud of this discovery that he requested that a 17 regular polygon be inscribed upon his tombstone (but it was not). Gauss later toasted Kästner, who was an amateur poet, as the best poet among mathematicians and the best mathematician among poets. In 1796, he settled Fermat's polygonal number theorem, the case that every positive integer can be written as the sum of three triangular numbers $t_n = n(n+1)/2$. In his *Disquisitiones Arithmeticae*, published in 1798, he collected work conducted by his predecessors, enriching and blending it with his own into a unified whole. The book is regarded by many as the true beginning of the theory of numbers.

The fundamental theorem of algebra, which states that every algebraic equation with one unknown has a root, was first proved by Gauss in 1797 as part of his doctoral dissertation completed in 1799. This theorem had challenged the world's finest mathematicians, such as Jean le Rond d'Alembert (1717–1783, France), Euler, Lagrange, and Pierre Simon de Laplace (1749–1827, France), for at least 200 years. Gauss' proof used advanced mathematical concepts from outside the field of algebra. To this day, no purely algebraic proof has been discovered. Gauss returned to the theorem many times and in 1849 published his fourth and last proof, in which he extended the coefficients of the unknown quantities to include complex numbers. Today, students often meet the fundamental theorem of algebra in a first course on complex variables, where it can be established as a consequence of some of the basic properties of complex analytic functions. In 1800, Gauss formulated the rule for determining the date of Easter, which enabled him to place his birthday on 30 April. Although the concept of the determinant of a matrix is due to Seki Kowa (1642–1708, Japan) in 1683, the term was first introduced by Gauss in 1801. He used this to "determine" the properties of certain kinds of functions. Interestingly, the term matrix is derived from a Latin word for "womb" because it was viewed as a container of determinants.

In the last decades of the eighteenth century, many astronomers searched for a new planet between the orbits of Mars and Jupiter, where Bode's (Johann Elert Bode, 1747–1826, Germany) Law (1772) suggested that there ought to be one. The first and largest of the numerous minor planets known as asteroids was discovered by Giuseppe Piazzi (1746–1826, Italy) in that region in 1801, and was named Ceres. Unfortunately, the tiny new planet was difficult to see under even the best of circumstances, and it was soon lost in the light of the sky near the Sun. The sparse observational data posed the problem of calculating the orbit with sufficient accuracy to locate Ceres again after it had moved away from the Sun. The astronomers of Europe attempted this task without success for many months. Finally, Gauss was attracted by the challenge; with the aid of his method of least squares and the procedure that we now call *Gaussian elimination*, and his unparalleled skill at numerical computation, he determined the orbit. He told the astronomers where to look with their telescopes, and there it was. He had succeeded in rediscovering Ceres after all the experts had failed. This achievement brought him fame, an increase in his pension from the Duke, and in 1807 an appointment as Professor of Astronomy and first director of the new observatory at Göttingen. His treatise *Theoria Motus Corporum Coelestium*, published in 1809, remained the Bible of planetary astronomers for over a century. Its methods for dealing with perturbations later led to the discovery of Neptune. Gauss thought of astronomy as his profession and pure mathematics as his recreation, and from time to time he published a few of the fruits of his private research. His great work on theta functions (1808), hypergeometric series (1812), general ellipsoids (1813), mechanical quadrature (1814), and continuous perturbations (1818) belongs to this period. This was a typical Gaussian effort, packed with new ideas in analysis that have kept mathematicians busy ever since.

From the 1820s on, Gauss became actively interested in geodesy. In the paper *Disquisitiones generales circa superficies curvas* (1827) he founded the intrinsic differential geometry of general curved surfaces. In this work he introduced curvilinear coordinates, obtained the fundamental quadratic differential form, and formulated the concepts of Gaussian curvature and integral curvature. Extensions of these concepts opened the doors to Riemannian geometry, tensor analysis (developed by Elwin Bruno Christoffel, Germany; Gregorio Ricci-Curbastro, 1853–1925, Italy; and Tullio Levi-Civita), and the ideas of Einstein. Another great work from this period was his 1831 paper on biquadratic residues. Here he extended some of his early discoveries in number theory with the aid of a new method, his purely algebraic approach to complex numbers. He defined these numbers as ordered pairs of real numbers with suitable algebraic operations, and in so doing laid to rest the confusion that still surrounded the subject and prepared the way for the later algebra and geometry of n-dimensional spaces. He defined complex integers (now called Gaussian integers) as complex numbers $a + ib$, with a and b being ordinary integers; he introduced a new concept of prime numbers, in which 3 remains prime but $5 = (1 + 2i)(1 - 2i)$ does not; and he proved the unique factorization theorem for these integers and primes. The ideas of this paper inaugurated algebraic number theory, which has grown steadily since. In 1831 he expressed his "horror of the actual infinite" as follows, "I protest against the use of infinite magnitude as something completed, which is never permissible in mathematics. Infinity is merely a way of speaking, the true meaning being a limit which certain ratios approach indefinitely close, while others are permitted to increase without restriction".

From the 1830s on, Gauss was increasingly occupied with physics, and he enriched every branch of the subject that he touched. In the theory of surface tension, he developed the fundamental idea of conservation of energy and solved the earliest problem in the calculus of variations involving a double integral with variable limits. In optics, he introduced the concept of the focal length of a system of lenses and invented the Gauss wide-angle lens (which is relatively free of chromatic aberration) for telescope and camera objectives. In collaboration with his friend and colleague Wilhelm Eduard Weber (1804–1891, Germany), he built and operated an iron-free magnetic observatory, founded the Magnetic Union for collecting and publishing observations from many places in the world, and invented the electromagnetic telegraph and the bifilar magnetometer. There are many references to his work in Maxwell's famous *Treatise on Electricity and Magnetism* (1873). In his preface, James Clerk Maxwell (1831–1879, UK) says that Gauss "brought his powerful intellect to bear on the theory of magnetism and on the methods of observing it, and he not only added greatly to our knowledge of the theory of attractions, but reconstructed the whole of magnetic science as regards the instruments used, the methods of observation, and the calculation of results, so that his memoirs on Terrestrial Magnetism may be taken as models of physical research by all those who are engaged in the measurement of any of the forces in nature". In 1839 Gauss published his fundamental paper on the general theory of inverse square forces, which established potential theory as a coherent branch of mathematics. He had been thinking about these matters for many years; among his discoveries were the divergence theorem (also called Gauss' theorem) of modern vector analysis, the basic mean value theorem for harmonic functions, and the very powerful statement that later became known as "Dirichlet's principle" (after Peter Gustav Lejeune Dirichlet, 1805–1859, France), which was finally proved by Hilbert in 1899.

His scientific diary, a little booklet of 19 pages, is one of the most precious documents in the history of mathematics. It was unknown until 1898, when it was found among family papers in the possession of one of Gauss' grandsons. It extends from 1796 to 1814 and consists of 146 very concise statements of the results of his investigations, which often occupied him for weeks or months. All of this material makes it abundantly clear that the ideas Gauss conceived and worked out in considerable detail, but kept to himself, would have made him the most insurmountable mathematician of all time had he published them. For example, the theory of functions of a complex variable was one of the major accomplishments of nineteenth-century mathematics, and the central facts of this discipline are Augustin-Louis Cauchy's (1789–1857, France) integral theorem (1827) and the Brook Taylor (1685–1731, England) and Pierre-Alphonse Laurent (1813–1854, France) expansions of an analytic function (1831 and 1843). In a letter written to his friend Friedrich Wilhelm Bessel (1784–1846, Germany) in 1811, Gauss explicitly states Cauchy's theorem and then remarks, "This is a very beautiful theorem whose fairly simple proof I will give on a suitable occasion. It is connected with other beautiful truths which are concerned with series expansions". Therefore, he knew Cauchy's theorem, and possibly both series expansions, many years earlier. However, for some reason the suitable occasion for publication did not come. This may be due to comments he made to Farkas (Wolfgang) Bolyai (1775–1852, Romania), a close friend from his university years with whom he maintained a lifelong correspondence: "It is not knowledge but the act of learning, not possession but the act of getting there, which grants the greatest enjoyment. When I have clarified and exhausted a subject, then I turn away from it in order to go into darkness again". As it was, Gauss wrote a great deal, but to publish every fundamental discovery he made in a form satisfactory to himself would have required several long lifetimes. Another prime example is non-Euclidean geometry. From the time of Euclid to the boyhood of Gauss, the postulates of Euclidean geometry were universally regarded as necessities of thought. Yet there was a flaw in the Euclidean structure that had long been a focus of attention: the so-called parallel postulate. This postulate was thought not to be independent of the others, and many had failed in their efforts to prove it as a theorem. Gauss joined in these efforts at the age of fifteen and also failed. But his failure was different, for he soon came to the shattering conclusion, which had escaped all his predecessors, that the Euclidean form is not the only possible geometry. He worked intermittently on these ideas for many years, and by 1820 he was in full possession of the main theorems of non-Euclidian geometry (the term was coined by him). But he did not reveal his conclusions, and in 1829 and 1832 Lobachevsky and Johann Bolyai (1802–1860, Romania), son of Wolfgang, published their independent work on this subject. One reason for Gauss' silence in this case is that the intellectual climate in

Germany at the time was totally dominated by the philosophy of Kant, and one of the basic tenets of this philosophy was the idea that Euclidian geometry is the only possible way of thinking about space. Gauss knew that this idea was totally false, but he valued his privacy and quiet life. In 1829 he wrote to Bessel "I shall probably not put my very extensive investigations on this subject (the foundations of geometry) into publishable form for a long time, perhaps not in my lifetime, for I dread the shrieks we would hear from the Boeotians if I were to express myself fully on this matter". The same thing happened with his theory of elliptic functions (called 'elliptic' because these functions exist in the expression for finding the length of an arc of an ellipse), a very rich field of analysis that was launched primarily by Abel in 1827 and also by Jacobi in 1828–1829. Gauss had published nothing on this subject, and claimed nothing, so the mathematical world was filled with astonishment when it gradually became known that he had found many of the results published by Abel and Jacobi before they were born. Abel was spared this devastating knowledge by his early death in 1829, but Jacobi was compelled to swallow his disappointment and go on with his work. The facts became known partly through Jacobi himself. His attention was caught by a cryptic passage in the *Disquisitiones*, whose meaning can only be understood if one knows something about elliptic functions. He visited Gauss on several occasions to verify his suspicions and tell him about his most recent discoveries; each time, Gauss pulled a 30-year-old manuscript out of his desk and showed Jacobi what Jacobi had just shown him. The depth of Jacobi's chagrin is understandable. At this point in his life, Gauss was indifferent to fame and was actually pleased to be relieved of the burden of preparing the treatise on the subject, which he had planned for a long time. After a week's visit with Gauss in 1840, Jacobi wrote to his brother, "mathematics would be in a very different position if practical astronomy had not diverted this colossal genius from his glorious career". The Royal Society of Göttingen published a collection of his works in several volumes.

Gauss, despite an aversion to teaching, continuously gave lectures until he died on 23 February 1855, due to several heart attacks. He was buried at St. Albans Cemetery in Göttingen next to the unmarked grave of his mother. Gauss took complete care of his mother, who became totally blind for the last four years of her life. The King of Hanover had a memorial coin struck with the dedication "Georgius V Rex Hannoverae Mathematicorum Principi". Also, Wolfgang Sartorius von Walterhausen (1809–1876, Germany) said in his obituary " Gauss always strove to give his investigations the form of finished works of art. He did not rest until he had succeeded, and hence he never published a work until it had achieved the form he wanted. He used to say that when a fine building was finished, the scaffolding should no longer be visible" ("You know that I write slowly. This is chiefly because I am never satisfied until I have said as much as possible in a few words, and writing briefly takes far more time than writing at length"). Gauss' brain was preserved and studied by the leading neuroscientist Rudolf Friedrich Johann Heinrich Wagner (1805–1864, Germany). He found his brain was heavier than average, with very notable convolutions, which were the sources of his intelligence. Gauss' brain was accidentally switched with the physician Conrad Heinrich Fuchs' (1803–1855, Germany), and was mislabeled for 150 years, which has been corrected.

Apart from science he had two wives and six children; his main interests were history and world literature, international politics, and public finance. He owned a large library of about 6000 volumes in many languages, including Greek, Latin, English, French, Russian, Danish, and German. His acuteness in handling his own financial affairs (the analysis and prediction of financial markets) is shown by the fact that although he started with virtually nothing, he left an estate over a hundred times as great as his average annual income during the last half of his life. Once, in 1828, he visited Berlin, and once, in 1854, he made a pilgrimage to be present at the opening of the railway from Hanover to Göttingen. He saw his first railway engine in 1836, but other than these quiet adventures, until the last year of his life he never slept under any other roof than that of his own observatory. He was the last complete mathematician and has been named "the prince of mathematics". Gauss once asserted (if indeed he was) that "mathematics is the queen of the sciences, and the theory of numbers is the queen of mathematics". His friend Wolfgang Sartorius von Waltershausen (1809–1876, Germany) writes "As he was in his youth, so he remained through his old age to his dying day, the unaffectedly simple Gauss. A small study, a little work table with a green cover, a standing–desk painted white, a narrow sopha and, after his seventieth year, an arm chair, a shaded lamp, an unheated bedroom, plain food, a dressing gown and a velvet cap, these were so becoming all his needs". According to Kronecker, "The further elaboration and development of systematic arithmetic, like nearly everything else which the mathematics of our (nineteenth) century has produced in the way of original scientific ideas, is knit to Gauss". Today, Gauss is considered as a champion of applicable mathematics, but, ironically, Gauss received some criticism from his contemporaries for the lack of usefulness of his work. On 1 October 1993 the Deutsche Bundesbank issued a 10 Deutsche Mark note in honor of Gauss (a rare honor to a mathematician) in his trusty velvet cap, with a drawing of a town, presumably Göttingen, alongside. Superimposed is a representation of the normal or Gaussian curve of errors, together with its equation in modern form. They were withdrawn from circulation in 2002.

The following anecdotes about Gauss are often told:

Alexander von Humboldt asked Laplace who was the greatest mathematician in Germany, and Laplace replied Johann Friedrich Pfaff (1765–1825, Germany). "But what about Gauss" the astonished von Humboldt asked, as he was backing Gauss for the position of director at the Göttingen observatory. "Oh", said Laplace, "Gauss is the greatest mathematician in the world". (A two-hour movie *Measuring the World*, which deals with the lives of von Humboldt and Gauss, was released in 2012.)

The Paris Academy in 1816 proposed the proof (or disproof) of Fermat's Last Theorem as its prize problem for the period 1816–1818. Some tried to entice Gauss into competing, but Gauss resisted, replying "I am very much obliged for your news concerning the Paris prize. But I confess that Fermat's Theorem as an isolated proposition has very little interest for me, because I could easily lay down a multitude of such propositions, which one could neither prove nor dispose of".

The Berlin ICM 1998 ended in a surplus, which DMV decided to use in creating a new international award in mathematics (administered by the DMV) to be awarded jointly with the IMU in the same manner as the other awards, but with no age restriction for the prize winner. The focus of this award was set to honor scientists whose mathematical research has had an impact outside mathematics—either in technology, in business, or simply in people's everyday lives. The award received its name from the most versatile mathematician, Gauss. It was announced during the opening ceremony of the ICM 2002 in commendation of the 225th anniversary of Gauss' birth. Naming this award after Gauss was more than appropriate. The Gauss Prize consists of a gold medal and a monetary award of EUR 10,000. This award broadened the range of the IMU awards, now including the influence of mathematics on other disciplines. The front side of the Gauss Medal contains a portrait of Gauss dissolved into a barcode of lines. The back side of the medal has horizontal and vertical lines crossed by a curve. The disk and the square, two elements connected by the curve, symbolize both the least squares method and the discovery of Ceres' orbit.

The front of the Gauss Medal.

The back of the Gauss Medal.

33. Niels Henrik Abel (1802–1829, Norway) and Abel Prize

He was a brilliant Norwegian mathematician whose tragic death at age 26 of tuberculosis was an inestimable loss for mathematics. Along with Gauss and Cauchy, Abel was one of the pioneers in the development of modern mathematics. He was one of six children in the family of a poor country minister. At 16, influenced by a perceptive teacher, he read the works of Newton, Euler, and Lagrange. As a comment on this experience, he inserted the following marginal remark in one of his later mathematical notebooks: "It appears to me that if one wants to make progress in mathematics, one should study the masters and not the pupils". When Abel was only eighteen, his father died and left the family destitute. They subsisted on the aid of friends and neighbors, and somehow Abel, helped by contributions from several professors, managed to enter the University of Oslo in 1821. His earliest research was published in 1823 and included his solution of the classic tautochrone problem (the problem of finding the curve down which a bead placed anywhere will fall to the bottom in the same amount of time) by means of an integral equation. He devoted much of his early life to the study of algebraic solutions of equations and gave the first rigorous proof that the general fifth-order equation cannot be solved by purely by rational operations, and extractions of n-th roots, on the coefficients. This disposed of a problem that had baffled mathematicians for almost 300 years. He published his proof in a small pamphlet at his own expense. Later, Abel spent some time in Berlin and wrote his classic study of the binomial series, in which he founded the general theory of convergence and gave the first satisfactory proof of the validity of this series expansion. He also inspired August Leopold Crelle (1780–1855, Germany) to launch the prestigious *Journal für die reine und angewandte Mathematik*, which was the world's first periodical devoted wholly to mathematical research. The first three volumes of this journal contained 22 of Abel's articles. He had sent his pamphlet on the fifth-degree equation to Gauss, hoping that it would serve as a kind of scientific passport. However, for some reason Gauss put it aside without looking at it, for it was found uncut among his papers after his death 30 years later. Abel felt that he had been snubbed, and without visiting Gauss went from Berlin to Paris. Soon after his arrival in Paris, he finished his great *Mémoire sur une Propriété Générale d'une Classe Très Étendue des Fonctions Transcendantes*, which he regarded as his masterpiece. This work contains the discovery about integrals of algebraic functions now known as Abel's theorem and is the foundation for the later theory of abelian integrals, abelian functions, and much of algebraic geometry. Abel submitted his masterpiece to the French Academy with the hope that it would bring him to the notice of the French mathematicians. He waited for a reply in vain until he could no longer afford to stay and he was forced to return to Berlin. His manuscript was given to Cauchy and Legendre for examination; Cauchy took it home, mislaid it, and forgot all about it. It was not published until 1841, when again the manuscript was lost before the proof sheets were read. The original finally turned up in Florence in 1952. In Berlin, Abel finished his first revolutionary article on elliptic functions, a subject he had been working on for several years, and then went back to Norway deeply in debt. He had expected to be appointed to a professorship at the university on his return, but once again his hopes were dashed. He made a living by tutoring, and for a brief time he held a substitute teaching position. During this period, he worked incessantly, mainly on the theory of elliptic functions, which he had discovered to be the inverses of elliptic integrals. This theory quickly took its place as one of the major fields of nineteenth-century analysis, with many applications to number theory, mathematical physics, and algebraic geometry. Meanwhile, Abel's fame had spread to all of the mathematical centers of Europe, and he stood among the elite of the world's mathematicians but in his isolation was unaware of it. On the occasion of the centenary of his death in 1929, Abel was commemorated on Norwegian stamps. In 1948, Norges Bank printed Abel's portrait on the obverse of the NOK 500 banknote. Further, Abel's memory was kept alive in subsequent banknote and stamp issues. In 2000, during the "World Mathematical Year", Abel was Norway's leading logo.

Norwegian mathematician Sophus Lie (1842–1899), when he learned that Alfred Nobel's plans for annual prizes would not include a prize in mathematics, initiated the concept of Abel's Prize; however, he was not successful in procuring sufficient funds. Then, during the centenary celebration of Abel in 1902, King Oscar II (1829–1907) of Sweden and Norway indicated his willingness to finance the creation of a mathematics prize to complement the Nobel Prizes, but the establishment of the prize was prevented by the dissolution of the union between Norway and Sweden in 1905. Finally, in 2002 the Abel Prize was established by the Norwegian Government and is managed by the NASL. The prize was intended to give annually to outstanding international mathematicians, which is their own equivalent of a Nobel Prize. The IMU strongly supports the Abel Prize; its selection committee is appointed by the NASL and nominated by the IMU and EMS. The Abel Prize is awarded by the King of Norway, and it is different from the Fields Medal in several ways: it is awarded annually, it can be awarded to up to three living mathematicians at a time, there are no restrictions on the area of maths, no restrictions on age, and no restrictions on geography, and in 2019 the prize money was increased to NOK 7.5 million from 6 million. The Abel Prize also consists of glass plaque designed by Norwegian artist Henrik Haugan. A book series presenting Abel Prize laureates and their research was commenced in 2010. The first four volumes cover the years 2003–2007, 2008–2012, 2013–2017, and 2018–2022, respectively, in [2–5].

The Abel Prize logo in glass.

The complete list of laureates from 2003 to 2024 is as follows:
2003. Jean-Pierre Serre
2004. Michael Francis Atiyah
2004. Isadore Manuel Singer
2005. Peter David Lax
2006. Lennart Axel Edvard Carleson
2007. Sathamangalam Ranga Iyengar Srinivasa Varadhan
2008. Jacques Tits
2008. John Griggs Thompson
2009. Mikhail Gromov Boksitogorsk (born 1943, Russia)
2010. John Torrence Tate Jr.
2011. John Willard Milnor
2012. Endre Szemerédi
2013. Pierre René Deligne
2014. Yakov Grigorevich Sinai
2015. John Forbes Nash Jr.
2015. Louis Nirenberg
2016. Andrew John Wiles
2017. Yves François Meyer (born 1939, France)
2018. Robert Phelan Langlands
2019. Karen Keskulla Uhlenbeck (first woman to win an Abel Prize)
2020. Hillel Furstenberg (born 1935, Germany–Israel–USA)
2020. Gregori Aleksandrovitch Margulis
2021. László Lovász
2021. Avi Wigderson
2022. Dennis Parnell Sullivan
2023. Luis Angel Caffarelli
2024. Michel Pierre Talagrand (born 1952, France)

34. Srinivasa Ramanujan (1887–1920, India) and Ramanujan Prize

He was a famous mathematical prodigy, born and raised in the southern Indian Brahmin family of Ayyangars near the city of Madras. His father, Srinivasa, was a clerk in a cloth shop. His mother, Komalatammal, contributed to the family income by singing at a local temple. In his elementary school class, the teacher was explaining the concept of division (sharing) through an example: if three bananas are divided among three children, then each child will get one banana; if four bananas are divided among four children, then each child will get one banana; if five bananas are divided among five children, and so on. Then the teacher generalized the idea of sharing x bananas among x children. Ramanujan claimed that when x is equal to zero, each child will get one banana. He explained to his classmates that zero divided by zero could be anything, since the zero of the denominator may be any number times the zero of the numerator. Ramanujan studied at the local English-language school, displaying his talent and interest for mathematics. At 13 he mastered a textbook used by college students. When he was 15, a university student lent him a copy of George Shoobridge Carr's (1837–1914, UK) *Synopsis of Pure Mathematics*. Ramanujan decided to work out most of the 6165 results in this book, stated without proof or explanation, writing on papers that were later collected to form notebooks. He graduated from high school in 1904, winning a scholarship to the University of Madras. He enrolled in a fine arts curriculum, neglected every subject but mathematics, and lost his scholarship. He failed the university examination four times from 1904 to 1907, doing well only in mathematics. During this time, he filled his notebooks with original writings, sometimes rediscovering work that had already been published and at other times making new discoveries. Without a university degree, it was difficult for Ramanujan to find a decent job. To survive, he had to depend on the goodwill of his friends. He tutored students in mathematics, but his unconventional ways of thinking and failure to stick to the syllabus caused problems. He was married to a nine-year old bride, Janaki Ammal, as per his parents' wishes, but she did not come to live with him until 1912. Needing to support himself and his wife, he moved to Madras and sought a job. He showed his notebooks of mathematical writings to his potential employers, but the books bewildered them. However, a professor at the Presidency College recognized his genius and supported him for a while, and in 1912 he found work as an accounts clerk, earning a small salary. Ramanujan continued his mathematical work during this time and published his first paper on Bernoulli numbers in 1911 in the *Journal of the Indian Mathematical Society*. He found that the denominators of Bernoulli numbers are divisible by 6. He realized that his work was beyond that of the other Indian mathematicians, and so he began writing to leading English mathematicians. The first mathematicians he contacted, Ernest William Hobson (1856–1933, UK) and Henry Frederick Baker (1866–1956, UK), turned down his requests for help. But in January 1913 he wrote to Hardy, who was inclined to turn Ramanujan down, but the mathematical statements in his letter, although stated without proof, puzzled Hardy. He decided to examine them closely with the help of his colleague and collaborator, Littlewood. They decided, after careful study, that Ramanujan was probably a genius, since his statements "could only be written down by a mathematician of the highest class, they must be true, because if they were not true, no one would have the imagination to invent them". Hardy arranged a scholarship for Ramanujan, bringing him to England in 1914. At first Ramanujan refused to travel, but in the end he decided to go, which was attributed to the divine intervention of the family goddess Namagiri. Hardy personally tutored him in mathematical analysis, and they collaborated for five years, proving significant theorems regarding the number of partitions of integers. During this time, Ramanujan made important contributions to number theory and also worked on continued fractions, infinite series, and elliptic functions. Unfortunately, in 1917 Ramanujan became extremely ill. At the time, it was thought that he had trouble with the English climate and had contracted tuberculosis. It is now thought that he suffered from a vitamin deficiency, brought on by Ramanujan's strict vegetarianism and the food shortage in wartime England. His illness was certainly exacerbated by Hardy's high expectations and his own strict work ethic. During this period, he became severely depressed. He threw himself on the track of an approaching train in London and badly injured his knee. Miraculously, his life was spared. Observing Ramanujan's failing health, Hardy worked relentlessly to have him elected an FRS of London. In 1918 Ramanujan became one of the youngest to achieve this honor. He returned to India in 1919 and continued to perform mathematics even while he was confined to his bed by debilitating pain. On 12 January 1920 he wrote to Hardy about his discovery of *mock theta functions*, which, according to George Neville Watson (1886–1965, UK), was a very significant achievement. On 26 April 1920, at the age of 32, Ramanujan fell unconsciousness and died, and the world lost one of its mathematical legends. Appreciating Ramanujan, historian Eric Temple Bell (1883–1960, USA) in the 1930s remarked that he was *a gift from Heaven*, and Polish American mathematician Mark Kac (1914–1984) said he was *a magician rather than an ordinary genius*.

According to Hardy, "the limitations of Ramanujan's knowledge were as startling as its profundity". "Here was a man who could work out modular equations and theorems of complex multiplication, to orders unheard of, whose mastery of continued fractions was beyond that of any mathematician in the world, who had found for himself the functional equation of the zeta–function, and the dominant terms of the many of the most famous problems in the analytic theory of numbers; and he had never heard of a doubly periodic function or of Cauchy's theorem, and had indeed but the vaguest idea of what a function of a complex variable was."

Ramanujan was a simple, religious man; he always attributed his mathematical talent to his family deity, Namagiri. He considered mathematics and religion to be linked. He said, "an equation for me has no meaning unless it expresses a thought of God". He belongs to the school of hyper-pure mathematicians that regard mathematics as a game that involves the manipulation of symbols according to given rules. He intuitively stated many complicated results and attributed these to his goddess. He was endowed with an astounding memory and remembered the idiosyncrasies of the first 10000 integers to such an extent that each number became like a personal friend to him. Once, Hardy went to see Ramanujan when he was in a nursing home and remarked that he had traveled in a taxi with a rather dull number, 1729, at which Ramanujan exclaimed, "No, Hardy, 1729 is a very interesting number. It is the smallest number that can be expressed as the sum of two cubes ($1729 = 1^3 + 12^3 = 9^3 + 10^3$), and the next such number is very large". His life can be summed up in his own words, "I really love my subject".

In 1976, George Eyre Andrews (born 1938, USA), Atherton Professor of Mathematics at Pennsylvania State University, came across one hundred and thirty pages of scrap paper in a library at Cambridge University that were filled with notes representing Ramanujan's work during the last year of his life in Madras. These pages are now known as Ramanujan's *Lost Notebook*, and they contain about 4000 formulas and other work. According to Richard Allen Askey (1933–2019, USA), who collaborated with Andrews, "The work of that one year, while he was dying, was the equivalent of the lifetime work of a very great mathematician. What he accomplished was unbelievable. If it were in a novel, nobody would believe it". Ramanujan's formulas keep mathematicians busy to this day, waiting to be deciphered and proved. Many of these formulas were given in their final form without any intermediate steps. This is quite consistent with the ancient Indian tradition, in which great mathematicians merely used to state their results, leaving their students and followers to provide commentaries. His 1914 paper on "Modulus functions and approximation to π" was used recently to compute π to a level of accuracy never before attained. As Robert Kanigel (born 1946, USA) wrote in his book *The Man Who Knew Infinity: A Life of the Genius Ramanujan* (Charles Scribner's Sons, New York, 1991), "What makes Ramanujan's work so seductive is not the prospect of its use in the solution of real–world problems, but its riches, beauty and mystery–its sheer mathematical loveliness". There are many institutions and a temple in India where different portraits and busts of Ramanujan can be found. During 1985–1997, Bruce Carl Berndt (born 1939, USA) meticulously edited Ramanujan's original notebooks in five volumes, published by Springer-Verlag.

Since 2005, the Ramanujan Prize has been awarded annually, usually to one researcher from a developing country who is less than 45 years of age on 31 December of the year of the award and who has conducted outstanding research in a developing country. Researchers working in any branch of the mathematical sciences are eligible. The Prize carries a USD 10,000 cash award. It was originally instituted by the ICTP and IMU, who play a similar role to the case of Abel's Prize. The prize is supported by the Ministry of Science and Technology (India) and the NASL through the Abel Memorial Fund, with the cooperation of the IMU. The winner is invited to the ICTP to receive the prize and deliver a lecture. Past recipients of the Ramanujan Prize are listed below:

2005. Marcelo Miranda Viana da Silva (born 1962, Brazil)
2006. Sujatha Ramdorai (born 1962, India–Canada)
2007. Jorge Lauret (born 1969, Argentina)
2008. Enrique Ramiro Pujals (born 1967, Brazil–USA)
2009. Ernesto Lupercio (born 1970, Mexico)
2010. Shi Yuguang (born 1969, China)
2011. Philibert Nang (born 1967, Gabon)
2012. Fernando Codá Marques (born 1979, Brazil–USA)
2013. Tian Ye (born 1971, China)

2014. Miguel Nicolás Walsh (born 1987, Argentina)
2015. Amalendu Krishna (born 1971, India–USA)
2016. Chenyang Xu (born 1981, China–USA)
2017. Eduardo V. Teixeira (born 1976, Brazil–USA)
2018. Ritabrata Munshi (born 1976, India)
2019. Pham Hoang Hiep (born 1982, Vietnam)
2020. Carolina Bhering de Araujo (born 1976, Brazil)
2021. Neena Gupta (born 1984, India)
2022. Mouhamed Moustapha Fall (born 1981, Senegal)
2023. Not awarded
2024. Ruochuan Liu (China)

35. Madrid ICM 2006

This Congress was held in Madrid, Spain, during 22–30 August 2006. The Congress was attended by 3425 participants (1330 from Spain) from an all-time record of 108 countries. During the opening ceremony IMU President John Ball praised the effort of the Spanish mathematical community for the organization of the Congress. He proposed Manuel de León Rodríguez (born 1953, Spain) as President of the congress and said "Mathematics has a strong record of service, freely given. We see this in the time and care spent in the refereeing of papers and other forms of peer review. We see it in the running of mathematical societies and journals, in the provision of free mathematical software and teaching resources, and in the various projects world-wide to improve electronic access to the mathematical literature, old and new. We see it in the nurturing of students beyond the call of duty". He also gave the quote "Mathematicians do not own mathematics". Carlos Andradas Heranz (born 1956, Spain) was appointed as the Vice-President General, and three Vice-Presidents were appointed: Carles Casacuberta, Eduardo Casas (born 1957, Spain), and Pedro Gil Álvarez (born 1947, Spain). After a few formal lectures there was a medal and prize awarding ceremony. The Fields Medal Committee consisted of John Macleod Ball (Chairman), Enrico Arbarello (born 1945, Italy), Jeff Cheeger (born 1943, USA), Donald Andrew Dawson (born 1937, Canada), Gerhard Huisken (born 1958, Germany), Curtis Tracy McMullen, Aleksei Nikolaevich Parshin (1942–2022, Russia), Thomas Crawford Spencer (born 1946, USA), and Michéle Vergne (born 1943, France, woman). The President of the IMU and the Chairman of the Fields Medal Committee announced the unanimous decision on the four winners of Fields Medals: Andrei Yuryevich Okounkov (born 1969, Russia–USA). Grigori Yakovlevich Perelman (born 1966, Russia). [He declined to accept the Medal. This was first time in the history of the medal an awardee had refused to accept the prize. Two months before, John Ball visited Perelman in St. Petersburg and attempted to persuade him to accept the medal, even suggesting that he need not attend the congress and receive the medal later. But Perelman's decision was definite.] Terence Chi-Shen Tao (born 1975, Australia–USA). Wendelin Werner (born 1968, Germany–France). The Rolf Nevanlinna Prize Committee consisted of Margaret H. Wright (born 1944, USA) [Chairwoman], Samson Abramsky (born 1953, England), Franco Brezzi (born 1945, Italy), Gert-Martin Greuel (born 1944, Poland), and Johan Hastad (born 1960, Sweden). The award was granted to Jon Michael Kleinberg (born 1971, USA). The Gauss Prize Committee consisted of Martin Grötschel (Chairman), Robert Eugene Bixby (born 1945, USA), Frank den Hollander (born 1956, the Netherlands), Stéphane Georges Mallat (born 1962, France), and Ian Hugh Sloan (born 1938, Australia). The Gauss Prize was awarded to Kiyosi Ito. The King of Spain Juan Carlos I (born 1938) presided over the opening ceremony. He also presided over the Honor Committee and presented the medals and prizes to the award winners. For health reasons, Ito was unable to be present at the award ceremony, but his daughter Junko Ito (born 1954, Japan–USA), Professor of Linguistics at the UC, Santa Cruz, accepted the prize on behalf of her father. Later, John Ball personally took the Gauss Medal to Kyoto and presented it to Kiyoshi Ito.

The work of the laureates was reported in a series of twenty-minute laudations. Giovanni Felder (born 1958, Switzerland) spoke on Andrei Okounkov's work: "for his contributions bridging probability, representation theory and algebraic geometry". The work of Andrei Okounkov has revealed profound new connections between different areas of mathematics and has brought new insights into problems arising in physics. John William Lott (born 1959, USA) spoke on the work of Grigori Perelman: "for his contributions to geometry and his revolutionary insights into the analytical and geometric structure of the Ricci flow". His work from 2002 to 2003 brought groundbreaking insights into the study of evolution equations and their singularities. Most significantly, his results provide a way of resolving two outstanding problems in topology: the Poincaré conjecture and the Thurston Geometrization Conjecture. Charles Fefferman spoke on the work of Terence Tao: "for his contributions to partial differential equations, combinatorics, harmonic analysis and additive number theory". He is considered as a supreme problem-solver whose spectacular work has had an impact across several mathematical areas. He combines sheer technical power, an other-worldly ingenuity for hitting upon new ideas, and a startlingly natural point of view that leaves other mathematicians wondering, "Why didn't anyone see that before"? Charles Michael Newman (born 1946, USA) spoke on the work of Wendelin Werner: "for his contributions to the development of stochastic Loewner evolution (after Oded Schramm, 1961–2008, Israel–USA), the geometry of two-dimensional Brownian motion, and conformal field theory". The work of Wendelin Werner and his collaborators represents one of the most exciting and fruitful interactions between mathematics and physics in recent times. John Edward Hopcroft (born 1939, USA) spoke on the work of Jon Kleinberg: "for deep, creative and insightful contributions to the mathematical theory of the global information environment". Kleinberg's work contained plenty of concrete practical applications, such as improving the effectiveness of web search engines or Internet routing. Hans Föllmer (born 1941, Germany) gave a forty-five minutes lecture on "The Work of Kiyoshi Ito and Its Impact": "for laying the foundations of the theory of stochastic differential equations and stochastic analysis", which found a wide range of applications outside of mathematics, including areas such as engineering, physics, biology, economics, finance, and the size of populations of living organisms.

The opening ceremony included a video showing the ancient relation of mathematics to art and culture in Spain and a five-minute computer graphics video entitled The Borromean Rings (three simple closed curves in three-dimensional space that are topologically linked and cannot be separated from each other but that break apart into two unknotted and unlinked loops when any one of the three is cut or removed) about the new logo created by John Matthew Sullivan (born 1963, USA–Germany) for the IMU. There were 20 one-hour plenary lectures (which included Michéle Vergne), 169 invited talks of forty-five minutes distributed in 20 sections, and about 1000 short communications and posters. There was a record number of 64 satellite conferences associated with the ICM, and 28 of these took place outside Spain. There was a round-table discussion "Are Pure and Applied Mathematics Drifting Apart"? and a panel discussion "Should Mathematicians Care about Communicating to Broad Audiences?: Theory and Practice"? A special commemorative edition of the works of Archimedes was published on the occasion of the 2006 congress. It included a facsimile of a sixteenth-century manuscript from the Library of the Monastery of El Escorial containing the works *On the Sphere and Cylinder*, *Measurement of the Circle*, and *Quadrature of the Parabola*. During the closing ceremony John Ball stated the decisions taken at the General Assembly of the IMU held in Santiago de Compostela on the selection of the new EC of the IMU for the period 2007–2010, László Lovász (President), Zhi-Ming Ma and Claudio Procesi (born 1941, Italy) as Vice-Presidents, Martin Grötschel as Secretary, and Mohammed Salah Baouendi (born 1937, Tunisia–USA), Manuel de León Rodríguez, Ragni Piene, Cheryl Elisabeth Praeger (born 1948, Australia, woman), Victor Anatolyevich Vassiliev, Marcelo Viana, and John Ball as members, and about the next Congress in 2010 in Hyderabad (India). Indian representative Rajat Tandon (born 1947, India) in his speech said the following: Hyderabad, like Madrid, is a wonderful composition of the old and the new. This city, founded more than 400 years ago, houses teeming bazaars, old jewelry and fine craftsmen, old forts and mausoleums. Cosmopolitan in its population you find people of all faiths living and learning together here. Two hundred years ago this city expanded to the twin cities of Hyderabad and Secunderabad with the addition of a cantonment area and today greater Hyderabad is a conglomeration of three cities in one with the modern Cyberabad area which is second only to Bangalore (now Bengaluru) as the information technology heart of India. An important feature of the closing ceremony was an exhibition to commemorate the 25 ICMs held from the first in Zurich in 1897 to the Madrid congress in 2006.

35.1. Andrei Yuryevich Okounkov

He was born in Moscow, USSR (now Russia). In 1993, Okounkov received first degree from Moscow State University. He continued there and obtained a candidate's degree (equivalent to a Ph.D.) in 1995. The title of his thesis was *Admissible Representation of Gelfand Pairs Associated with the Infinite Symmetric Group*, written under the supervision of Alexander Kirillov and Grigori Olshanski (born 1949, Russia). Prior to his Ph.D. degree, in 1994 he had published research papers: *Thoma's Theorem and Representations of an Infinite Bisymmetric Group* and *On the Representation of Orbits in the Form of the Sum of Elementary Orbits*, both in Russian. After his Ph.D. for a few months he joined Dobrushin Mathematical Laboratory at the Institute for Problems of Information Transmission at the RAS as a Research Fellow. Then, the academic year 1996–1997 he spent at the Mathematical Science Research Institute in Berkeley, which was financially supported by a grant from the NSF, USA. During this period, he wrote the paper *Proof of a Conjecture of Goulden and Jackson* (in which he proved an integral formula involving Jack polynomials), which was published in 1997 in the *Canadian Journal of Mathematics*. In 1997, Okounkov joined the University of Chicago as an Instructor, a role he continued for three years. During this period he also spent some time at the IAS, Princeton. He was also appointed as an Assistant Professor and Associate Professor at UC, Berkeley, held a Sloan Research Fellowship in 2000, and a Fellowship from the David and Lucile Packard Foundation (established in 1964) in 2001. In 2002, Okounkov was appointed as a Professor at Princeton University. He left Princeton in 2010 to take up a professorship of mathematics at Columbia University in New York and continues there. His main interest is in representation theory and its applications to algebraic geometry, mathematical physics, probability theory, and special functions. Okounkov, along with Rahul Pandharipande (born 1969, India–Switzerland), Nikita Alexandrovich Nekrasov (born 1973, Russia), and Davesh Maulik (USA), has formulated well-known conjectures relating the Gromov–Witten invariants and Donaldson–Thomas (Winsley Thomas) invariants of threefolds. He has published more than 90 research papers and supervised 10 doctoral students. Okounkov has received several honors and awards, including the EMS Prize in 2004, Fields Medal in 2006, AMS Colloquium Lecturer in 2007, Chern Visiting Professor in 2011, and a Fellow of the AAAS in 2016. According to him "Mathematics is both a personal and collective endeavour: while ideas are born in individual heads, the exchange of ideas is just as important for progress". In appreciation of Okounkov, Andrew Wiles said "One of his greatest strengths is his amazing versatility. He works in many different fields of mathematics and succeeds in taking results from one area and applying them in a seemingly quite different field".

35.2. Grigori Yakovlevich Perelman

He was born in Leningrad, USSR (now St. Petersburg, Russia), to Jewish parents. His father Yakov Perelman was an electrical engineer, and his mother Lubov Lvovna was a teacher of mathematics at a technical institute. When Grigori was a young child, his father gave him logical and other maths problems to think about, he received a lot of books to read, and he was taught how to play chess. By the time he was ten years old, his mother recognized her son's talent in mathematics and set him up in various math clubs in St. Petersburg. Not only did she challenge Grigori with math and logic puzzles constantly, but she also provided a window into a recreational world, as his personal violin and tennis tutor. His mathematical education continued at the Leningrad Secondary School 239, a specialized school with advanced mathematics and physics programs. Grigori excelled in all subjects except physical education. In January 1982, he won a gold medal (and a special prize) being a member of the Soviet team at the IMO hosted in Budapest, achieving a perfect score. This gave him automatic entry to Leningrad State University in autumn 1982. There he was particularly influenced by Victor Abramovich Zalgaller (1920–2020, Russia–Israel) and Aleksandr Danilovic Aleksandrov (1912–1999, Russia). Before graduating in 1987, he published three papers in Russian: *Realization of abstract k-skeletons as k-skeletons of intersections of convex polyhedra in* R^{2k-1} in 1985, *A remark on Helly's theorem* in 1986, and *k-radii of a convex body* in 1987. Because he was a Jew, for graduate study his achievements were not good enough to get admission directly to the Leningrad branch of the Steklov Mathematics Institute; rather for this he needed a strong recommendation from Aleksandr Aleksandrov. In 1990, Grigori defended his thesis *Saddle Surfaces in Euclidean Spaces*, written under the supervision of Aleksandr Aleksandrov and Yuri Dmitrievich Burago (born 1936, Russia). Before obtaining his doctorate degree in 1989, he published in Russian one of the main results of his thesis in the paper *An example of a complete saddle surface in* R^4 *with Gaussian curvature bounded away from zero*, whose English translation was published in 1992. In 1991, Grigori won the Young Mathematician Prize of the Saint Petersburg Mathematical Society for his work on Aleksandrov's spaces of curvature bounded from below. Next, he spent several months at the IHES, working with Gromov on Aleksandrov spaces. His first major 58-page paper, written jointly with Burago and Gromov, *A D Aleksandrov spaces with curvatures bounded below*, was published in 1992. In 1992, Grigori spend the autumn semester at the Courant Institute, on a postdoctoral fellowship, and the spring 1993 semester at Stony Brook, again funded by a fellowship. In 1993, he accepted a two-year Miller Research Fellowship at UC, Berkeley. During 1994–1995, he published seven exceptional papers. Specifically, he proved the Soul Conjecture, which had been an open problem for the previous 20 years. In 1995, he was offered positions from several prestigious universities (including Princeton and Stanford), but in the summer he preferred to return to the St. Petersburg branch of the Steklov Mathematics Institute, accepting a research position. In November 2002, March 2003, and July 2003, Grigori posted three preprints to arXiv, giving sketchy proofs of the Poincaré conjecture (and the more powerful geometrization conjecture of Thurston: each of certain three-dimensional topological spaces has a unique geometric structure). The Poincaré conjecture had been a famous open problem in mathematics for the past century. In April 2003, on invitation he gave a short series of lectures on his work at MIT, Stony Brook, Columbia University, Princeton University, and New York University. He turned down all offers of professorships that were made to him, in fact becoming annoyed at the pressure some put on him to accept. After his work several mathematicians have published proofs with the details filled in, which come to several hundred pages. In 2006, he was awarded a Fields Medal and an EMS prize; however, he refused to accept both (the only person so far to have done so). In 2006, he also declined to accept the invitation to be a plenary speaker at the IMU. On 18 March 2010, it was announced that Grigori had met the criteria to receive the first Clay Millennium Prize for resolution of the Poincaré conjecture, but on 1 July 2010, he rejected the prize of USD one million by saying I'm not interested in money or fame; I don't want to be on display like an animal in a zoo. I'm not a hero of mathematics. I'm not even that successful; that is why I don't want to have everybody looking at me". In an interview he said "You cannot cheapen mathematics with such meretricious frippery as a prize awarded by some stupid committee that does not understand my work"! He moved back home to live in the basement of his mother's apartment, where he plays ping-pong against a wall all day. He has declined requests for interviews since 2006 and entirely abandoned mathematics. In a 2006 article in *The New Yorker* , he said that he was disappointed with the ethical standards of the field of mathematics. Jean-Paul Sartre (1905–1980, France) declined the Nobel Prize in Literature (1964) by saying that receiving a prize is like the kiss of death because if it is not well assimilated it can annihilate people. Unfortunately, in some cases this is true.

35.3. Terence Chi-Shen Tao

He was born in Adelaide, Australia. Tao was a child prodigy: at the age of two he attempted to teach a 5-year-old child mathematics and English; when he was three and a half years old his parents sent him to a private school but, six weeks later, they realized that he was not ready for schooling and also that the teachers did not know how to teach someone like him; his parents put him in school again when he was five years old; and at the age of eight he scored 760 on the mathematics section of the SAT. When Tao was nine years old, his father took him on a trip to meet some of the world's top mathematicians; they went to the IAS, Princeton, where Tao was interviewed by Charles Fefferman and Enrico Bombieri. At the age of nine he also took university-level mathematics courses. Tao competed in the IMO in 1986, 1987, and 1988, winning bronze, silver, and gold medals, respectively. At thirteen, he was the youngest gold medalist in the history of the competition, and he holds this record to this day. In 1989, at the age of fourteen he began full-time university studies at Flinders University. At the age of 15, Tao wrote his first book *Solving mathematical problems: A personal perspective*. He was awarded a Bachelor of Science with Honours in 1991 and a Master of Science in 1992 defending the thesis *Convolution operators generated by right-monogenic and harmonic kernels*, written under the supervision of Garth Gaudry (1941–2012, Australia). He was awarded the University Medal by Flinders University and a Fulbright Postgraduate Scholarship to enable him to undertake research in the United States. In 1992, he joined Princeton University as a graduate student under the supervision of Elias Stein and completed his Ph.D. on his thesis *Three Regularity Results in Harmonic Analysis* at the age of twenty-one. In 1996, he published four research papers, *Weak-type endpoint bounds for Riesz means*, *On the almost-everywhere convergence of wavelet summation methods*, *Harmonic convolution operators on Lipschitz graphs*, and *On the Structure of Projective Group Representations in Quaternionic Hilbert Space*. During 1996–1998, he worked at UCLA as an Assistant Professor, and became full Professor in 2000, the youngest person to hold that rank at the university. He is also the James and Carol Collins Chair in the College of Letters and Sciences. Tao's areas of research include harmonic analysis, partial differential equations, combinatorics, number theory, and signal processing. He has almost 400 publications and has supervised 22 doctoral students. He has received numerous number of honors and awards, including the following: Sloan Foundation and Packard fellowships during 1999–2001 and 1999–2006; Salem Prize in 2000; Bôcher Prize in 2002; Clay Research Award in 2003; Levi Leonard Conant Prize in 2005; Australian Mathematical Society Medal in 2005; Fields Medal in 2006; Shanmugha Arts, Science, Technology & Research Academy (SASTRA) Ramanujan Prize in 2006; elected to the Australian Academy of Sciences in 2006; MacArthur Fellowship and Ostrowski Prize in 2007; elected a FRS of London in 2007; elected to the United States NAS in 2008; Alan Tower Waterman Award in 2008; elected to AAAS in 2009; King Faisal Prize in 2010; Nemmers Prize in 2010; Polya Prize in 2010; Crafoord Prize in 2012; Breakthrough Prize in Mathematics in 2014; Riemann Prize in 2019; the Princess of Asturias Award for Technical & Scientific Research in 2020; Johann Bolyai International Mathematical Prize by the Hungarian Academy of Sciences in 2020; the United Sigma Intelligence Association Award for Mathematics in 2021; the Education and Research Award by Advance Global Australian Awards in 2022; Global Australian of the Year Award in 2022; and Grande Médaille of the FAS in 2023. His most famous result is the Green–Tao theorem (with Ben Joseph Green, born 1977, UK), which states that there exist arbitrarily long arithmetic progressions of prime numbers. Tao currently lives with his wife Laura and two children in Los Angeles, California.

35.4. Wendelin Werner

He was born in Cologne, Germany, but his parents moved to France when he was nine months old. Wendelin acwuired French nationality at the age of nine. After a classe préparatoire at Lycée Franco-Allemand de Buc located in Buc, Yvelines, in the Paris metropolitan area, he studied at the ENS from 1987 to 1991. Then he joined the Université Pierre-et-Marie-Curie and under the supervision of Jean-François Le Gall (born 1959, France) secured his doctorate degree in 1993. The title of Wendelin's thesis was *Quelques propriétés du mouvement brownien plan* (Some properties of plane Brownian motion). During 1991–1997, he was a researcher at the CNRS and also held a two-year Leibniz Fellowship to continue at the University of Cambridge. From 1997 to 2013 he was appointed as a Professor at the University of Paris-Sud 11; in addition from 2005 to 2013 he taught at the ENS. Next, he was a Professor at the ETH Zurich from 2013 to 2023. Wendelin is currently Rouse Ball Professor of Mathematics at the University of Cambridge and the University of Oxford. He has made remarkable contributions in the following fields: random processes such as self-avoiding random walks, Brownian motion, Schramm–Loewner evolution (Charles Loewner, 1893–1968, Czech Republic–USA), and related theories in probability theory and mathematical physics. He has almost 100 publications and has supervised 13 doctoral students. Wendelin has received several awards and honors, including the Rollo Davidson (1944–1970, England) Prize in 1998, Prix Paul Doistau-Émile Blutet in 1999, EMS Prize in 2000, Fermat Prize in 2001, Grand Prix Jacques Herbrand in 2003, Michel Loéve Prize in 2005, Polya Prize in 2006, Fields Medal in 2006, a member of the FAS in 2008, Heinz Gumin Prize in 2016, and elected a Foreign Member of the Royal Society in 2020. Besides mathematics Wendelin played a role in the 1982 film *La Passante du Sans-Souci* (*The Passante of Sans-Souci*) and involved himself with political issues, publishing an open letter to President Nicolas Sarkozy (born 1955) of France in February 2009. The letter criticizes the policies of Sarkozy's government, which have, in his opinion, led to a breakdown in trust between the government and researchers.

35.5. Jon Michael Kleinberg

He was born in Boston, Massachusetts, USA, to a mathematics professor father and a computer consultant mother. In 1993, he completed his undergraduate degree in computer science at Cornell University and in 1996 his doctorate, also in computer science, at MIT. The title of his thesis was *Approximation Algorithms for Disjoint Paths Problems*, written under the supervision of Michel Xavier Goemans (born 1964, Belgium–USA). Since 1996 he has been a Professor in the Department of Computer Science at Cornell, as well as a visiting scientist at IBM's Almaden Research Center. His research focuses on algorithms and networks, the roles they play in large-scale social and information systems, and their broader societal implications. His work has been supported by an NSF Career Award, an Office of Naval Research Young Investigator Award, a MacArthur Foundation Fellowship, a Packard Foundation Fellowship, a Simons Investigator Award, a Sloan Foundation Fellowship, a Vannevar Bush (1890–1974, USA) Faculty Fellowship, and grants from Facebook, Google, Yahoo, the Air Force Office of Scientific Research, and the Army Research Office. His younger brother Robert David Kleinberg is also a Professor of Computer Science at Cornell University. Jon Kleinberg is best known for his HITS algorithm, which identifies good authorities and hubs for a topic by assigning two numbers to a page: an authority and a hub weight. These weights are defined recursively. A higher authority weight occurs if the page is pointed to by pages with high hub weights. He is also known for his work on algorithmic aspects of the small-world experiment. He has more than 100 publications, including two textbook entitled *Algorithm Design*, co-authored with Éva Tardos (born 1957, Hungary–USA), and *Networks, Crowds, and Markets: Reasoning About a Highly Connected World*, co-authored with David Alan Easley (born 1950s, USA), and has supervised eight doctoral students. He has received several awards, including the Rolf Nevanlinna Prize in 2006, ACM-Infosys Foundation Award in 2008, Harvey Prize in 2013, and Allen Newell Award in 2014. He is a member of the United States NAS, the National Academy of Engineering, and the AAAS and a Fellow of the ACM and the APS.

35.6. Kiyosi Ito

He was born in the town of Hokusei-cho in Mie Prefecture, Japan. Kiyosi Ito excelled in his studies as a youth; then he studied mathematics in the Faculty of Science of the Imperial University of Tokyo. Since he was a student, he was attracted to the fact that statistical laws reside in seemingly random phenomena. In 1938, Kiyosi Ito graduated from the Imperial University of Tokyo and in the following year he joined the Cabinet Statistics Bureau and worked there until 1943. In 1940, his first paper *On the probability distribution on a compact group* appeared jointly with Yukiyosi Kawada. In 1942, he published two papers *Differential equations determining a Markoff process* and the famous *On stochastic processes I (Infinitely divisible laws of probability)*, which took several years to find its significance. In 1943, Kiyosi Ito was appointed an Assistant Professor at Nagoya Imperial University, and from the Imperial University of Tokyo obtained his Ph.D. in 1945 for his thesis *On Stochastic Processes* written under the supervision of Shokichi Iyanaga. During these two years he published a series of six articles, *On the ergodicity of a certain stationary process; A kinematic theory of turbulence; On the normal stationary process with no hysteresis; A screw line in Hilbert space and its application to the probability theory; On Student's test*; and especially *Stochastic integral*, in which he defined the stochastic integral and laid the foundations of Ito calculus. All these works were conducted and published during the years of extreme difficulty in Japan caused by World War II. He continued to advance his work on stochastic analysis with many important papers on the topic. Among them were *On a stochastic integral equation* in 1946, *On the stochastic integral* in 1948, *Stochastic differential equations in a differentiable manifold* in 1950, *Brownian motions in a Lie group* in 1950, and *On stochastic differential equations* in 1951. In 1952, he became a Professor at the University of Kyoto and remained affiliated there until his retirement in 1979 (with long periods away from Japan). His most well-known text, *Probability Theory*, appeared in 1953. During 1954–1956, Kiyosi Ito was at the IAS, Princeton, on a Fulbright fellowship. In 1957, he published an important book *Essentials of Stochastic Processes* (in Japanese, which was translated into English in 1999). In 1960, he visited the Tata Institute of Fundamental Research in Bombay, India, where he gave a series of lectures surveying his own work and that of others on Markov processes, Levy processes, Brownian motion, and linear diffusion. During

1961–1964, he worked as a Professor at Stanford University, from 1966 to 1969 as a Professor at Aarhus University (Denmark), and during 1969–1975 as a Professor at Cornell University. Then he returned to Japan and became the Director of the RIMS at Kyoto University. After his retirement, he became Professor Emeritus at Kyoto University. Kiyosi Ito published around 80 research articles and supervised nine doctoral students. He was the recipient of the Asahi Prize in 1977, Fujiwara Prize in 1985, Wolf Prize in 1987, Kyoto Prize in 1998, and (inaugural) Gauss Prize in 2006 (for his lifetime achievements). He also received honorary doctorates from the universities of Warwick, England, and ETH. Kiyosi Ito was a member of the Japan Academy and a Foreign Member of the Académie des Sciences in France and the United States NAS. In October 2008, he was honored with Japan's Order of Culture, and an awards ceremony for the Order of Culture was held at the Imperial Palace. Kiyosi Ito died on 10 November 2008 in Kyoto, Japan, at age 93, of respiratory failure.

36. Shiing-Shen Chern (1911–2004, China–USA) and Chern Medal

He was born in Xiushui, Jiaxing, China, into a family of two sons and two daughters. He was educated at home as well as from time to time attending Chia-hsing elementary school from the winter of 1917 until 1920. He learned Chinese from his aunt and mathematics from his father. In 1920, he joined Xiushui Middle School; then in 1922 his family moved to Tianjin, and Chern spent the four years 1922–1926 there at Fulun High School. During these four years he took great interest in mathematics, particularly algebra, geometry, and trigonometry. After graduating in 1926, he enrolled at Nankai University in Tianjin and was awarded a diploma and Bachelor of Science fegree in mathematics in 1930. The same year Chern was appointed as an assistant in the Department of Mathematics at Tsing Hua University, Peking (now Beijing), and from 1931 he started performing research as a graduate student (he was the only graduate student in mathematics to enter the university). In 1932, Chern published his first research article in the *Tsinghua University Journal*. In the summer of 1934, Chern graduated from Tsing Hua University with a master's degree (the first ever master's degree in mathematics issued in China). In 1934, Tsing Hua University offered him a scholarship for three years to study in the United States, but he made a special request that he be allowed to go to the University of Hamburg (Germany). In 1935, his first paper *Triads of rectilinear congruences with generators in correspondence* appeared in the *Tuhoku Journal of Japan*. After two years, in 1936, he received a Doctor of Sciences degree from the University of Hamburg for his dissertation *Eine Invariantentheorie der Dreigewebe aus r-dimensionalen Mannigfaltigkeiten im* R_{2r} (An invariant theory of tri-tissues of r-dimensional manifolds in R_{2r}), written under the supervision of Wilhelm Johann Eugen Blaschke (1885–1962, Austria–Germany). For the third year of his scholarship, he went to Paris to work with Élie Cartan. In 1937, Chern left Paris to become Professor of mathematics at Tsing Hua University. In 1939, he married Zheng Shih-ning (1915–2000, China), and they had a son and a daughter. During 1943–1945, Chern was a member of the IAS, Princeton, and in 1946 he returned to China to become acting director of the Institute of Mathematics at the Academia Sinica in Nanjing. In 1949, he returned to the USA and joined the University of Chicago as a full Professor, where he collaborated with André Weil. This time he brought his family with him. In 1960, Chern moved to UC, Berkeley, became a naturalized citizen of the United States in 1961, retiring officially in 1979, and then became an Emeritus Professor. He helped found and was the Director of the MSRI, Berkeley (1981–1984). In 1999, at the age of 88, he returned to China, where he made his home in Tianjin, where the Chern Institute of Mathematics of Nankai University had been set up in 1985. Chern's wife died in January 2000 in Tianjin, and he died at his home in Tianjin at the age of 93 from heart failure following a heart attack. Chern is considered as a foremost educator whose research mainly in differential geometry developed ideas that now play a major role in mathematics and in mathematical physics. He is remembered for the Chern class, Chern–Gauss–Bonnet theorem (Pierre Ossian Bonnet, 1819–1892, France), Chern–Simons theory (James Harris Simons, 1938–2024,

USA), Chern–Simons form, Chern–Weil theory, Chern–Weil homomorphism, Chern's conjecture, Chern's conjecture (differential geometry), Chern–Bott formula, and Chern–Lashof theory (Richard Kenneth Lashof, 1922–2010, USA). Chern supervised 43 doctoral students, including Fields medalist Shing-Tung Yau and Nobel Prize winner Chen-Ning Yang, and published more than 300 research articles, including several very influential books: *Topics in Differential Geometry* (1951), *Differential Manifolds* (1953), *Complex Manifolds* (1956), *Complex manifolds Without Potential Theory* (1979), *Minimal Submanifolds in a Riemannian Manifold* (1968), *Selected Papers, Vol I–IV* (1978, 1989, 1989, and 1989), *Lectures on Differential Geometry* (1999), *An Introduction to Riemann-Finsler Geometry* (2000), and *Riemann Finsler Geometry* (2005). Chern was the recipient of many international honors: Chauvenet Prize in 1970, National Medal of Science in 1975, Humboldt Prize in 1982, Steele Prize in 1983, Wolf Prize in 1983, ForMemRS in 1985, Lobachevsky Medal in 2002, and Shaw Prize in 2004. He was elected/selected Academician, Academia Sinica (1948); Honorary Member, Indian Mathematical Society (1950); Honorary Fellow, Tata Institute of Fundamental Research (1950); member of the United States NAS (1961); Fellow, AAAS (1963); Vice-President of the AMS (1963–1964); Corresponding Member, Brazilian Academy of Sciences (1971); Associate Founding Fellow, The World Academy of Sciences (1983); Foreign Fellow, RSL (1985); Honorary Fellow, LMS (1986); Corresponding Member, Accademia Peloritana, Messina, Sicily (1986); Honorary Life Member, New York Academy of Sciences (1987); Foreign Member, Accademia dei Lincei (1989); Foreign Member, Académie des sciences (1989); Member, APS (1989); Foreign Member, Chinese Academy of Sciences (1994); and Member, RAS (2001). He was awarded an honorary doctorate by the University of Chicago in 1969, Chinese University of Hong Kong in 1969, ETH Zurich in 1982, Stony Brook University in 1985, University of Hamburg in 1971, Nankai University in 1985, University of Notre Dame in 1994, Technische Universität Berlin in 2001, and Hong Kong University of Science and Technology in 2003. The asteroid 29552 Chern is named after him.

In memory of Shiing-Shen Chern, the IMU established the Chern Medal in 2010 to an individual whose accomplishments warrant the highest level of recognition for outstanding achievements in the field of mathematics. All living, natural persons, regardless of age or vocation, are eligible for the medal. The Chern Medal, like other medals, is awarded every four years on the occasion of the ICM. The medal was established based on a generous grant from the Chern Medal Foundation (CMF). It consists a monetary award of USD 500,000 (half of the monetary award will be donated to organizations of the recipient's choice), for the support of research, education, or other outreach programs in the field of mathematics, and a medallion. The medal is 18KT green-gold-plated with 24-karat gold, with a diameter of 2.5 inch, and packaged in a cherry wood box. The obverse side of the medal features the text "CHERN MEDAL" and his portrait; Chern's Chinese signature is to the left of the portrait, while his English signature sits to the right, and the text "1911–2004" indicates the years of his birth and passing, respectively. The reverse side of the medal displays the generalized Gauss–Bonnet theorem (formula). The selection committee is chosen by the EC of the IMU, and only the name of the Chair of the Committee is made public.

The front of the Chern Medal.

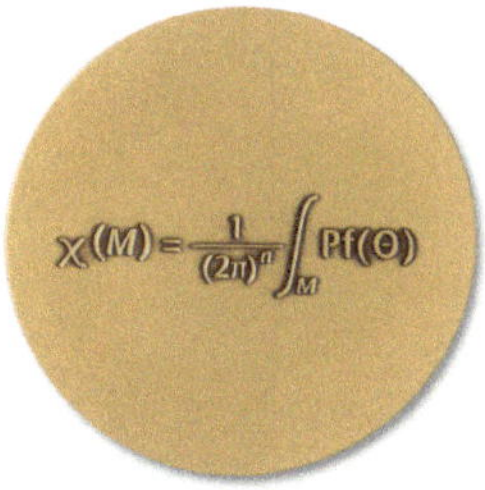

The back of the Chern Medal.

37. Bhaskara II or Bhaskaracharya (Working 486) and Leelavati Award

He was born in Bijapur district, Karnataka, India, and was actively working in 486 AD. He was the son of Chudamani Maheshvar. Bhaskaracharya was the head of the astronomical observatory at Ujjain. His celebrated work *Siddhanta Siromani* (*Crown of Treatises*) consists of four parts, namely, *Leelavati, Bijaganitam, Grahaganitam*, and *Goladhyaya*. The first two deal exclusively with mathematics and the last two address astronomy. His popular text *Leelavati* (named after his daughter) was written in 486 AD and was translated into Persian in 1587. During British rule, the British government banned it due to suspicions that it was being used to practice occult practices and spread superstitions among the population. According to legend, Bhaskaracharya had calculated that his daughter Leelavati (one who is full of grace and charm) might propitiously marry only at one particular hour on a given day. However, on that day just before the wedding the eager girl bent over the water clock and unknowingly dropped a pearl, which stopped the water clock. Before the mishap was noticed, the auspicious hour had passed. To console the unhappy girl, the father gave her name to the book. Bhaskaracharya's contributions to mathematics include a proof of the Pythagorean theorem; solutions of quadratic, cubic, and quartic indeterminate equations; integer solutions of linear and quadratic indeterminate equations; a cyclic Chakravala method for solving indeterminate equations, which was rediscovered by William Viscount Brouncker (1620–1684, Ireland) in 1657; solutions of Pell's equations (after John Pell, 1611–1685, U.K.); solutions of Diophantine equations of the second order, such as $61x^2 + 1 = y^2$ (this equation was posed in 1657 by Fermat, but its solution was unknown in Europe until the time of Euler in the 18th century); solutions of quadratic equations with more than one unknown, including negative and irrational solutions; a preliminary concept of infinitesimal calculus, along with notable contributions towards integral calculus; a concept of differential calculus, after discovering the derivative and differential coefficient; a statement of Rolle's theorem; derivatives of trigonometric functions and formulas; and work on spherical trigonometry, including a number of trigonometric results such as $\sin(a \pm b) = \sin a \cos b \pm \cos a \sin b$, and the following two remarkable identities:

$$\sqrt{a \pm \sqrt{b}} = \sqrt{[a + \sqrt{a^2 - b}]/2} \pm \sqrt{[a - \sqrt{a^2 - b}]/2}.$$

He conceived the modern mathematical convention that when a finite number is divided by zero, the result is infinity. He speculated on the nature of the number $1/0$ by stating that it is "like the Infinite, Invariable God who suffers no change when old worlds are destroyed or new ones created, when innumerable species of creatures are born or as many perish". Bhaskaracharya postulated that the Earth had a gravitational force. In astronomy, his studies included lunar and solar eclipses, latitudes of the planets, the sunrise equation, the Moon's crescent, cosmography, and geography. Bhaskaracharya's greatness lies in making mathematics highly irresistible and attractive. We list here some of his stimulating problems, which are in verse form:

A beautiful pearl necklace belonging to a young lady was torn in a love quarrel and the pearls were all scattered on the floor. One third of the number of pearls was on the bed, one–fifth was under the bed, one–sixth was found by the pretty lady, one–tenth was collected by the lover, and six were left hanging on the thread. Tell me the total number of pearls in the necklace (30).

One person has three hundred coins and six horses. Another has ten horses (each) of similar value as well as a debt of one hundred coins. They are of equal worth. What is the price of a horse? (100).

The square–root of half of a swarm of bees went to a rose–bush to suck honey, followed by eight–ninths of the entire swarm. One lady bee was caught in a lotus flower which closed at night. She was humming in response to the humming call of a male bee. O lady, tell me the number of bees in the swarm (72).

A snake's hole is at the foot of a pillar which is 15 cubits high, and a peacock is perched on its summit. Seeing a snake at a distance of thrice the pillar's height, gliding toward his hole, he pounces obliquely upon him. Say quickly at how many cubits from the snake's hole do they meet, both proceeding an equal distance? (20).

Inside a forest, a number of apes equal to the square of one–eighth of the total apes in a pack are playing noisy games. The remaining 12 apes, who are of a more serious disposition, are on a nearby hill and are irritated by the shrieks coming from the forest. What is the total number of apes in the pack? (16 and 48).

A single bee (out of a swarm of bees) was seen in the sky; 1/5 of the remainder (of the swarm), and 1/4 of the remainder (left thereafter) and again 1/3 of the remainder (left thereafter), and a number of bees equal to the square–root of the numerical value of the swarm were seen in lotuses; two bees were on a mango tree. How many bees were there? (16).

One says, "Give me a hundred, friend, I shall then become twice as rich as you". The other replies, "If you give me ten, I shall be six times as rich as you". Tell me what is the amount of their (respective) capitals? (40, 170).

What is that number, O learned man, which being multiplied by twelve and increased by the cube of the number is equal to six times the square of the number added with thirty–five (5).

What is that number which being multiplied by 200 and added to the square of the number, and then multiplied by 2 and subtracted from the fourth power of the number, will become one myriad less unity (9999)? Tell that number if thou be conversant with the operations of analysis (11).

The Leelavati Prize was confirmed by the IMU in 2010 to accord high recognition and great appreciation for outstanding contributions to increasing public awareness of mathematics as an intellectual discipline and the crucial role it plays in diverse human endeavors. It was sponsored by Indian Multinational Information Technology Company (Infosys), which offers business consulting, information technology, and outsourcing services. The initial planning was only for a one-time international award; however, it was so well received during the closing ceremony at the ICM 2010 and in the mathematical press that the IMU decided to turn the Leelavati Prize into a recurring four-yearly award and the award ceremony a regular feature of every ICM closing ceremony. The prize carries a cash prize of INR 1,000,000 together with a citation.

38. Hyderabad ICM 2010

This Congress was held in Hyderabad, India, during 19–27 August 2010. In spite of the Mumbai terrorist attacks during 26–29 November 2008, and rumored fears of diseases such as malaria, the Congress was attended by 2941 participants from 85 countries. On the morning of 19 August, the Congress was inaugurated by the the President of India, Honorable Pratibha Devisingh Patil (born 1934). In her short speech she emphasized the contributions of mathematics to society and the many contributions of India to the subject. Her speech was beautifully crafted and showed an appreciation for the mathematical sciences that one sometimes feels is lacking in other national leaders. The President of the Congress was Madabusi Santanam Raghunathan, Vice-President Shrikrishna Gopalrao Dani (born 1947, India), and Secretary Rajat Tandon. After the inauguration, Madabusi Raghunathan welcomed all the participants, which was followed by the President of the IMU László Lovász. In his brief address he mentioned the great contributions of Indian mathematicians, particularly, of Bhaskara II and Ramanujan, and Indians' role in the progress of computational science. Next there was an address from the Chief Minister Konijeti Rosaiah (1933–2021) of Andhra Pradesh. He welcomed the audience and talked about Hyderabad's higher educational institutions, specifically Osmania University, which was established in 1887. He mentioned several prominent mathematicians from Andhra Pradesh: Subbaramiah Minakshisundaram (1913–1968), Calyampudi Radhakrishna Rao (1920–2023), Chandrasekharan, and Kollagunta Gopalaiyer Ramanathan (1920–1992). Then, there was the medal and prize awarding ceremony. The Fields Medal Committee consisted of László Lovász (Chairman), Corrado de Concini (born 1949, Italy), Yakov Matveevich Eliashberg (born 1946, USSR–USA), Peter Gavin Hall (1951–2016, Australia), William Timothy Gowers, Ngaiming Mok (born 1956, Hong Kong, China), Stefan Müller (born 1962, Germany), Peter Clive Sarnak, and Karen Keskulla Uhlenbeck. Martin Grötschel announced the names of four winners with citations, László Lovász handed over the checks, and the medals were presented by the President of India: Elon Lindenstrauss (born 1970, Israel) "for his results on measure rigidity in ergodic theory, and their applications to number theory"; Ngô Bảo Châu (born 1972, Vietnam–France) "for his proof of the Fundamental Lemma in the theory of automorphic forms through the introduction of new algebro-geometric methods"; Stanislav Konstantinovich Smirnov (born 1970, Russia) "for the proof of conformal invariance of percolation and the planar Ising model in statistical physics"; and Cédric Patrice Thierry Villani (born 1973, France) "for his proofs of nonlinear Landau damping and convergence to equilibrium for the Boltzmann equation". The Rolf Nevanlinna Prize Committee consisted of Ravindran Kannan (born 1953, India) [Chairman], Stanley Joel Osher (born 1942, USA), Olivier Pironneau (born 1945, France), Madhu Sudan, and Emmerich Welzl (born 1958, Austria). Ravindran Kannan announced the name of the winner Daniel Alan Spielman (born 1970, USA) "for smoothed analysis of Linear Programming, algorithms for graph-based codes and applications of graph theory to Numerical Computing", the check was given by Pertti Esko Juhani Mattila (born 1948, Finland), and the medal was presented by the President of India. After the awards of the medals, the President of India left. Then László Lovász commemorated the mathematicians who had died since the previous ICM, including Henri Cartan, Vladimir Arnold, and Kyosi Ito. He also announced the name of Ingrid Daubechies as the next President of the IMU (first woman), South Korea as the country for the next ICM, and Berlin as the new permanent office of the IMU. Finally, after the speech of Martin Grötschel, the President of the Congress Madabusi Raghunathan announced the closing of the morning session (break for the lunch).

In the afternoon of 19 August, there were laudations of the works of the awardees. Hillel Furstenberg said the following for Lindenstrauss: His work continues a tradition of interaction between dynamical systems theory and diophantine analysis; there is both power and beauty in the mathematical work of Lindenstrauss. James Greig Arthur spoke for Ngô Bảo Châu: His proof of the Fundamental Lemma (from Langlands's program) is a profound and beautiful argument, built on insights mathematicians have contributed for over thirty years. Harry Kesten (1931–2019, Germany–USA) talked about Stanislav Smirnov: His ingenious and astonishing work on the existence and conformal invariance of scaling limits or continuum limits of lattice models in statistical physics. Horng-Tzer Yau (born 1959, Taiwan–USA) shared the following for Cédric Villani: His fundamental connection between entropy and its dissipation which involves rigorous mathematical analysis which is not just a display of powerful analytic skill, but also leads to deep insights into nature. Villani has developed a general theory, hypercoercivity, which applies to broad systems of equations. Gil Kalai (born 1955, Israel) said the following for Daniel Spielman: His groundbreaking contributions in theoretical computer science and mathematical programming and his work has profound connections to the study of polytopes and convex bodies, to error-correcting codes, expanders, and numerical analysis. Then, the Gauss Prize and Chern Medal were awarded. The Gauss Prize Committee consisted of Wolfgang Dahmen (born 1949, Germany) [Chairman], Rolf Jeltsch (1945–2024, Switzerland), Servet Martinez Aguilera (born 1952, Chile), and William R. Pulleyblank (Canada–USA). The Gauss Prize was awarded to Yves François Meyer "for his fundamental contributions to number theory, operator theory and harmonic analysis, and his pivotal role in the development of wavelets and multiresolution analysis". The Chern Medal Committee consisted of Phillip Augustus Griffiths (Chairman), Robert Leamon Bryant (born 1953, USA), Gerd Faltings, Fanghua Lin (born 1959, China–USA), and Wendelin Werner. The Chern Medal and a monetary award of USD 500000 were awarded to Louis Nirenberg "for his role in the formulation of the modern theory of non-liner elliptic partial differential equations and for mentoring numerous students and post-docs in this area". Ingrid Daubechies spoke about Yves Meyer: He has made numerous contributions to mathematics, in particular in number theory, harmonic analysis, partial differential equations, wavelets, and singular integral operator theory. Yan Yan Li (China-USA) spoke about his Ph.D. Supervisor Louis Nirenberg: He is one of the most outstanding analysts of the twentieth century. For more than half a century, he has been a world leader in partial differential equations—a master of inequalities and regularity theory—with fundamental contributions in geometry, complex analysis, and fluid dynamics. The academic program for the day ended with the Abel Lecture on *Large Deviations* (sponsored by the Norwegian Academy of Sciences) by Srinivasa Varadhan, for which Rangachari Parthasarathy was the chair.

There were 20 one-hour plenary invited speakers (12 from USA, 1 from India, and 4 women), 177 invited talks of forty-five minutes distributed in 20 sections, and plenty of short communications and poster sessions: on 21 August alone there were 77 short communications and 132 poster sessions. There were also several satellite conferences. During the closing ceremony Leelavati Prize was presented. The Leelavati Prize Committee consisted of Mudumbai Seshachalu Narasimhan (Chairman), John Macleod Ball, László Lovász, Jacob Palis Jr., and Madabusi Santanam Raghunathan. The prize was awarded to Simon Lehna Singh (born 1964, England) "for his outstanding contributions to public outreach in mathematics by an individual". Then, Radha Charan Gupta (1935–2024, India) was awarded the Kenneth Ownsworth May (1915–1977, USA–Canada) Prize, which was actually conferred in 2009 during the 23rd International Congress of History of Science and Technology in Budapest, Hungary. Gupta's work focused on the history of mathematics in India, particularly the development of trigonometry, including interpolation rules and infinite series for trigonometric functions. In 2023, he was honored with the Padma Shri Award (the fourth-highest civilian award of the Republic of India). Next, László Lovász spoke about the decisions taken at the General Assembly of the IMU held recently in Bangalore (now Bengaluru): The selection of the new EC of the IMU for the period 2011–2014, Ingrid Daubechies (President), Christiane Rousseau (born 1954, France–Canada) and Marcelo Viana as Vice-Presidents, Martin Grötschel as Secretary, and Manuel de León Rodríguez, Long Yiming (born 1948, China), Cheryl Elisabeth Praeger, Vasudevan Srinivas (born 1958, India), John Francis Toland (born 1949, UK), Wendelin Werner, and László Lovász as members, and about the next Congress in 2014 in Seoul (South Korea). Korean representative Hyungju Park (born 1964) in his speech gave thanks to the decision of the IMU to hold the next conference in Korea and described the progress Korea has made in education, especially in mathematics from 1981. He talked about the research centers the National Institute for Mathematical Sciences (NIMS) and Korean Institute of Advanced Studies (KIAS). He also promised support to 1000 participants from the developing countries. Finally, Madabusi Raghunathan declared the Congress closed. One of the "special activities" of the ICM 2010 was the Emmy Noether Lecture by Idun Reiten (born 1942, Norway) entitled *Cluster Categories*.

38.1. Elon Lindenstrauss

He was born in Jerusalem, Israel, to a mathematics professor father Joram Lindenstrauss (1936–2012, Israel) and a computer scientist mother Naomi Lindenstrauss, both at the Hebrew University of Jerusalem. Elon's sister Ayelet Lindenstrauss is also a mathematician. In 1988, Elon represented Israel in the IMO held in Canberra, Australia, and won a bronze medal. He was enlisted to the Israeli Defense Forces Talpiot program and studied at the Hebrew University of Jerusalem, where he earned his Bachelor of Science in mathematics and physics in 1991, his master's degree in mathematics in 1995, and his Ph.D. in 1999 for his thesis entitled *Entropy Properties of Dynamical Systems*, written under the supervision of Benjamin Weiss. During 1999–2001, Elon was at the IAS in Princeton, and from 2001 to 2003, he was Gábor Szegö Assistant Professor of Mathematics at Stanford University. Then for two years, 2003–2005, he was a visiting member at the Courant Institute of Mathematical Sciences in New York. During the same period he was also a Long-Term Prize Fellow at the Clay Mathematics Institute. Next Elon joined Princeton University in 2004 as a Professor and stayed there until 2010, and concurrently he was a Professor at the Hebrew University of Jerusalem from the beginning of 2008. In 2024, Elon was appointed a permanent faculty member in the School of Mathematics of the IAS, Princeton. Elon is a leading authority in the field of ergodic theory, dynamical systems, and their applications to number theory. His major breakthroughs include the development of the theory of mean topological dimension, the proof of quantum unique ergodicity for arithmetic surfaces, and the characterization of the set of possible exceptions to the celebrated Littlewood conjecture in Diophantine approximation. He has published more than 65 research papers and supervised eight doctoral students. Elon has received several awards, inlcuding the Blumenthal Award in 2001, Salem Prize in 2003, EMS Prize in 2004, Fermat Prize in 2009, Erdös Prize in 2009, and Fields Medal in 2010 (first Israeli). He has been elected to the Academia Europaea (2012) and Israel Academy of Sciences and Humanities (2012). Elon is a editorial board member of the *Duke Mathematical Journal* and *Journal d'Analyse Mathématique*. In 1997, he married Abigail and they have three children.

38.2. Ngô Bảo Châu

He was born in Hanoi, North Vietnam, in an intellectual family. His father Ngo Huy Can (born 1941, Vietnam) is the Head of the Hydro-Pneumatic Dynamics Department, Institute of Weapons, General Department of Defense Industry, and his mother Tran Luu Van Hien (Vietnam) is a physician and Associate Professor at the Central Hospital of Traditional Medicine in Hanoi. He started his education at an experimental elementary school that had been founded by a revolutionary pedagogue, but then his father enrolled him in the special classes for gifted students in mathematics at Trung Vuong Middle School. Châu in 1988 and 1989 participated in the 29th and 30th IMO and became the first Vietnamese student to win two IMO gold medals, of which the first one was won with a perfect score. In 1990, Châu was offered a scholarship by the French Government for undergraduate study at the Paris VI University. In 1992, he entered the ENS, and he received a doctorate degree from the University of Paris-South in 1997. The title of his thesis was *Le lemme fondamental de Jacquet et Ye en égales caractéristiques* (The fundamental lemma of Jacquet and Ye in equal characteristics), written under the supervision of Gérard Laumon. He became a member of the CNRS at Paris 13 University from 1998 to 2005 and defended his habilitation degree there in 2003. During 2005–2010, Châu was a Professor at the University of Paris-South, and from 2007 to 2010 he held a concurrent appointment as a member of the IAS, Princeton. In 2010, he joined the University of Chicago as a Professor of Mathematics, and since 2023 he has been serving as the Chair of the department. Châu is best known for proving the fundamental lemma for automorphic forms (proposed in 1984 by Robert Langlands and Diana Frost Shelstad, born 1947, Australia). He has published more than 30 research articles and supervised 11 doctoral students. Châu was the co-author of the Vietnamese children's book *Ai and Ky in the Land of the Invisible Numbers*. He is the recipient of several honors and awards: Clay Research Award in 2004, Oberwolfach Prize in 2007, Sophie Germain Prize in 2007, Fields Medal in 2010 (the first Vietnamese), and Legion of Honour in 2011. In 2012, he became a Fellow of the AMS and in 2021 an Honorary Member of the LMS. Châu is a editorial board member of the journals *Grundlehren der mathematischen Wissenschaften*, *Compositio Mathematica*, *Acta Mathematica Vietnamica*, and *Vietnam Journal of Mathematics*. He married Nguyen Bao Thanh at the age of 22, and they have three children.

38.3. Stanislav Konstantinovich Smirnov

He was born in Leningrad, Soviet Union. Smirnov graduated from the special mathematics high school Saint Petersburg Lyceum 239 in 1987. During his high school years, he won two gold medals with perfect scores in IMO 1986 and 1987. He received his undergraduate and master's degrees in mathematics from Saint Petersburg State University in 1992, where he worked under Victor Petrovich Havin (1933–2015, USSR). In 1996, he defended his Ph.D. thesis entitled *Spectral Analysis of Julia Sets* at Caltech, primarily with Nikolai Georgievich Makarov (born 1955, Russia–USA). During 1996–1998, Smirnov held research positions at Yale University, the MPIM at Bonn, and the IAS, Princeton. He moved to Sweden in 1998 and became Professor at the Royal Institute of Technology in Stockholm and researcher at the Swedish Royal Academy of Sciences in 2001. In 2003, Smirnov become a Professor in the Analysis, Mathematical Physics, and Probability group at the University of Geneva, Switzerland, and continues there. Concurrently in 2010, he became the Founding Director of the Chebyshev Laboratory at Saint Petersburg State University, and in 2014 he was appointed the Director of the National Centre of Competence in Research SwissMAP funded by the Swiss NSF. He has made significant contributions in several different fields: probability theory and stochastic processes, statistical mechanics, the structure of matter, dynamical systems and ergodic theory, functions of a complex variable, measure and integration, global analysis, analysis on manifolds, calculus of variations and optimal control, optimization, functional analysis, approximations and expansions, and potential theory. He has published more than 50 research papers and supervised six doctoral students. His distinctions include the St. Petersburg Mathematical Society Prize in 1997, Clay Research Award in 2001, Salem Prize in 2001, Göran Gustafsson (1919–2003, Sweden) Research Prize in 2001, Rollo Davidson Prize in 2002, EMS Prize in 2004, and Fields Medal in 2010. He received an honorary doctorate from Joseph Fourier University (2012) and was elected Fellow of the AMS (2013) and Academia Europaea (2013).

38.4. Cédric Patrice Thierry Villani

He was born in Brive-la-Gaillarde, France. Villani took preparatory classes at the Lycée Louis-le-Grand in Paris and then joined the ENS in Paris and studied there from 1992 to 1996. After passing the agrégation in mathematics and obtaining a degree in data envelopment analysis in numerical analysis from Sorbonne University, he was an agrégé préparateur from 1996 to 2000. At the University of Paris-Dauphine, in 1998, he defended his doctorate thesis entitled *Contribution á l'étude mathématique des équations de Boltzmann et de Landau en théorie cinétique des gaz et des plasmas* (Contribution to the mathematical study of the Boltzmann and Landau equations in the kinetic theory of gases and plasmas), written under the supervision of Pierre-Louis Lions. In 2000, he became a Professor at the ENS de Lyon and then at the Université Claude Bernard Lyon 1, where he remained until 2010. He was director of the Institut Henri Poincaré from 2009 to 2017. He is now Professor at the University of Lyon. He also had various visiting positions at Georgia Tech (Fall 1999), UC, Berkeley (Spring 2004), and the IAS, Princeton (Spring 2009). He has made fundamental contributions in partial differential equations, Riemannian geometry, mathematical physics, and optimal transport theory. Specifically, he is well known for his work on the Boltzmann equation, kinetic theory, Landau damping, the Otto–Villani theorem (Felix Otto, born 1966, Germany), and the proof of Carlo Cercignani's (1939–2010, Italy) conjecture. Villani has published more than 100 research papers and supervised six doctoral students. He has received several awards and honors, including the Peccot–Vimont Prize and Cours Peccot of the Collége de France in 2003, EMS Prize in 2008, Fermat Prize in 2009, Knight of the National Order of Merit in 2009, Henri Poincaré Prize in 2009, Fields Medal in 2010, Knight of the Legion of Honor in 2011, member of the FAS in 2013, Doob Prize in 2014, ordinary member of the Pontifical Academy of Sciences in 2016, and Fellow of the International Science Council in 2022. He has been also a leading French politician since 2017.

38.5. Daniel Alan Spielman

He was born in Philadelphia, USA. Spielman began his primary education in The Philadelphia School and then Germantown Friends School. In 1992, he received his Bachelor of Arts degree in mathematics and computer science from Yale University. Then, he moved to MIT, and in 1995 received his Ph.D. degree in applied mathematics defending his thesis entitled *Computationally Efficient Error-Correcting Codes and Holographic Proofs*, written under the supervision of Michael Fredric Sipser (born 1954, USA). He spent a year as an NSF Mathematical Sciences Postdoctoral Fellow in the Computer Science Department at UC, Berkeley, and then taught in the Applied Mathematics Department at MIT until 2005. Then, he moved to Yale University as a Professor of Applied Mathematics and Computer Science. In 2012, he was part of the inaugural class of Simons Investigators, being provided with USD 660,000 for five years for curiosity-driven research. In 2018, he became the John William Sterling (1844–1918, USA-Canada) Professor of Computer Science. He has also been the Co-Director of the Yale Institute for Network Science since its founding and is chair of the newly established Department of Statistics and Data Science. Spielman's main research interests include the design and analysis of algorithms, graph theory, network science, machine learning, digital communications, scientific computing, and the Kadison–Singer problem (after Richard Vincent Kadison, 1925–2018, USA, and Isadore Manuel Singer). Spielman has published over 60 research papers and supervised 10 doctoral students. The awards he has received include the following: ACM Doctoral Dissertation Award in 1995, IEEE Information Theory Paper Award in 2002, Gödel Prize in 2008 and 2015, Fulkerson Prize in 2009, Rolf Nevanlinna Prize in 2010, MacArthur Fellowship in 2012, Pólya Prize in 2014, Michael and Sheila Held

Prize in 2021, and Breakthrough Prize in Mathematics in 2023. He is a Fellow of the ACM (2010) and a member of the United States NAS (2017).

38.6. Yves François Meyer

He was born in Paris, France. Yves Meyer studied at the Lycée Carnot in Tunis (largest city in Tunisia). When he was a student in high school, Jean-Pierre Kahane visited Tunis and gave a talk to a general audience on his research on trigonometric series. Yves Meyer was fascinated by the personality of Jean-Pierre Kahane and his influential lecture. He decided to specialize in mathematics. In 1957, he won the French General Student Competition (Concours Gnéral) in Mathematics and was placed first in the entrance examination for the ENS in Paris. Yves Meyer graduated in 1960, and then he performed military service as a high school teacher to avoid the Algerian War (1954–1962). In 1963 he married Anne Limpaler, and they have two children. In the same year he was appointed as a teaching assistant in the Department of Mathematics of the University of Strasbourg. He wrote twelve chapters on the results he had obtained for his thesis entitled *Idéaux Fermés de L1 dans Lesquels une Suite Approche l'Identité* (L1 Closed Ideals in Which a Suite Approaches Identity). With the official approval of Jean-Pierre Kahane, Yves Meyer submitted his work to the University of Strasbourg in 1966 and obtained his doctorate degree. In the same year he was appointed to a temporary position at the Faculty of Sciences of the Université at Paris-Sud and soon became Professor. He continued there until 1980, when he joined École Polytechnique for six years as a Professor. During (1985–1995), he was a Professor at the Université Paris-Dauphine. From 1995 to 1999, he was a senior researcher at the CNRS. Yves Meyer was a Professor at the ENS de Cachan during 1999–2003. In 2008 he retired, becoming Professor Emeritus at the ENS de Cachan. Yves Meyer has made major contributions in different areas, for example Diophantine approximations, Charles Pisot (1910–1984, France) and Salem numbers, solution of the Calderón conjecture (after Alberto Pedro Calderón, 1920–1998, Argentina), and quasicrystals, and he founded the mathematical theory of wavelets. He has written more than 215 research papers and supervised 37 doctoral students. He has also written influential books: *Nombres de Pisot, nombres de Salem, et analyse harmonique* (1970), *Algebraic Numbers and Harmonic Analysis* (1972), *Ondelettes et opérateurs* (1990), and *Wavelets and Operators* (1993). Yues Meyer has been awarded major prizes: Salem Prize in 1970, Gauss Prize in 2010, Abel Prize in 2017, and Princess of Asturias Award in 2020. He was elected to the Académie des Sciences (1993), elected as an International Member of the United States NAS in 2014, and elected a Foreign Member of the Spanish Academy of Exact, Physical, and Natural Sciences in January 2018. He was also elected as a Foreign Honorary Member of the AAAS in 1994, a Fellow of AMS in 2013, and a member of the Royal Norwegian Academy of Sciences and Letters.

38.7. Louis Nirenberg

He was born in Hamilton, Ontario, Canada, to Ukrainian Jewish immigrants. Nirenberg attended Baron Byng High School in Montreal, where he had excellent teachers. After graduating from the school, he entered McGill University, completing his Bachelor of Science in both mathematics and physics in 1945. After graduating he took a summer job at the National Research Council of Canada in Montreal. In Montreal he came to know Sara Paul (Canada), the wife of Ernest Courant (1920–2020, Germany–USA), the eldest son of Richard Courant (1888–1972, Poland–Germany–USA). Sara asked Richard Courant where Nirenberg should apply to study theoretical physics, the subject he wanted to continue in his higher education. The advice came back that Nirenberg should first complete a master's degree in mathematics at New York University and then go on to study physics. Nirenberg went for an interview with Richard Courant and Kurt Friedrichs at New York University and they offered him an assistantship. In 1947, he obtained a master's degree in mathematics from New York University and remained there working for his doctorate. In 1949, he obtained his doctorate in mathematics under the direction of James Johnston Stoker (1905–1992, USA). The title of his thesis was *The Determination of a Closed Convex Surface Having Given Line Elements*. In his thesis he resolved a question in differential geometry, first asked, and partially solved, by Hermann Weyl around 1916: Given a Riemannian metric on the unit sphere, with positive Gauss curvature, can you embed this 2-sphere isometrically into 3-space as a convex surface? After completing his doctorate, Nirenberg was appointed as a Research Assistant at New York University, becoming one of the early members of the Institute of Mathematical Sciences and Mechanics (it was renamed the Courant Institute in 1964). He was made an Assistant Professor in 1951, then Associate Professor, Full Professor in 1957, and Professor Emeritus in 1999 at the Courant Institute, where he remained for the rest of his career. He continued to carry out mathematical research until the age of 87, and died at the age of 94. He is recognized throughout the world specially for linear and nonlinear partial differential equations, harmonic analysis, differential geometry, functional analysis, complex analysis, the set of Garliardo–Nirenberg inequalities (Emilio Gagliardo, 1930–2008, Italy), the John–Nirenberg inequality (Fritz John, 1910–1994, Germany–USA), the concept of a pseudo-differential operator, regularity of free boundary problems, the Minkowski problem in two dimensions, the existence of smooth solutions of equations of Monge–Ampére type, singular sets for the Navier–Stokes equations, and the list continues. He published 185 research papers and supervised 45 doctoral students. His publications include notable collaborators such as Shmuel Agmon (born 1922, Israel), Henri Berestycki (born 1951, France), Haïm Brézis, Luis Caffarelli, Avron Douglis (1918–1995, USA), and YanYan Li. Nirenberg has been awarded many prizes and given many honors in his distinguished career: Sloan Fellow during 1958–1960, Guggenheim Fellow during 1966–1967 and 1975–1976, Bôcher Prize in 1959, Crafoord Prize in 1982, Jeffery–Williams Prize in 1987, Steele Prize in 1994 and 2014, National Medal of Science in 1995, Chern Medal in 2010, and Abel Prize in 2015. He served the AMS in several roles. He was a member of the Council during 1963–1965, gave the AMS Colloquium Lectures in 1974, and was Vice-President of the Society in 1976–1977. He was also elected to the United States NAS, the APS, the AAAS, the Accademia dei Lincei, the French Académie des Sciences, the Accademia Mediterranea della Scienze, the Istituto Lombardo, the Accademia Scienze e Lettere, and the Ukrainian Academy of Sciences. He was also awarded honorary doctorate degrees from McGill University (1986), the University of Pisa (1990), and the Université de Paris IX Paris-Dauphine (1990). To honor his 65th, 70th (June and July), 75th, and 80th birthdays, conferences were, respectively, organized in Trento, Venice, Florence, Hsinchu (Taiwan), and Toledo.

38.8. Simon Lehna Singh

He was born in Wellington, Somerset, UK, in a Sikh family. His parents emigrated from the Punjab in India to Britain in 1950. He is an author who has specialized in writing about mathematical and scientific topics in an accessible manner. He attended Wellington School and then went to Imperial College London and completed a Bachelor of Science in physics. He was active in the student union, becoming President of the Royal College of Science Union. In 1983, Singh was a part of the UA2 experiment at the Conseil européen pour la Recherche Nucléaire (European Council for Nuclear Research), in short CERN, Geneva. In 1987, Singh taught science at The Doon School (Dehradun, India), an independent all-boys' boarding school in India. In 1990 he joined the BBC's Science and Features Department, where he was a producer and director working on programs such as *Tomorrow's World* and *Horizon*. In 1991, he completed a Ph.D. in particle physics at the University of Cambridge while working at CERN. The title of his thesis was *Heavy Flavour Physics at the CERN $P\bar{P}$ Collider*. In 1996, he directed *Fermat's Last Theorem*, a BAFTA (The British Academy Film Awards) award-winning documentary about the world's most notorious mathematical problem. In 1997, he published his first book *Fermat's Last Theorem* (also published in 1998 as *Fermat's Enigma* in the USA), which became the first book about mathematics to become a No 1 bestseller in the UK. In 2000, Singh published his second book *The Code Book*, which provides a history of codes and codebreaking, which brought him back to television. He presented *The Science of Secrecy*, a five-part series for Channel 4. Singh's third book *Big Bang: The Origin of the Universe* was published in 2005, which is a very comprehensive summary of physical sciences, leading to astronomy and eventually to cosmology. In 2008, he published his fourth book *Trick or Treatment? Alternative Medicine on Trial* with Edzard Ernst (born 1948, Germany–UK), which evaluates the scientific evidence for alternative medicines such as acupuncture, homeopathy, herbal medicine, and chiropractic, and briefly covers 36 other treatments. In 2013, his book The Simpsons and Their Mathematical Secrets was published, which is based on the premise that "many of the writers of The Simpsons are deeply in love with numbers, and their ultimate desire is to drip-feed morsels of mathematics into the subconscious minds of viewers". He has received several honors and awards: Science Writing Award in 2006, Kelvin Prize in 2008, HealthWatch Award in 2010, and the Leelavati Award in 2010. In 2003 Singh was awarded an Honorary Degree of Doctor of Letters by Loughborough University, in 2005 he was given an Honorary Degree in mathematics by the University of Southampton, in 2006 he was awarded an Honorary Doctor of Design degree by the University of the West of England, in 2008 he was awarded a degree of Doctor of Science by Royal Holloway, University of London, in 2011 he was awarded a Doctor of Science degree by the University of Kent in Canterbury, and in June 2012 Singh was awarded an Honorary Degree of Doctor of Science by The University of St. Andrews. In 2007 he married the journalist and broadcaster Anita Anand (born 1972, England); they have two sons.

39. Seoul ICM 2014

This Congress was held in Seoul, South Korea, during 13–21 August 2014. The Congress was attended by 4680 regular participants from 120 countries. The Congress invited and supported 1000 mathematicians from developing countries to participate, many of whom would not have been able to attend otherwise. The Congress Travel Fellowship Fund was established to help cover the costs of these participants, which were estimated to be between USD 1500 and USD 2500 per person. There were also 51 satellite conferences (35 in Korea). The opening ceremony on the first day of the Congress began with an opening address and a welcoming address by the Chairman of the Seoul ICM Organizing Committee Hyungju Park, and Ingrid Daubechies, the President of the IMU. Park Geun-hye (born 1952), then the President of South Korea, attended the ceremony. Ingrid Daubechies announced that each of the Fields medalists and Rolf Nevanlinna Prize winners would be introduced by a short movie. The medals were awarded by the President of Korea. Myung-Hwan Kin, the President of the Korean Mathematical Society, and Sug Woo Shin (Korea–USA) assisted the award ceremony. The Fields Medal Committee consisted of Ingrid Daubechies (chair), Luigi Ambrosio (born 1963, Italy), David Eisenbud (born 1947, USA), Kenji Fukaya (born 1959, Japan), Étienne Ghys (born 1954, France), Benedict Hyman Gross (born 1950, USA), Dame Frances Clare Kirwan, Jáos Kollár, Maxim Lvovich Kontsevich, Michael Struwe (born 1955, Germany), Ofer Zeitouni (born 1960, Israel), and Günter Matthias Ziegler (born 1963, Germany). The winners of the Fields Medals were Artur Avila Cordeiro de Melo (born 1979, Brazil–France), Manjul Bhargava (born 1974, Canada–USA), Martin Hairer (born 1975, Austria–UK), and Maryam Mirzakhani (1977–2017, Iran–USA) [first woman to receive a Fields Medal]. Ingrid Daubechies read the citations for each medalist. Artur Avila: For his profound contributions to dynamical systems theory, which have changed the face of the field, using the powerful idea of renormalization as a unifying principle. Manjul Bhargava: For developing powerful new methods in the geometry of numbers, which he applied to count rings of small rank and to bound the average rank of elliptic curves. Martin Hairer: For his outstanding contributions to the theory of stochastic partial differential equations, and in particular for the creation of a theory of regularity structures for such equations. Maryam Mirzakhani: For her outstanding contributions to the dynamics and geometry of Riemann surfaces and their moduli spaces. The Rolf Nevanlinna Prize Committee consisted of Avi Wigderson (Chairman), Thierry Coquand (born 1961, France), Yurii Nesterov (born 1956, Russia), Jaikumar Radhakrishnan (born 1964, India), Éva Tardos, and Leslie Gabriel Valiant. The winner of the Rolf Nevanlinna Prize was Subhash Khot (born 1978, India–USA). Ingrid Daubechies read the citation for him: Subhash Khot is awarded the Nevanlinna Prize for his prescient definition of the "Unique Games" problem, and leading the effort to understand its complexity and its pivotal role in the study of efficient approximation of optimization problems; his work has led to breakthroughs in algorithmic design and approximation hardness, and to new exciting interactions between computational complexity, analysis and geometry.

The Gauss Prize Committee consisted of Alfio Quarteroni (born 1952, Italy) [Chairman], Weinan E (born 1963, China–USA), Andrés Weintraub Pohorille (born 1942, Chile), and Aad van der Vaart (born 1959, the Netherlands). The winner of the prize was Stanley Joel Osher. The citation was read by Alfio Quarteroni: For his influential contributions to several fields in applied mathematics and for his far-ranging inventions that have changed our conception of physical, perceptual, and mathematical concepts, giving us new tools to apprehend the world. The Chern Medal Committee consisted of Robert Leamon Bryant (Chairman), Kazuo Murota (born 1955, Japan), Felix Otto, Alain-Sol Sznitman (born 1955, France–Switzerland), and Claire Voisin (born 1962, France). Ingrid Daubechies announced the winner Phillip Augustus Griffiths and read the citation: For his groundbreaking and transformative development of transcendental methods in complex geometry, particularly his seminal work in Hodge theory and periods of algebraic varieties. After the award ceremony, the President of South Korea welcomed the participants, congratulated all seven prize winners, and said "the study of mathematics enjoys the longest history within academia and its magnificent legacy has been with us throughout the entire history of humanity. From ancient times when humanity still lived without letters people started to calculate and measure. Indeed, mathematics transformed the life of humanity as universal language, going beyond regions and nations, and serving as the basis of human logical thinking." The Leelavati Award Committee consisted of David Bryant Mumford (Chairman), Oh Nam Kwon (born 1961, South Korea), Guillermo Martínez (born 1962, Argentina), Madabusi Raghunathan, and Srinivasa Varadhan. Ingrid Daubechies announced the winner Adrián Arnoldo Paenza (born 1949, Argentina): For his decisive contributions to changing the mind of a whole country, namely, Argentina, about the way it perceives mathematics in daily life, and in particular for his books, his TV programs, and his unique gift of enthusiasm and passion in communicating the beauty and joy of mathematics. She also said the prize would be awarded during the closing ceremony. Ingrid Daubechies also announced that Phillip Griffiths had designated the Chern Award money, USD 250000, to the African Mathematics Millennium Science Initiative (AMMSI). Finally, Martin Grötschel, the Secretary of the IMU, thanked all committees for their diligent work and announced the decisions of the General Assembly, which was held on 11 August in Gyeongju (Korea): the selection of new the EC of the IMU for the period 20015–2018, Shigefumi Mori (President), Alicia Dickenstein (born 1955, Argentina) and Vaughan Frederick Randal Jones as Vice-Presidents, Helge Holden (born 1956, Norway) as Secretary, and Benedict Gross, Hyungju Park, Christiane Rousseau, Vasudevan Srinivas, John Francis Toland, Wendelin Werner, and Ingrid Daubechies as members, and also for the next ICM in 2018 the venue Rio de Janeiro, Brazil.

There were 19 one-hour plenary lectures (which included one woman, Vera Serganova, born 1960, Russia); 5 special lectures, Emmy Noether Lecture by Georgia McClure Benkart (1947–2022, USA) entitled *Connecting the McKay Correspondence and Schur-Weyl Duality*, Manjul Bhargava's lecture on *Rational Points on Elliptic and Hyperelliptic Curves*, Martin Hairer's lecture on *Singular Stochastic PDEs*, Subhash Khot's lecture on *Hardness of Approximation*, and Adrián Arnoldo Paenza's lecture on *I Want to Play with Mathematics*; 179 invited talks of forty-five minutes distributed in 19 sections; and about 615 short communications. There were laudations of the works of the awardees. Étienne Ghys talked for Artur Avila: "He leads and shapes the field of dynamical systems. With his collaborators, he has made essential progress in many areas, including real and complex one-dimensional dynamics, spectral theory of the one-frequency Schrödinger operator, flat billiards and partially hyperbolic dynamics". Benedict Hyman Gross said the following for Manjul Bhargava: "His work is based both on a deep understanding of the representations of arithmetic groups and a unique blend of algebraic and analytic expertise". Ofer Zeitouni spoke for Martin Hairer: "He created an abstract theory of regularity structures for stochastic partial differential equations (SPDEs). This allows Taylor-like expansions around any point in space and time. The new theory allowed him to construct systematically solutions to singular nonlinear SPDEs as fixed points of a renormalization procedure. Hairer was thus able to give, for the first time, a rigorous intrinsic meaning to many SPDEs arising in physics". Curtis Tracy McMullen spoke for Maryam Mirzakhani: "She has made stunning advances in the theory of Riemann surfaces and their moduli spaces, and led the way to new frontiers in this area. Her insights have integrated methods from diverse fields, such as algebraic geometry, topology and probability theory". Sanjeev Arora (born 1968, India–USA) said the following for Subhash Khot: "He has brought new clarity to the study of approximation algorithms for NP-hard problems, and opened new avenues of research. Several of these concerns and his Unique Games Conjecture, which has led to optimal in inapproximability results that exactly characterize the approximability of the problem". Ronald Paul (born 1968, USA), Jean-Michel Morel (born 1953, France), Guillermo Sapiro (born 1966, Uruguay), Chi-Wang Shu (born 1957, China–USA), and Wotao Yin (USA) summarized the work of Stanley Joel Osher: "He contributed in the areas of high-resolution shock capturing methods, level set methods, partial differential equation based methods in computer vision and image processing, and optimization. His numerical analysis contributions, including the Engquist-Osher scheme, total variation diminishing schemes, entropy conditions, essentially non-oscillatory and weighted essentially non-oscillatory schemes, and numerical schemes for Hamilton-Jacobi type equations have revolutionized the field. His level set contributions include new level set calculus, novel numerical techniques, fluids and materials modeling, variational approaches, high codimension motion analysis, geometric optics, and the computation of discontinuous solutions to Hamilton-Jacobi equations. On optimization, he introduced Lev Meerovich Bregman (1941–2023, Russia-Israel) algorithms and applied them to problems in a variety of contexts such as image processing, compressive sensing, signal processing, and machine learning". Mark Lee Green (born 1947, USA) summarized the major accomplishments of his thesis supervisor Phillip Augustus Griffiths: "Algebraic equivalence $\neq$ homological equivalence; Geometry of periodic domains; Non-rationality of the cubic 3-fold; Holomorphic maps; Brill-Noether problem; Infinitesimal variation of Hodge structure; Homotopy theory of Kähler manifolds; Exterior differential systems; Conservation laws of exterior differential systems; Isometric embedding; Tangent space to algebraic cycles; and Mumford-Tate groups".

The closing ceremony started with a lecture by Hyungju Park. He presented an overview of the nine-day Congress and spoke about the participation of almost 20,000 high school students in the Congress. Ingrid Daubechies conferred the Leelavati Award to Adrián Arnoldo Paenza. Then, Shigefumi Mori, newly elected President of the IMU, thanked the Nomination Committee. For the success of the Seoul Congress, he thanked the members of the EC and Executive Organizing Committee. Next, for the ICM 2018 in Rio de Janeiro, Brazil, Marcelo Silva, the Chairman of the Organizing Committee, thanked the General Assembly for approving the bid to hold the ICM 2018 for the first time in the southern hemisphere. He said "Ours is a young region of the world, where the Congress can and will be a powerful tool to disseminate Mathematics in the whole society, especially around the younger generations". He finsihed his talk with the invitation "See you soon in Rio de Janeiro". Finally, Ingrid Daubechies thanked the Program Committee, Prize Selection Committees, and plenary and invited speakers, especially the Local Organizing Committee, and all the participants.

39.1. Artur Avila Cordeiro de Melo

He was born in Rio de Janeiro, Brazil. His father taught him to read and write when he was three years old. At the age of five he was reading mathematics books; at the age of six he began his schooling at Colégio de São Bento in Rio de Janeiro, but started to read more advanced books; and at the age of 16, Avila won a gold medal at the 1995 IMO (Toronto, Canada) and received a scholarship from the IMPA to start a Master of Science degree while still attending high school in Colégio de São Bento and Colégio Santo Agostinho in Rio de Janeiro. For his master's degree Avila was advised by Elon Lages Lima (1929–2017, Brazil), and he completed his master's in 1997. At the age of 19, Avila began writing his doctoral thesis on the theory of dynamical systems. In 2001, at the IMPA, he defended his Ph.D. thesis entitled *Bifurcations of Unimodal Maps: The Topologic and Metric Picture*, written under the supervision of Welington Celso de Melo (1946–2016, Brazil). During 2001–2013 Avila was a Maître de Conférence Associé at the Collége de France, from 2003 to 2008 he was a Chargé de recherche at the CNRS, from 2006 to 2009 he was a Research Fellow of the Clay Mathematics Institute, attached to the IMPA, CNRS UMI 2294, since 2008 he has been the Directeur de recherche at the CNRS, from 2009 to 2018 he was attached to the Institut de Mathématiques de Jussieu-Paris Rive Gauche, since 2018 he has been a Professor at the University of Zurich, and also since 2009 he has been an extraordinary researcher at the IMPA, CNRS. His first major research paper of 100 pages *Regular or Stochastic Dynamics in Real Analytic Families of Unimodal Maps, Inventiones Mathematicae* (2003), 451-550, was jointly published with Welington de Melo and Misha Lyubich (born 1959, Ukraine). By 2004 he had eleven papers in print. In March of 2005, Avila proved the conjecture of the ten martinis posed by Barry Simon (born 1946, USA) and four months later proved the Zorich–Kontsevich (Vladimir Antonovich Zorich, 1937–2023, Russia) conjecture. He has published over 90 research papers and supervised seven doctoral students. He has been awarded several prizes and awards, including the bronze medal of the CNRS in 2006, Salem Prize in 2006, EMS Prize in 2008, Grand Prix Jacques Herbrand of the FAS in 2009, Michael Brin Prize in Dynamical Systems in 2011, International Association of Mathematical Physics Early Career Award in 2012, Prize of the Brazilian Mathematical Society in 2013, TWAS Prize in 2013, Fields Medal in 2014 (the first Latin American and lusophone),

TWAS-Lenovo Science Prize in 2015, and Knight of the Legion of Honor in 2015. In 2013, he became a member of the Brazilian Academy of Sciences and in 2019 Foreign associate of the United States NAS. Avila is a member of *World Minds*.

39.2. Manjul Bhargava

He was born to an Indian family in Hamilton, Ontario, Canada, but grew up and attended school primarily on Long Island, New York. His mother Mira Bhargava is a well-known mathematician and is a mathematics teacher at Hofstra University. He inherited his mathematical skills from his mother, who was also his first teacher of mathematics. Manjul Bhargava completed all of his high school mathematics course and also the computer science course by the age of 14. He attended Plainedge High School in North Massapequa and graduated in 1992 as the class valedictorian. Manjul Bhargava then started studying at Harvard University and obtained his Bachelor of Arts degree in 1996. He then pursed graduate studies at Princeton University, where he completed a doctoral dissertation titled *Higher Composition Laws* under the supervision of Andrew Wiles and received his Ph.D. in 2001, with the support of a Hertz Fellowship. His breakthrough thesis surprised the mathematical community by generalizing the classical Gauss composition law for quadratic forms to many other situations. He was a visiting scholar at the IAS, Princeton, during 2001–2002 and at Harvard University in 2002–2003. In 2003, he joined Princeton University as a tenured Full Professor. In 2010, he was appointed as the Stieltjes Professor of Number Theory (after Thomas Joannes Stieltjes, 1856–1894, the Netherlands) at Leiden University. He was also appointed as an Adjunct Professor at the Tata Institute of Fundamental Research, University of Hyderabad, and Indian Institute of Technology, Bombay. Currently he is Professor of Mathematics at Princeton University. Manjul Bhargava has made several contributions to mathematics, especially to number theory, including fourteen new Gauss-style composition laws; determination of the asymptotic density of discriminants of quartic and quintic number fields; proofs of the first-known cases of the Cohen–Lenstra–Martinet (Jacques Martinet, born 1939, France) heuristics for class groups; proof of the 15 theorem, including an extension of the theorem to other number sets such as odd numbers and prime numbers; proof of the 290 theorem; the Bhargava factorial, providing an answer to a decades-old question of George Pólya; proof that the average rank of all elliptic curves over **Q** (when ordered by height) is bounded; proof that most hyperelliptic curves over **Q** have no rational points; and proof of the Birch and Swinnerton–Dyer conjecture for a positive proportion of elliptic curves. He has published more than 55 research papers and supervised 13 doctoral students. Manjul Bhargava has been the recipient of numerous awards, including the Hoopes Prize in 1996, Morgan Prize in 1996, Merten M. Hasse Prize in 2003, Blumenthal Award in 2005, SASTRA Ramanujan Prize in 2005, Clay Research Award in 2005, Cole Prize in 2008, Fermat Prize in 2011, Infosys Prize in 2012, Fields Medal in 2014, and Padma Bhushan (the third highest civilian award of India) in 2015. In November 2002, he was named one of *Popular Science* magazine's "Brilliant 10"; in 2009, he was awarded the Face of the Future award at the India Abroad Person of the Year ceremony in New York; in 2012, he was named an inaugural recipient of the Simons Investigator Award; in 2013, he was elected to the United States NAS; in 2017, he was elected as a member of the AAAS;

in 2018, he was named as the inaugural occupant of The Distinguished Chair for the Public Dissemination of Mathematics at The National Museum of Mathematics (this is the first visiting professorship in the United States dedicated exclusively to raising public awareness of mathematics); and in 2019, he was elected an FRS of London. Manjul Bhargava beyond mathematics is an excellent Indian musical player and admirer of Sanskrit poetry and ancient Indian history. He has even performed in some concerts. According to him "All kinds of creative thoughts come together when I think about all three" "Mathematics, music, and poetry". Manjul Bhargava is a name that resonates with brilliance in the world of mathematics.

39.3. Martin Hairer

He was born in Geneva, Switzerland. Hairer received his high school diploma in June 1994 from the Collége Claparéde, Geneva, and then he entered a school science competition with sound editing software that was developed into Amadeus. He continued to maintain the software in addition to his academic work. His software was widely used as of 2020. After obtaining his high school diploma, he entered the University of Geneva, where he received his Bachelor of Science degree in mathematics in July 1998, Master of Science in physics in October 1998, and Ph.D. in physics in November 2001. The title of thesis was *Comportement Asymptotique d'Equations Dérivées Partielles Stochastiques* (Asymptotic Behavior of Stochastic Partial Differential Equations), written under the supervision of Jean-Pierre Eckmann (born 1944, Switzerland). During 2002–2004, Hairer was a Postdoctoral Fellow at the Mathematics Research Centre, University of Warwick. Later in 2004, he joined the University of Warwick as a Lecturer/Assistant Professor, and in 2006 was promoted to an Associate Professor. During 2009–1010, Hairer was an Associate Professor at the Courant Institute. In 2010, he returned to the University of Warwick and joined as a Professor, and in 2014 became Regius Professor of Mathematics. From 2017, Hairer has been the Chair of Probability and Stochastic Analysis at Imperial College London and also from 2022 Chair of Probability and Partial Differential Equations at École Polytechnique Fédérale de Lausanne. Hairer's work is on variants of Hörmander's theorem, systematization of the construction of Lyapunov functions for stochastic systems, the development of a general theory of ergodicity for non-Markovian systems, multiscale analysis techniques, the theory of homogenization, the theory of path sampling and theory of rough paths, and regularity structures. His name appears in HairerSoft and he develops Macintosh software. He has published more than 125 research papers and supervised 10 doctoral students. Hairer has received several awards and honors, including the Editors' Choice Award, Macworld 2007, Whitehead Prize in 2008, Philip Leverhulme Prize in 2008, Royal Society Wolfson Research Merit Award in 2009, Leverhulme Research Leadership Award in 2012, Fermat Prize in 2013, Fröhlich Prize in 2014, Fields Medal in 2014, Breakthrough Prize in Mathematics in 2021, King Faisal Prize in 2022, and the Erwin Schrödinger Medal in 2022. He has been elected FRS of London (2014) and is a Fellow of the AMS (2015), member of the Austrian Academy of Sciences (2015), member of the Academy of Sciences Leopoldina (2015), member of the Academia Europaea (2015), Honorary Knight Commander of the Order of the British Empire (2016), Foreign member of the

Polish Academy of Sciences (2017), and Substantive Knight Commander of the Order of the British Empire (2019). He married a fellow mathematician Li Xue-Mei in 2003.

39.4. Maryam Mirzakhani

She was born in Tehran, Iran. Mirzakhani started her education at Tehran Farzanegan School, which is administered under the National Organization for Development of Exceptional Talents. In her junior and senior years of high school, she won the gold medal for mathematics in the Iranian National Olympiad; this allowed her to bypass the national college entrance exam. In 1994, Mirzakhani became the first Iranian woman to win a gold medal at the IMO in Hong Kong, scoring 41 out of 42 points. Next year she became the first Iranian to achieve the full score and to win two gold medals in the IMO in Toronto. Mirzakhani and Roya Beheshti Zavareh (born 1977, Iran), who won a silver medal in the IMO in 1994, became close friends and in 1999 wrote a book *Elementary Number Theory, Challenging Problems* (in Persian). In 1999, Mirzakhani received her Bachelor of Science in Mathematics from Sharif University of Technology. During the same time her simple proof of the theorem of Schur (Ernst Viktor Axel Schur, 1891–1930, Estonia–Germany) received recognition from the AMS. Immediately after completing her Bachelor of Science she headed to graduate school at Harvard University, where she was supervised by the Fields Medalist Curtis Tracy McMullen. In 2004, she defended her Ph.D. thesis *Simple Geodesics on Hyperbolic Surfaces and the Volume of the Moduli Space of Curves*. After completing her Ph.D., she became a Research Fellow at the Clay Mathematics Institute and later joined Princeton University as a Professor. Mirzakhani joined the faculty of Stanford University in 2009, where she served as a Professor of mathematics until her premature death in 2017 due to breast cancer. In 2008, she married Jan Vondrák (Czech Republic), who is a theoretical computer scientist and applied mathematician, currently working as a Professor of Mathematics at Stanford University. They had a daughter, Anahita, in 2011. Her research topics included complex dynamics of geometric structures with particular emphasis on moduli spaces and Riemann surfaces, Teichmüller theory, hyperbolic geometry, ergodic theory, and symplectic geometry. In particular, she proved the long-standing conjecture that William Thurston's earthquake flow on Teichmüller space is ergodic. In her short life she published 24 research papers and supervised two doctoral students. Mirzakhani was awarded the Blumenthal Award in 2009, Satter Prize in 2013, Clay Research Award in 2014, and Fields Medal in 2014 (first woman to win the prize, as well as the first Iranian). The President Hassan Rouhani (born 1948) of Iran congratulated her for winning the Fields Medal. She was elected Foreign Associate to the FAS (2015) and elected to the APS (2015), the United States NAS (2016), and the AAAS (2017), and Asteroid 321357 Mirzakhani was named in her memory. In 2019, to promote women in mathematics, the Breakthrough Prize Foundation announced that the Maryam Mirzakhani New Frontiers Prize had been created to be awarded to outstanding women in the field of mathematics each year. The USD 50,000 award will be presented to early-career mathematicians who have completed their Ph.D. within the past two years. In addition, upon her death, several Iranian newspapers, along with President Hassan Rouhani, offered their condolences and praised Mirzakhani's scientific achievements. Rouhani said in his message that "the unprecedented brilliance of this creative scientist and modest human being, who made Iran's name resonate in the world's scientific forums, was a turning point in showing the great will of Iranian women and young people on the path towards reaching the peaks of glory and in various international arenas". Numerous obituaries and tributes were published in the days following Mirzakhani's death. Various establishments have also been named after Mirzakhani to honor her life and achievements.

39.5. Subhash Khot

He was born in Ichalkaranji, Maharashtra, India. In 1994 and 1995, Khot represented India at the IMO and received silver medals. In 1995, he achieved the highest score countrywide in the (highly difficult) IIT Joint Entrance Examination. He obtained his bachelor's degree in computer science from the IIT Bombay in 1999. Khot received his master's degree in computer science from Princeton University in 2001 and Doctorate Degrees in 2003 under the supervision of Sanjeev Arora. His doctoral dissertation was titled *New Techniques for Probabilistically Checkable Proofs and Inapproximability Results*. During 2003–2004, Khot was a member of the School of Mathematics at the IAS and during 2004–2007 Assistant Professor at the College of Computing at Georgia Tech. In 2007, he joined the Courant Institute of Mathematical Sciences as an Associate Professor; he was promoted to a Professor in 2011, and from 2016 he became Julius Silver Professor. During 2011–2013 Khot was a Visiting faculty at University of Chicago. Khot has contributed to the field of computational complexity and is best known for his unique games conjecture made in 2002, which is the most studied conjecture in theoretical computer science. His work draws connections between optimization and geometry. He has published more than 135 research papers. Khot was awarded the Microsoft Research New Faculty Fellowship Award in 2005, Waterman Award in 2010, Rolf Nevanlinna Prize 2014, MacArthur Fellow in 2016, Simons Investigator Award in 2016, was elected an FRS of London in 2017, and was inducted into the United States NAS in 2023. He cherishes the memories of his high school principal and lifelong mentor Shri Gogate Sir.

39.6. Stanley Joel Osher

He was born in Brooklyn, New York, USA. He obtained his Bachelor of Science in 1962 from Brooklyn College, Master of Science in 1964 from New York University, and Ph.D. in 1966 from the same university. The title of his thesis was *Similarity Properties of Certain Volterra Operators on* $L_p[0,1]$, written under the supervision of Jacob Theodore Schwartz. During 1966–1968, he was Associate Mathematician at Brookhaven National Laboratories; during 1968–1970, Assistant Professor at UC Berkeley; during 1970–1975, Associate Professor at SUNY Stony Brook and then Professor from 1975 to 1977; and in 1977 he joined UCLA as a Professor of Mathematics, where he remains. He is also attached to the Institute for Pure and Applied Mathematics and the California NanoSystems Institute (CNSI) at UCLA. Stanley Osher mainly focuses on mathematical analysis, algorithms, the level set method, applied mathematics, and image processing. His mathematical analysis study integrates concerns from other disciplines, such as regularization and nonlinear systems. Stanley Osher combines subjects such as mathematical optimization, minification, and deblurring with his study of algorithms. His level set method research incorporates elements of level sets, curvature, the signed distance function, and vector fields. His research investigates the connection between applied mathematics and topics such as scale space that intersect with issues in inverse problems. The concepts of his image processing study are interwoven with issues in bounded variation and pattern recognition. He has published more than 500 research articles in mathematics and more then 425 in computer science. He has also supervised 64 doctoral students. He has also jointly published books: *Level Set Methods and Dynamic Implicit Surfaces* in 2003, *Geometric Level Set Methods in Imaging, Vision, and Graphics* in 2003, and several conference proceedings. Each of his joint papers *Fronts propagating with curvature-dependent speed: Algorithms based on Hamilton-Jacobi formulations* and *Nonlinear total variation based noise removal algorithms* have been cited by more than 20000 times. He has received several honors and awards, including the following: Fulbright Fellow (1971), Sloan Fellow (1972–1974), Smithsonian Environmental Research Center Fellowship (1982), US–Israel Binational Science Foundation Fellow (1986), NASA Public Service Group Achievement Award (1992), Computational Mechanics Award, Japan Society of Mechanical Engineering (2002), International Council for Industrial and Applied Mathematics Pioneer Prize (2003), SIAM Kleinman Prize (2005), member of the United States NAS (2005), Docteur Honoris Causa, ENS in Cachan, France (2006), Computational and Applied Sciences Award, US Association for Computational Mechanics (2007), John Tinsley Oden (1936–2023, USA) Medal (2007), International Cooperation Award, International Congress of Chinese Mathematicians (2007), honorary doctoral degree, Hong Kong Baptist University (2009), Fellow of SIAM (2009), Fellow of the AAAS (2009), Fellow of the AMS (2013), John von Neumann Lecture Prize from the SIAM (2013), Gauss Prize (2014), William Benter Prize in Applied Mathematics (2016), member of the National Academy of Engineering (2018), and Research.com Leader Award (2022, 2023, and 2024). Stanley Osher has been very successful in receiving numerous prestigious research grants, has given several invited talks at many institutions of the world, and has served as a member of editorial boards of several international journals.

39.7. Phillip Augustus Griffiths

He was born in Raleigh, North Carolina, USA. In 1959, Phillip Griffiths graduated with a Bachelor of Science from Wake Forest College in Winston-Salem, North Carolina. In 1958, while he was still an undergraduate, he married Ann Lane Crittenden; they had two children. After graduating from Wake Forest, he went to Princeton University to undertake research. Phillip Griffiths received his Ph.D. in 1962 after completing a doctoral dissertation, entitled *On certain homogeneous complex manifolds*, under the supervision of Donald Spencer. Before completing his thesis, he had spent the summer of 1961 at Berkeley working with Shiing-Shen Chern. During 1962–1964, Phillip Griffiths was Miller Fellow at UC, Berkeley. From 1964 to 1967, he was a faculty member at UC, Berkeley. In 1967, Phillip Griffiths and Ann Crittenden divorced. During 1967–1968, he was a Visiting Professor at Princeton University, and then he was appointed as a Professor. In 1968, he married Marian

Folsom Jones; they had two children. From 1972 to 1983, Phillip Griffiths was a Professor at Harvard University. The year 1975–1976 he spent at UC, Berkeley. In 1983, he was offered the Dwight Parker Robinson Professorship at Harvard University, but the same year he was named Provost and James Buchanan Duke (1856–1925, USA) Professor of Mathematics at Duke University. During 1991–2003, Phillip Griffiths was the Director of the IAS, Princeton, during 2004–2009 he was Professor of Mathematics, and from 2009 he has continued as Emeritus Professor. He has made significant contributions, mainly in the fields complex algebraic geometry, complex differential geometry, variations of Hodge structure, algebraic cycles, and the geometry of partial differential equations. He has more than 170 publications and has supervised 37 doctoral students. In 2003, his *Selected Works of Phillip Augustus Griffiths with Commentary* in four volumes (respectively, on analytic geometry, on algebraic geometry, on variations of Hodge structures, and on differential systems), containing 2598 pages, was compiled by Maurizio Cornalba (born 1947, Italy), Mark Lee Green, and Wilfried Schmid (born 1943, Germany–USA). He has also published several very influential books, including *Entire Holomorphic Mappings in One and Several Complex Variables* (1976), *Principles of Algebraic Geometry* (1978), *Rational Homotopy Theory and Differential Forms* (1981), *Exterior Differential Systems and the Calculus of Variations* (1983), *Topics in Transcendental Algebraic Geometry* (1984), *Differential Systems and Isometric Embeddings* (1987), *Introduction to Algebraic Curves* (1989), *Exterior differential systems and Euler-Lagrange partial differential equations* (2003), and *Mumford-Tate groups and domains: their geometry and arithmetic* (2012). Phillip Griffiths has served as an editor for seven major journals: *Advances in Function Theory*; *Annals of Math. Studies*; *Annals of Mathematics*; *Selecta Mathematica*; *Duke Mathematical Journal*; *Compositio Mathematica*; and the *Journal of Differential Geometry*. He has received a host of honors, including the AMS Steele Prize in 1971, Dannie Heineman Prize in 1979, Brouwer Medal in 2008, Wolf Prize in 2008, AMS Steele Prize for Lifetime Achievement 2014, and Chern Medal 2014. Phillip Griffiths was elected to the United States NAS in 1979, the APS in 1992, the AAAS in 1995, and the APS in 1996. In 2012 he became a Fellow of the AMS. He has also received Honorary Degrees from Wake Forest University (1973), Angers University in France (1979), the University of Peking (1983), and the University of Oslo (2002).

39.8. Adrián Arnoldo Paenza

He was born in Buenos Aires, Argentina, to a middle-class family who always encouraged him to pursue different activities to find his interests, such as ice skating or playing the piano. At the age of 14, he joined the Faculty of Exact and Natural Sciences at the University of Buenos Aires, where he received a Ph.D. degree in mathematics in 1979 under the supervision of Miguel E. Herrera (1938–1984, Argentina), and between 1986 and 1997 he was an Associate Professor in the mathematics department of that institution. At the age of 16, he had his first job as a journalist and received the Martin Fierro Award (television and radio awards in Argentina) for the best journalistic program on several occasions (every year 2004–2006 and 2007–2012). He also worked in the major radio stations and on all five air channels in Argentina and was a contributor to the three national newspapers: *Clarn*, *Página12*, and *La Nación*. Paenza was also the winner of the Konex Award in the Audiovisual Sports Journalism category in 1997 and 2007. His children's book series, started in 2006, *Matemáica ...¿Estás ahí? (Mathematics... Are You There?)*, about numbers, characters, problems, and curiosities, has been a bestseller in Argentina. In fact, more than 600,000 copies have been sold and it is still on the best-seller lists. The series wants to bring maths closer to people and entertain them. His other books are *Wrong Door* (2014); *What, Are These Also Mathematics?* (2011); *M47HS 4 EVERY1* (2012); *Mathemagic* (2013); *Detectives* (2015); *Strange Things Happen in Robotland* (2016); *Future Maths* (2017); *Who Loses, Wins* (2017); *Maths is Wonderful* (2017); *Maths is a Festival* (2018); *Is there a mathematician in the house?* (2018); *Danger! Explicit maths ahead* (2019); and *Incredible Mathematics* (2021). His books have also been published in Spain, Russia, Italy, the Czech Republic, Brazil, and Portugal. In 2014 he received the Leelavati Award for his work in the dissemination of mathematics.

40. Rio de Janeiro ICM 2018

This Congress was held in Rio de Janeiro, Brazil, during 1–9 August 2018. The Congress was attended by 3018 (792 from Brazil) participants from 114 countries. The Congress invited and supported 630 mathematicians from developing countries to participate, many of whom would not have been able to attend otherwise. In addition, 250 domestic travel grants were offered to mathematicians based in Brazil. The opening ceremony of the Congress began with an address from the Chairman of the Rio de Janeiro ICM Organizing Committee Marcelo Viana. He welcomed the participants and thanked the IMU for having the first ICM in the southern hemisphere. He also nominated Jacob Palis Jr. to be the Honorary President of the Congress, which was accepted through a round of applause. Marcelo Viana also acknowledged the presence of 576 gold medalists of the Brazilian Mathematical Olympiad. Then the President of the IMU Shigefumi Mori welcomed the participants. Next, Shigefumi Mori, on behalf of respective committees, announced the names of the medal and prize winners. The Fields Medal committee comprised Shigefumi Mori (chair), Héléne Esnault (born 1953, France–Germany), Eduard Feireisl (born 1957, Czech Republic), Alice Guionnet (born 1969, France), Nigel James Hitchin, John Willard Morgan (born 1946, USA), Hee Oh (born 1969, South Korea), Andrei Yuryevich Okounkov, Madabusi Santanam Raghunathan, Kenneth Alan Ribet (born 1948, USA), and Terence Chi–Shen Tao. The four Fields Medal winners were Caucher Birkar (born 1978, Iran–UK) "for the proof of the boundedness of Fano varieties and for contributions to the minimal model program"; Alessio Figalli (born 1984, Italy) "for contributions to the theory of optimal transport and its applications in partial differential equations, metric geometry, and probability; Peter Scholze "for his having transformed arithmetic algebraic geometry over p-adic fields; and Akshay Venkatesh (born 1981, India–Australia) "for his synthesis of analytic number theory, homogeneous dynamics, topology, and representation theory, which has resolved long-standing problems in areas such as the equidistribution of arithmetic objects". The Rolf Nevanlinna Prize winner was selected by the following committee: Tony Fan-Cheong Chan (born 1952, Hong Kong–USA) [chair], Manindra Agrawal (born 1966, India), Emmanuel Jean Candés (born 1970, France–USA), Shafi Goldwasser, Nicholas John Higham (1961–2024, England), and Jon Michael Kleinberg. The winner was Constantinos Costis Daskalakis (born 1981, Greece–USA) "for transforming our understanding of the computational complexity of fundamental problems in markets, auctions, equilibria, and other economic structures. His work provides both efficient algorithms and limits on what can be performed efficiently in these domains". The Gauss Prize Committee comprised Björn Engquis (chair), Mara Jesús Esteban Galarza (born 1956, Spain), Motoko Kotani (born 1960, Japan), Martin Andreas Nowak (born 1965, Austria–USA), Andrew Stuart (born 1962, UK–USA), Lloyd Nicholas Trefethen (born 1955, USA–UK), and Bin Yu (born 1969, China–USA). The Gauss Prize winner was David Leigh Donoho (born 1957, USA) "for his fundamental contributions to the mathematical, statistical and computational analysis of important problems in signal processing". The Chern Medal recipient was decided by the following committee: Caroline Mary Series (born 1951, UK) [chair], Jordan Stuart Ellenberg (born 1971,

USA), Gerhard Huisken, Michio Jimbo, and Benot Perthame (born 1959, France). The Chern Medal winner was Masaki Kashiwara "for his outstanding and foundational contributions to algebraic analysis and representation theory sustained over a period of almost 50 years". The Leelavati Prize Committee comprised Gert-Martin Greuel (chair), Shihoko Ishii (born 1950, Japan), Andrés Navas Flores (Chile), Sun Sook Noh (South Korea), and Simon Lehna Singh. The Leelavati Prize winner was Ali Nesin (born 1956, Turkey) "for his outstanding contributions towards increasing public awareness of mathematics in Turkey, in particular for his tireless work in creating the *Mathematical Village* as an exceptional, peaceful place for education, research and the exploration of mathematics for anyone". The Fields Medals and Rolf Nevanlinna Prize were awarded by Shigefumi Mori during the opening ceremony on 1 August; the Gauss prize was awarded by Michael Röckner (born 1956, Germany), President of the German Mathematical Society; the Chern Medal was handed out by Robert Leamon Bryant on 4 August, preceding the social dinner; and the Leelavati Prize was presented by Shigefumi Mori during the closing ceremony on 9 August.

The final item of the opening ceremony was the IMU Status Report by Helge Holden, Secretary General of the IMU. He also announced two important decisions of the 18th General Assembly of the IMU in São Paulo, Brazil. The EC for the term 2019–2022 would comprise Carlos Eduardo Kenig (President), Nalini Joshi (born 1958, Burma–Australia), and Loyiso Gordon Nongxa (born 1953, South Africa) as Vice-Presidents, Helge Holden as Secretary General, and Luigi Ambrosio, Andrei Yuryevich Okounkov, Paolo Piccione (born 1964, Italy–Brazil), Trivandrum Ramakrishnan Ramadas (born 1955, India), Gang Tian (born 1958, China), and Günter Matthias Ziegler as members. For the first time, the EC had a representative from Africa, and also all five continents were represented in the EC. He also reported that for the next Congress there were two bids, one from France and the other from Russia, with the venue St. Petersburg. The IMU General Assembly accepted the bid from Russia.

The work of the winners of Fields Medals, the Chern Medal, and the Leelavati Prize was summarized by Christopher Derek Hacon (born 1970, UK–Italy–USA) in the lecture "Caucher Birkar's work in birational algebraic geometry"; Luis Angel Caffarelli in the lecture "Alessio Figalli: His contributions to geometry and analysis"; Michael Rapoport (born 1948, Austria) in the lecture "The work of Peter Scholze"; Peter Clive Sarnak in the lecture "On the work of Akshay Venkatesh"; Pierre Schapira (born 1943, France) in the lecture "Fifty years of mathematics with Masaki Kashiwara"; and Gert-Martin Greuel in the lecture "Ali Nesin and the Nesin Mathematics Village". There were also eight special lectures: the Abel Lecture by Michael Francis Atiyah entitled *Arithmetic physics*; Emmy Noether Lecture by Sun-Yung Alice Chang entitled *Conformal geometry on four manifolds*; Rolf Nevanlinna Prize Lecture by Constantinos Costis Daskalakis entitled *Equilibria, fixed points, and computational complexity*; Gauss Prize Lecture by David Donoho entitled *From blackboard to bedside*; Fields Medal Lecture by Alessio Figalli entitled *Regularity of interfaces in phase transitions via obstacle problems*; Chern Medal Lecture by Masaki Kashiwara entitled *Crystal bases and categorifications*; Leelavati Prize Lecture by Ali Nesin entitled *Simple memories from a simple mathematics lecturer*; and Fields Medal Lecture by Akshay Venkatesh entitled *Cohomology of arithmetic groups*.

There were 21 one-hour plenary lectures, 176 invited talks of forty-five minutes distributed in 19 sections, 408 short communications, and 240 posters. On 9 August, during the closing ceremony Marcelo Viana gave detailed statistics of the number of participants, travel grants, the lectures program (which included five public lectures, which were attended by 5790) and award ceremonies, and expressed deep gratitude to his colleagues in the Organizing Committee. Then there was Leelavati Prize award ceremony. Finally, Shigefumi Mori gave a report on the General Assembly and the future of the IMU and thanked the Organization Committee and the participants.

40.1. Caucher Birkar

He is a Kurd born during the brutal eight-year Iran–Iraq War in Mariwan County, Kurdistan Province, Iran. He had five siblings (third of six children), and during his early years of school, his brothers taught him a lot of mathematics. After finishing high school, in 1996 Birkar entered the University of Tehran to study pure mathematics and earned a bachelor's degree in 1999. He was awarded the third prize in the 2000 International Mathematics Competition in London for university students and, shortly after, while still studying at the University, moved to the UK as a refugee and asked for political asylum. The British government placed him in Nottingham, where he met faculty members at the University of Nottingham, and he entered the university after his asylum request was granted (his birth name was Fereydoun Derakhshani, but after obtaining asylum his name was changed to Caucher Birkar, which translates in Kurdish to "migrant mathematician"). During 2001–2004 Birkar was a Ph.D. student at the University of Nottingham. As the most promising Ph.D. candidate, he received the Cecil King Travel Scholarship from the LMS in 2003. His official adviser there was Ivan Borisovich Fesenko (born 1962, Russia–UK–China), a number theorist; however, observing Birkar's interest in algebraic geometry, Fesenko encouraged him to attend math events outside the university. Fortunately, at a conference in 2002 in Cambridge, Birkar met Vyacheslav Vladimirovich Shokurov (born 1950, Russia), who ignited his interest in birational geometry. Birkar received his Ph.D. in 2004 from the University of Nottingham defending his thesis *Topics in modern algebraic geometry* under the supervision of Shokurov. After finishing his Ph.D., he moved to Warwick University to take up a postdoctoral research fellowship. After one year and a few months, he moved to Cambridge University in April 2006 with the same research fellowship. In autumn 2007 he was hired as a Lecturer at Cambridge. Birkar spent the academic year 2010–2011 in Paris at the Jussieu Mathematics Institute, with the support of the Fondation Mathématiques de Paris. Currently, he is a Professor at the Yao Mathematical Science Center, Tsinghua University, China. He has made significant contributions in algebraic geometry, particularly birational geometry. In 2006, he published the boundedness of Fano varieties, which is one of his most influential mathematical results. Jointly with Paolo Cascini (Italy–UK), Christopher Hacon, and James McKernan (born 1964, UK–USA), Birkar settled several conjectures, including the existence of log flips, finite generation of log canonical rings, and existence of minimal models for varieties of log general type. Jointly with De-Qi Zhang (China-Singapore), he also partially solved the Shigeru Iitaka conjecture on the effectivity of Iitaka fibrations induced by pluri-canonical systems on varieties with non-negative Kodaira dimension. He has published more than 35 research papers. Birkar has won various honors throughout his career: Leverhulme Prize in 2010, Prize of the Fondation Sciences Mathématiques de Paris in 2010, Moore Prize in 2016, Fields Medal in 2018, Whitehead Prize in 2018, FRS of London in 2019, and honorary doctorate of Salahaddin University-Erbil (Kurdish) in 2019. Birkar's Fields Medal was regrettably stolen after the ceremony in Rio, and news of the theft spread throughout the world. Thankfully, a few days later the committee gave him a replacement medal (he was the first person to receive the Fields Medal twice). At the time, Birkar stated "This has received significant media attention, making me more renowned than I would have been... And far more individuals than last week are aware of what a Fields Medal is". I just couldn't imagine that this would come true, he said after receiving the medal. "To go from the point that I didn't imagine meeting these people to the point where someday I hold a medal myself—I just couldn't imagine that this would come true". While he was completing his Ph.D. in Nottingham, he met Tarn (a girl from Thailand) and married; they have a son Zanko. According to Birkar "All these cultures make things more interesting to me. All these cultures give you a sense of pleasure". Zanko is a living example of this diversity because he is fluent in English, his mother's native Thai language, and his father's native Kurdish.

40.2. Alessio Figalli

He was born in Rome, Italy. Figalli's home was full of books on Greek history and mythology. When he was in high school, his parents wanted him to study the classics rather than science, which Figalli accepted willingly. However, he liked math from an early age, because he regarded it as an easy subject, something he was good at without having to work hard. Figalli turned toward serious math in his third year of high school. At the age of 18, he tried to enter the Scuola Normale Superiore of Pisa; while sitting in math classes with the top students in Italy, he realized he did not even know how to take a derivative. However, he quickly confronted the limits of his education and secured his master's degree in 2006 and doctorate in 2007 under the supervision of Luigi Ambrosio and Cédric Villani, both from the Scuola Normale Superiore of Pisa. The title of his thesis was *Optimal Transportation and Action-Minimizing Measures*. In 2007, he was appointed Chargé de recherche at the French National Centre for Scientific Research, and in 2008 he went to the École polytechnique as Professeur Hadamard. In 2009 he moved to the University of Texas in Austin as an Associate Professor. He became a Full Professor in 2011 and Robert Lee Moore (1882–1974, USA) Chair holder in 2013. Since 2016, he has been a Chaired Professor at ETH Zurich. Figalli has worked in the theory of optimal transport, with particular emphasis on the regularity theory of optimal transport maps and its connections to Monge–Ampére equations. He used optimal transport techniques to obtain improved versions of the anisotropic isoperimetric inequality and obtained several other important results on the stability of functional and geometric inequalities. Figalli also discussed the stability analysis of some Gagliardo–Nirenberg and logarithmic Hardy–Littlewood–Sobolev inequalities to obtain a quantitative rate of convergence for the critical mass Keller–Segel (Evelyn Fox Keller, 1936–2023, USA, and Lee Aaron Segel, 1932–2005, USA) equation. He also worked on Hamilton–Jacobi equations, Di Perna-Lions' theory, the Schrödinger equation, the Vlasov–Poisson equation, and the list continues. Figalli has written more than 170 research articles and supervised 11 doctoral students. In addition, he has written three books: *Optimal transportation and action-minimizing measures* (2008), *Partial differential equations and geometric measure theory: Cetraro* (2018), and *The Monge-Ampére equation and its applications* (2017). Figalli's results have provided a refined mathematical understanding of everything he has touched. He has been awarded several honors, including the Peccot–Vimont Prize in 2012, EMS Prize in 2012, Guido Stampacchia (1922–1978, Italy) Medal in 2015, Feltrinelli Prize in 2017, and Fields Medal in 2018. In 2018 he received a Doctorate Honoris Causa from the Université Côte d'Azur (France) and in 2019 from the Polytechnic University of Catalonia, Spain. His wife Mikaela Iacobelli (Italy) is also a mathematician; she joined ETH Zurich as a Professor of Mathematics in 2019.

40.3. Peter Scholze

He was born in Dresden, East Germany (now Germany), and grew up in Berlin. His father is a physicist, his mother is a computer scientist, and his sister studied chemistry. He attended the Heinrich-Hertz-Gymnasium, a state high school with a focus on mathematics and science in Berlin-Friedrichshain. He started teaching himself college-level mathematics at the age of 14. As a student, Scholze participated in the IMO, winning three gold medals (2005, 2006, and 2007) and one silver medal (2004). He studied at the University of Bonn and completed his bachelor's degree in three semesters (2009) and his master's degree in two further semesters (2010). He obtained his Ph.D. in 2012 under the supervision of Michael Rapoport. The title of his thesis was *Perfectoid Spaces* (a class of algebro-geometric objects living in the realm of p-adic geometry). In 2012, shortly after completing his Ph.D., he was made Full Professor at the University of Bonn, becoming at the age of 24 the youngest Full Professor in Germany. In fall 2014, Scholze was appointed the Chancellor's Professor at UC, Berkeley, where he taught a course on p-adic geometry. In 2018, he was appointed as a Scientific Member and one of the Directors of the MPIM in Bonn. He is known for his work in arithmetic geometry, algebraic geometry, and algebraic number theory. Peter Scholze is recognized as the leading mathematician of his generation in the field of arithmetic geometry. He, with Bhargav Bhatt, developed the theory of prismatic cohomology, which has been described as progress towards motivic cohomology by unifying singular cohomology, de Rham cohomology, l-adic cohomology, and crystalline cohomology. With Dustin Clausen (USA–Canada), he proposed a program for condensed mathematics. He has published more than 35 research papers and supervised five doctoral students. In 2020, with Jared Weinstein (USA), Scholze also published a book *Berkeley Lectures on p-adic Geometry*. He has been awarded several prizes: Prix and Cours Peccot in 2012, SASTRA Ramanujan Prize in 2013, Clay Research Award in 2014, Cole Prize in 2015, Fermat Prize in 2015, Ostrowski Prize in 2015, EMS Prize in 2016, Leibniz Prize in 2016, Berlin-Brandenburg Academy Award in 2016, and Fields Medal in 2018. He declined the USD 100,000 "New Horizons in Mathematics Prize" of the 2016 Breakthrough Prizes. It is interesting to note that Scholze was a student of Rapoport, who was a student of Deligne, who was a student of Grothendieck, who was a student of Schwartz; in this chain, Scholze, Deligne, Grothendieck, and Schwartz are all Fields medalists. In 2017, he became a member of the German Academy of Sciences Leopoldina. In 2019, Scholze received the Great Cross of Merit of the Order of Merit of the Federal Republic of Germany. In 2022, he became a Foreign Member of the Royal Society and was awarded the Pius XI Medal from the Pontifical Academy of Sciences. Scholze is married to a fellow mathematician and has a daughter.

40.4. Akshay Venkatesh

He was born in Delhi, India, in a Tamil Brahmin family. His family emigrated to Perth in Western Australia when he was just two years old. He attended Scotch College in Perth. His mother Svetha Venkatesh completed her Ph.D. after moving to Australia and became a computer scientist, whereas his father is a mechanical engineer. Akshay attended extracurricular training classes for gifted students in the state mathematical olympiad program, and in 1993, whilst aged only 11, he competed at the 24th International Physics Olympiad in Williamsburg, Virginia, USA, winning a bronze medal. The following year, he switched his attention to mathematics and, after placing second in the Australian Mathematical Olympiad, he won a silver medal in the sixth Asian Pacific Mathematics Olympiad, before winning a bronze medal at the 1994 IMO held in Hong Kong. Venkatesh completed his secondary education the same year, turning 13 before entering the University of Western Australia (UWA) for an honors course in mathematics as its youngest ever student. He completed the four-year course in three years and became, at 16, the youngest person to earn a bachelor's degree with first-class honors in pure mathematics from the university. In 1998, Venkatesh moved to the USA and joined Princeton University for his Ph.D. under the supervision of Peter Clive Sarnak, which he completed in 2002 (just at the age of 21). The title of his thesis was *Limiting Forms of the Trace Formula*. He was supported by the Hackett Fellowship for postgraduate study. He was then awarded a postdoctoral position at MIT, where he served as a Clarence Lemuel Elisha Moore instructor. Venkatesh then held a Clay Research Fellowship from the Clay Mathematics Institute from 2004 to 2006, and then became an Associate Professor at the Courant Institute of Mathematical Sciences. He was also a member of the IAS, Princeton, during 2005–2006. During 2008–2018, Venkatesh was a Full Professor at Stanford University. He was also a distinguished Visiting Professor at the IAS during 2017–2018. He became a permanent faculty member of the IAS, Princeton, in August 2018. His research interests are in the fields of counting, equidistribution problems in automorphic forms and number theory, and L-functions, in particular representation theory, locally symmetric spaces, ergodic theory, and algebraic topology. His recent work examines new algebraic structures related to the topology of locally symmetric spaces. He has published 55 research papers and supervised 12 doctoral students. According to Venkatesh "A lot of the time when you do math, you're stuck, but at the same time there are all these moments where you feel privileged that you get to work with it. You have this sensation of transcendence; you feel like you've been part of something really meaningful". He has received several honors: Salem Prize in 2007, SASTRA Ramanujan Prize in 2008, Aisenstadt Chair, Université de Montreal in 2010, Infosys Prize in 2016, Ostrowski Prize in 2017, Fields Medal in 2018 (second Australian and the second person of Indian descent to win the Fields Medal), and Honorary doctorate, University of Western Australia in 2019. Venkatesh married Sarah Paden (music teacher); they have two daughters.

40.5. Constantinos Costis Daskalakis

He was born in Athens, Greece. His grandparents resided in Crete (the largest and most populous of the Greek islands), where Daskalakis stayed during summer as a child. When Daskalakis was in third grade, his father bought an Amstrad CPC (home computers produced by Amstrad between 1984 and 1990), which Daskalakis stayed up all night with, attempting to learn how it worked. He attended Varvakeio High School (in Psychiko, a town and a suburb in Athens) and completed his undergraduate studies at the National Technical University of Athens (most prestigious among engineering schools in Greece), where in 2004 he received his Diploma in Electrical and Computer Engineering. He completed his undergraduate thesis *On the Existence of Pure Nash Equilibria in Graphical Games with Succinct Description* under the supervision of Stathis Zachos (born 1947, Athens, Greece). As an undergraduate, Daskalakis attained perfect scores in all but one of his classes, something which had not previously been achieved in the university's history. Then, Daskalakis joined UC, Berkeley, and received his Ph.D. degree in EECS in 2008. The title of his thesis was *The Complexity of Nash Equilibria*, written under the supervision of Christos Charilaos Papadimitriou (born 1949, Greece–USA). His thesis was awarded the 2008 ACM Doctoral Dissertation Award. After his Ph.D. he spent a year as a postdoctoral researcher in Jennifer Chayes's group at Microsoft Research, New England, and has been with the MIT faculty since 2009. He was appointed a tenured faculty in May 2015 and Full Professor in 2018. At MIT Daskalakis is a Professor of EECS, a member of the Computer Science and Artificial Intelligence Laboratory (CSAIL), an affiliate of the Laboratory for Information and Decision Systems and the Operations Research Center, and an investigator in the MIT Institute for Foundations of Data Science. He works on the theory of computation and its interface with game theory, economics, probability theory, statistics, and machine learning. He has resolved long-standing open problems regarding the computational complexity of the Nash equilibrium, the mathematical structure and computational complexity of multi-item auctions, and the behavior of machine learning methods such as the expectation–maximization algorithm. Daskalakis has obtained computationally and statistically efficient methods for statistical hypothesis testing and learning in high-dimensional settings, as well as results characterizing the structure and concentration properties of high-dimensional distributions. He has published more than 150 research papers and supervised 10 doctoral students. Daskalakis has been the recipient of several honors and awards, including the Kalai Prize in 2008, NSF Career Award in 2009, Sloan Foundation Fellowship in 2010, Spira Award in 2011, SIAM Outstanding Paper Prize in 2011, Microsoft Research Faculty Fellowship in 2012, Google Faculty Research Award in 2017, Rolf Nevanlinna Prize in 2018, ACM Grace Murray Hopper (1906–1992, USA) Award in 2019, Simons Investigator Award in 2018, Bodossaki Foundation Distinguished Young Scientists Award in 2019, and ACM Fellow in 2022. He also holds honorary doctorates from the University of Patras and the University of Piraeus, and was awarded the Golden Cross of the Order of the Redeemer by the Greek Presidency.

40.6. David Leigh Donoho

He was born in Los Angeles, California, USA. His father Paul Leighton Donoho (1931–2012, USA) was a Professor of Physics at Rice University in Houston, Texas. David attended Robert Edward Lee High School (now Margaret Long Wisdom High School) in Houston, graduating in 1974. When David was eleven years old, his father took a sabbatical and for a year the family went to Grenoble, France. He spent one year at school in Grenoble, finding France had a very intense mathematical culture, which had a great impact on his attitude towards mathematics. After completing high school he completed his undergraduate studies at Princeton University, completing his Bachelor of Arts degree in Statistics in 1978, Summa Cum Laude. His undergraduate thesis advisor was John Wilder Tukey (1915–2000, USA), the first Head of the Department of Statistics at Princeton. In 1979, Davis enrolled at Harvard University to study for a Ph.D. under the supervision of Peter Jost Huber (born 1934, Switzerland), one of the three main founders of robust statistics. He was awarded a Ph.D. in 1983 for his 418-page thesis entitled *A Tool for Research in Data Analysis*. In the thesis he described the design and implementation of a compact data analysis language. The uses of the language for constructing advanced systems for multivariate graphics were also described. David had already published six research articles before obtaining his Ph.D. In 1977 (summer) he worked as a Programmer for the University of Texas Marine Science Institute; during 1976–1978 as a Programmer for Statistics Department, Princeton University; during 1979–1983 as a Research assistant for Peter Huber; in 1983 as a Postdoctoral Fellow at the MSRI in Berkeley; during 1984–1990 in the Faculty of Department of Statistics, UC, Berkeley: NSF Postdoctoral Fellow 1983–1985, Assistant Professor 1984–1986, Associate Professor 1987–1990, and Professor 1990–1997; and from 1991–present as a Professor, Department of Statistics, Stanford University. David has made significant contributions in several different fields, including wavelets, information theory, mathematical statistics, emerging Internet applications, Internet appliances, Internet privacy and security models, wireless communications, signal and image processing, image and video coding, statistics of natural images, statistics of Internet traffic, inverse problems in geophysics, and extragalactic astronomy. He is best known for coining the term 'compressed sensing' while proposing a method for speeding up signal acquisition and reconstruction that today is used in MRI scanners by GE, Siemens, and Philips, serving millions of patients yearly. In recent years David and his postdocs and students have been studying large-scale covariance matrix estimation, large-scale matrix denoising, detection of rare and weak signals among many pure noise non-signals, compressed sensing and related scientific imaging problems, and, most recently, empirical deep learning. He has published more than 130 research papers and supervised 24 doctoral students. He has given several special lectures; has been Visiting Professor at several universities in France, Israel, the Netherlands, and England; and has 49 approved or filled US patents. David has received many honors and awards, including the Presidential Young Investigator Award during 1985–1991, Fellow Institute of Mathematical Statistics in 1990, MacArthur Fellow in 1991, Fellow AAAS in 1992, Committee of Presidents of Statistical Societies Presidents' Award in 1994, elected to the United States NAS in 1998, Sackler Fellow, Tel Aviv University, in 2000, Outstanding Achievement

Award, Soc. Photo. Instr. Eng. in 2000, von Neumann Lecture Prize 2001, SIGEST Best Paper, SIAM in 2001, appointed to the Bass Professorship in 2002, Information Theory Society Paper Award 2008, elected SIAM Fellow in 2009, Norbert Wiener Prize in 2010, elected Foreign Associate of the Académie des Sciences in 2010, Fellow of AMS in 2012, Shaw Prize in 2013, Gauss Prize in 2018, elected to the APS in 2019, and Jack St. Clair Kilby (1923–2005, USA) Signal Processing Medal in 2022. He has been awarded honorary doctorates from the University of Chicago (2009), the École Polytechnique Fédérale de Lausanne (2012), the University of Waterloo (2016), and Technion (2017). In 1984, David married Miriam Gasko (born 1945), also a statistician with a Ph.D. from Harvard; they have a son Daniel, born in 1985, who became a neurosurgeon and developed machine learning systems to make surgery safer. In 2022, David Donoho and his wife Gasko Donoho established the Donoho scholarship.

40.7. Masaki Kashiwara

He was born in Yūki, Ibaraki, Japan. He received his Master of Science degree in 1971 from the University of Tokyo. During 1971–1974, Kashiwara served as an Assistant at the RIMS at Kyoto University. In 1974, Kyoto University awarded him a Ph.D. degree. The title of his thesis was *On the maximality overdetermined system of linear differential equations*, written under the supervision of Mikio Sato (1928–2023, Japan). After completing his Ph.D. Kashiwara joined Nagoya University as an Associate Professor and remained until 1977. For the year 1977–1978, he was an Associate researcher at MIT. During 1978–1984, Kashiwara was an Associate Professor at the RIMS, Full Professor during 1984–2010, and Director during 2001–2003 and 2007–2009. From 2010, he has continued as a Professor Emeritus at the RIMS and also from 2019 as the Program-Specific Professor of KUIAS. Kashiwara has made significant contributions in algebraic analysis, microlocal analysis, D-module theory, Hodge theory, sheaf theory, and representation theory. Jointly with Mikio Sato, he established the foundations of the theory of systems of linear partial differential equations with analytic coefficients, introducing a cohomological approach that follows the spirit of the Grothendieck theory of schemes. There are several concepts and theorems named after Kashiwara, including the following: Kashiwara constructibility theorem, Kashiwara index theorem, Kashiwara–Malgrange filtration, Cauchy–Kowalevsky–Kashiwara theorem (Sofya Kovalevskaya, 1850–1891, Russia), Kashiwara operators, and Kashiwara crystal basis. He has published more than 265 research articles and supervised seven doctoral students. He has also written/edited several books: *Microfunctions and pseudo-differential equations* (1972), *Seminar on micro-local analysis* (1979), *Systems of microdifferential equations* (1983), *Introduction to microlocal analysis* (1986), *Foundations of algebraic analysis* (1986), *Algebraic analysis: papers dedicated to Professor Mikio Sato on the occasion of his sixtieth birthday* (1988), *Sheaves on manifolds: with a short history* (1990), *Moderate and formal cohomology associated with constructible sheaves* (1996), *Topological field theory, primitive forms and related topics* (1998), *Physical combinatorics* (2000), *MathPhys Odyssey 2001: integrable models and beyond: in honor of Barry M. McCoy* (2002), *Bases cristallines des groupes quantiques* (2002) in French, *D-modules and microlocal calculus* (2003), *Representation theory and complex analysis* (2004), *Categories and sheaves* (2006), and *Regular and irregular holonomic D-modules* (2016). In honor of the visit of Kashiwara to Strasbourg, a series of lectures by colleagues in the field was organized by Nalini Anantharaman (born 1976, France) during 3–6 April 2017. Kashiwara has received several honors and awards, including the Iyanaga Prize in 1981, Asahi Prize in 1988, Japan Academy Prize in 1988, member of the FAS in 2002, member of the Japan Academy in 2007, Fujihara Award in 2008, Kyoto Prize in 2018, Chern Medal in 2018, the Order of the Sacred Treasure, Gold and Silver Star in 2020, Frontiers of Science Award in 2023, and Kyoto Prefecture Culture Prize for Outstanding Contribution in 2024. He has also received a Doctor Honoris Causa from the University of Nancy in 1996 and the Universite Pierre et Marie Curie in 2005.

40.8. Ali Nesin

He was born in Istanbul, Turkey. His father Aziz Nesin (1915–1995, Turkey) was a famous Turkish writer and humorist and the author of more than 100 books, and his mother Meral Çelen (born 1934, Turkey) wrote three books, one a collection of short stories and the two others her memories. They married in 1956 and separated in 1967. After completing primary schooling, during 1967–1973 Ali Nesin went to the junior high school Lycée Saint-Joseph, Istanbul, and then during 1973–1977 to the high school Collége Champittet Lausanne—Switzerland. In 1977, he joined the Université Paris Diderot (at that time it was known as Paris 7) and in 1981 obtained a Maitrise és Arts degree (Master of Arts degree) in mathematics. In 1981, Ali Nesin enrolled at Yale University and in 1985 received his Ph.D. in mathematics. The title of his thesis was *Groups of Finite Morely Rank*, written under the supervision of Angus John Macintyre (born 1941, UK). In the academic year 1985–1986, Ali Nesin worked at UC, Berkeley, as an Instructor. In 1986, he returned to Turkey to complete his short-term military service. During that time, he was arrested and charged with "incitement to mutiny" after objecting to the same syringe being used to vaccinate numerous privates, but he was acquitted after the trial. However, this was only one of the minor accusations. In fact, he was accused of several undisciplinary acts, including trying to convince other soldiers not to go to military training. But all the accusations were grossly exaggerated. The main issue was to punish his father through him, as he was too famous to be touched. He was arrested along with Sevan Nişanyan (born 1956, Turkey–USA–Armenia). During 1987–1988 Ali Nesin worked at Notre Dame University as a Visiting Assistant Professor and during 1988–1991 at UC, Irvine, as an Assistant Professor, during 1991–1995 as an Associate Professor, and 1995 as a Full Professor. Ali Nesin also spent the 1993–1994 academic year at Bilkent University (Turkey) as a Visiting Professor. Upon the death of his father in 1995, he returned to Turkey for good, and in the same year took on the management of his father's Nesin Foundation. In 1996, he also joined the Department of Mathematics at Istanbul Bilgi University as Head and continued there until 2022; then just for one year he became the Head of the Department of Mathematics at Istinye University. During the academic year 2001–02, he also worked as a Visiting Lecturer at Lyon University (France). For ten years, Ali Nesin organized summer schools all over Turkey, driven by his belief that university mathematics education was inadequate. In 2007, with the support of Sevan Nişanyan, he established the Mathematics Village in Sirince, a village in the Selçuk area of Izmir. This non-profit institution, which is a global exemplar, opens its doors to over twenty thousand students every year. The village benefits from the voluntary support of respected academicians from Turkey and across the globe. In 2015, Ali Nesin and the Mathematics Village received the Vehbi Koç Award for "breaking the mold of mathematics education in Turkey and for an exceptional achievement in the field of creative education". In his speech at the award ceremony, Ali Nesin said that mathematics, philosophy, and art were not meant to bring money, but should be a way of life: "These things can't teach you what to think; they teach you how to think and to think about everything. They produce nothing, but are useful for everything. I give my students a problem to solve, and they think for two hours. The problem itself won't produce anything. But in order to persist in conjecture, conceptualize the problem correctly, explain the solution and solve the problem, you need to understand its challenges. This is useful for all things in life-in human relationships, in societal relationships and in your relationship with yourself". He also vowed that the award money would go to the construction of a Philosophy Village, also in Sirince. He has written more than 35 research articles, supervised several students, written monographs, undergraduate- and graduate-level mathematics books in Turkish, semi-academic books on mathematics for beginners (high schoolers and up), and mathematical books for high school students, edited mathematical books, and written and edited non-mathematical Books. In addition in Turkish he has written several popular books on mathematics, including *Mathematics and Nature* (2007), *Mathematics and Infinity* (2007), *Mathematics and Games* (2007), *Mathematics and Fear* (2008), *Mathematics and Donkeys with Camels* (2008), *Mathematics and Reality* (2009), *Mathematics Monster* (2010), *Mathematics and Art* (2012), and *Portraits of Mathematicians* (2013). He also works on oil painting, drawing, and portraiture; he has put his exhibits in several exhibitions in Turkey. During 2003–2013, he served as the Editor-in-Chief of *Matematik Dünyasi* (*The World of Mathematics*), a Turkish Mathematics Association magazine, and during 2009–2018, he was one of the editors of the *Turkish Journal of Mathematics*. Besides several honors and awards from the various organizations in Turkey, he received the Leelavati Prize in 2018. He is married to Özlem Beyarslan (who is also a Professor of Mathematics). Ali Nesin have five children, two with Özlem Beyarslan. Ali Nesin is an all in one.

41. Virtual ICM 2022

On 24 February 2022, Russia invaded Ukraine in a major escalation of the Russo-Ukrainian War. It caused tens of thousands of casualties. At meetings held over 24–27 February 2022, the EC of the IMU decided that the ICM 2022 and the 19th IMU General Assembly would not take place in Saint Petersburg, Russia, as originally planned. The General Assembly was then held on 3–4 July 2022 in Helsinki, Finland, and it was decided as the only feasible alternative to hold the ICM 2022 as a virtual event during 6–14 July, 2022 in Helsinki, Finland. They also decided that on 5 July there would be a live award ceremony in Helsinki, at which all the IMU prizes would be announced, and the IMU would hold the award ceremony as a live event. The Fields Medal committee comprised Carlos Eduardo Kenig (chair), Artur Avila Cordeiro de Melo, Camillo de Lellis (born 1976, Italy), Michael Jerome Hopkins (born 1958, USA), Antti Kupiainen (born 1954, Finland), Rahul Pandharipande, Alfio Quarteroni, Vera Serganova, Laure Saint-Raymond (born 1975, France), Richard Lawrence Taylor, Weiping Zhang (born 1964, China), and Tamar Debora Ziegler (born 1971, Israel). The four Fields Medal winners were Hugo Duminil-Copin (born 1985, France) "for solving longstanding problems in the probabilistic theory of phase transitions in statistical physics, especially in dimensions three and four"; June E Huh (born 1983, USA) "for bringing the ideas of Hodge theory to combinatorics, the proof of the Dowling-Wilson conjecture for geometric lattices, the proof of the Heron-Rota-Welsh conjecture for matroids, the development of the theory of Lorentzian polynomials, and the proof of the strong Mason conjecture"; James Alexander Maynard (born 1987, UK) "for contributions to analytic number theory, which have led to major advances in the understanding of the structure of prime numbers and in Diophantine approximation; and Maryna Sergiivna Viazovska (born 1984, Ukraine–France) "for the proof that the E_8 lattice provides the densest packing of identical spheres in 8 dimensions, and further contributions to related extremal problems and interpolation problems in Fourier analysis". The inaugural IMU Abacus Medal winner was selected by the following committee: James Weldon Demmel Jr. (born 1955, USA) [chair], Annalisa Buffa (born 1973, Italy), Meena Mahajan (born 1965, India), Amit Singer (Israel–USA), and Daniel Alan Spielman. The winner was Mark Braverman (born 1984, Russia–Israel–USA) "for his path-breaking research developing the theory of information complexity, a framework for using information theory to reason about communication protocols. His work has led to direct-sum theorems giving lower bounds on amortized communication, ingenious protocol compression methods, and new interactive communication protocols resilient to noise". The Gauss Prize Committee comprised Éva Tardos (chair), Liliana Borcea (born 1964, Romania–USA), Albert Cohen (born 1965, France), Bernd Sturmfels (born 1962, Germany–USA), and Tao Tang (born 1963, China). The Gauss Prize winner was Elliott Hershel Lieb (born 1932, USA) "for deep mathematical contributions of exceptional breadth which have shaped the fields of quantum mechanics, statistical mechanics, computational chemistry, and quantum information theory". The Chern Medal recipient was decided by the following committee: Yakov Matveevich Eliashberg (chair), Sun-Yung Alice Chang, Henri

Rene Darmon (born 1965, France–Canada), Alice Guionnet, and Hiraku Nakajima. The Chern Medal winner was Barry Charles Mazur "for his profound discoveries in topology, arithmetic geometry and number theory, and his leadership and generosity in forming the next generation of Mathematicians". The Leelavati Prize committee comprised Pavel Ilyich Etingof (born 1969, Russia–Ukraine–USA) [chair], Kannan Soundararajan (born 1973, India–USA), Tadashi Tokieda (born 1968, Japan–USA), Chandrashekhar Khare (born 1968, India–USA), and Michéle Artigue. The Leelavati Prize winner was Nikolai Nikolayevich Andreev (born 1975, Russia) "for his contribution to the art of mathematical animation and of mathematical model-building, in a style which inspires the young and the old alike, and which mathematicians around the world can adapt to their varied usesas well as for his indefatigable efforts to popularize genuine mathematics among the public via videos, lectures, and a prize-winning book". The ceremony was opened by the President of Finland Honorable Sauli Niinistö (born 1948). All four Fields medalists, the IMU Abacus Medalist, and the recipient of the Leelavati Prize were present in Helsinki; however, the recipients of the Gauss Prize and the Chern Medal participated in the ceremony remotely.

On 6th July, Carlos Eduardo Kenig, the President of the IMU, welcomed all the participants who were present in Helsinki and those who were participating online. He also stated that the Fields medalists and the IMU Abacus medalist were all present in Helsinki, so the recipients could give their ICM plenary talks in front of a live audience in Helsinki, and also that their lectures would be streamed via the virtual ICM platform for those who were not fortunate enough to be in Helsinki that day. He declared the 2022 virtual ICM open to all participants. The work of the winners of Fields Medals, the Chern Medal, and the Leelavati Prize was summarized by Martin Hairer in the lecture "The work of Hugo Duminil-Copin"; Gil Kalai in the lecture "The work of June E Huh"; Kannan Soundararajan in the lecture "The work of James Alexander Maynard"; Henry Cohn (USA) in the lecture "The work of Maryna Sergiivna Viazovska"; Ran Raz (born 1966, Israel) in the lecture "The work of Mark Braverman"; Rupert L. Frank (born 1978, Germany) in the lecture "The work of Elliott Hershel Lieb"; Henri Rene Darmon in the lecture "The work of Barry Charles Mazur; and Tadashi Tokieda in the lecture "Nikolai Nikolayevich Andreev and the art of mathematical animation and model-building". Except for Elliott Hershel Lieb, there were also lectures from the rest of th prize winners: Hugo Duminil-Copin talked on "100 years of the (critical) Ising model on the hypercubic lattice"; June E Huh talked on "Combinatorics and Hodge theory"; James Alexander Maynard talked on "Counting primes"; Maryna Sergiivna Viazovska talked on "On discrete Fourier uniqueness sets in Euclidean space"; Mark Braverman talked on "Communication and information complexity"; and Nikolai Nikolayevich Andreev talked on "Popularization of math: sketches of Russian projects and traditions". The Emmy Noether Lecture was given by Marie-France Vignéras (born 1946, France) on "Representations of p-adic groups over commutative rings". There were also four popular scientific expositions given by Andrei Yuryevich Okounkov.

There were 3 special plenary lectures by Kevin Mark Buzzard (born 1968, UK) on "What is the point of computers? A question for pure mathematicians', Frank Calegari (born 1975, Australia–USA) on "Reciprocity in the Langlands program since

Fermat's Last Theorem", and Frans Pretorius (born 1973 South African–Canada) on "A survey of gravitational waves", and there were 18 one-hour plenary lectures and 173 invited talks. On 14 July, during the closing ceremony Carlos Eduardo Kenig said "We have been very fortunate to be able to carry out in full this fantastic event despite the many obstacles that we have encountered along the way". He also thanked various committees and their elected members, speakers, and panelists. Then Helge Holden, the Secretary General of the IMU, discussed the COVID-19 pandemic, which changed the life of billions of people across the globe, and Russia's invasion of Ukraine on 24 February 2022. He also announced that the EC for the term 2022–2026 will comprise Hiraku Nakajima (President), Ulrike Tillmann, and Tatiana Toro as Vice-Presidents, Christoph Sorger (born 1964, France) as Secretary General, and Mouhamed Moustapha Fall, Nalini Joshi, JongHae Keum (born 1957, Korea), Paolo Piccione, Günter Matthias Ziegler, Tamar Debora Ziegler, and Carlos Eduardo Kenig as members. He also stated that the 20th GA will take place in New York City on 19–20 July 2026, while the ICM 2026 will be hosted in Philadelphia over 22–29 July 2026.

41.1. Hugo Duminil-Copin

He was born in Châtenay-Malabry, Île-de-France, France. His father was a middle school gym teacher and his mother a dancer before she became an elementary school teacher. In 2003, for preparatory classes, Hugo attended the Lycée Louis-Le-Grand in Paris. During 2006–2008, he studied at the ENS in Paris. In 2008, he joined Université de Genéve to conduct a Ph.D. under the supervision of Stanislav Konstantinovich Smirnov. He received his doctorate in 2011 for his dissertation *Phase transition in random-cluster and* $O(n)$*-models*. In 2012, he published five papers, four jointly in the *Annals of Mathematics*, *Probability Theory and Related Fields*, *Transactions of the AMS*, and the *Annals of Probability* and one independently in the *Journal of Physics A: Mathematical and Theoretical*. At the Université de Genéve, he was a postdoc during 2011–2013 and Assistant Professor during 2013–2014, and has been a Full Professor since 2014. In 2016, Hugo became Permanent Professor at the IHES, and since 2019 he has been a member of the Academia Europaea. Hugo has made significant contributions in statistical physics. He uses ideas from probability theory to study the critical behavior of various models on networks. His work focuses on identifying the critical point at which phase transitions occur, what happens at the critical point, and the behavior of the system just above and below the critical point. He has published more than 85 research papers and supervised two doctoral students. He has also published several books, surveys, and lecture notes. Hugo is also an editor of several prestigious journals, including *Probability and Mathematical Physics* (main editor), *Forum of Pi*, *Duke Mathematical Journal*, *Publications of IHES*, *Inventiones Mathematicae Communications in Mathematical Physics* (2016–2020), *Annals of Probability* (2016–2021), *Annales de l'Institut Henri Poincaré (B) Probabilités et Statistiques* (2015–2021), and *EMS Monographs in Mathematics*. He has given several plenary lectures at conferences and colloquia and commendable lectures such as the Charles River Lectures (2017), Takagi Lectures (2017), Princeton Minerva Distinguished Lecture Series (2019), ICTS Ramanujan Lectures (2023), Weiestrass Lecture (2023), and Leonardo da Vinci Lecture (2023). Hugo has been awarded several honors and awards, including the Vacheron-Constantin Prize in 2012, Rollo Davidson Prize in 2012, Oberwolfach Prize in 2013, Peccot Lectures at the Collége de France in 2015, Early Career Award of the International Association of Mathematical Physics in 2015, EMS Prize in 2016, Loéve Prize in 2017, New Horizons Prize in Mathematics in 2017, Jacques Herbrand Prize in 2017, Dobrushin Prize in 2019, Fields Medal in 2022, elected member of the European Academy of Sciences in 2023, member of the Council of Science and the Académie des Sciences de Paris in 2023, elected member of the Paris Academy of Sciences in 2023, and Frontiers of Science Award in 2023. He says "My priority is on the personal side, to spend time with my daughter and my wife".

41.2. June E Huh

He was born in Stanford, California, while his parents were completing graduate studies at Stanford University. His family returned to South Korea when June was about two years old. His father Myung-Hoe Huh was a Professor of Statistics at Korea University, Seoul Campus, while his mother In Young Lee was a Professor of Russian language at Seoul National University. In elementary school tests June earned very poor marks, which convinced him that he lacked the inborn talent to excel in mathematics. Later when June was in high school, he became bored and exhausted by the constant routine of relentless studying, so he dropped out to become a poet. Huh matriculated at Seoul National University in 2002. Initially, he wanted to become a science journalist and decided to major in physics and astronomy but compiled a poor attendance record and had to repeat several courses. Finally, he obtained Bachelor of Science degree in 2007 from Seoul National University in physics and astronomy and mathematics. Then he came in contact with Heisuke Hironaka, who went to Seoul National University as a Visiting Professor. June attended his course on algebraic geometry, specifically on singularity theory, which stimulated June's interest in research-level math. June proceeded to complete a master's degree in 2009 in mathematics at Seoul National University. During this period, he visited Heisuke Hironaka several times and worked as his personal assistant. In 2009, he managed to get admission to the University of Illinois Urbana-Champaign to conduct his Ph.D. studies, but then he was transferred to the University of Michigan in 2011. He received his Ph.D. in 2014 (at the age of 31) for his thesis *Rota's conjecture and positivity of algebraic cycles in permutohedral varieties*, written under the supervision of Mircea Immanuel Mustaţǎ (born 1971, Romania–USA). He was awarded the Sumner Byron Myers (1910–1955) Prize for his Ph.D. thesis. During 2014–2019, June was a Clay Fellow at the Clay Mathematics Institute, during 2014–2017 a Veblen Fellow at the IAS, Princeton, during 2017–2019 a Visiting Professor at the IAS, during 2019–2020 a Fernholz Visiting Professor at the IAS, and during 2020–2021 a Professor at Stanford University, and since 2021 he has been a Professor at Princeton University. June has also been a Distinguished Professor at the KIAS since 2022. He is especially noted for noting the linkages between algebraic geometry and combinatorics. He has written more than 25 innovative research papers and supervised one doctoral student. He has been awarded the Blavatnik Award for Young Scientists in 2017, New Horizons in Mathematics Prize in 2019, Samsung Ho-Am Prize in Science for Physics and Mathematics in 2021, Fields Medal in 2022, and MacArthur Fellowship in 2022. Huh is married to Nayoung Kim, whom he met during his studies while attending Seoul National University. She completed her Ph.D. in mathematics in 2014. The couple has two sons. June says "I'm very good at finding stuff, that's one of my special abilities".

41.3. James Alexander Maynard

He was born in Chelmsford, Essex, England, to Chris Maynard and Gill Maynard, both language teachers. Maynard attended King Edward VI Grammar School, Chelmsford, England. After completing his bachelor's and master's degrees at Queens' College, Cambridge, in 2009, Maynard obtained his Doctor of Philosophy from Balliol College, Oxford, in 2013 under the supervision of Roger Heath-Brown (born 1952, UK). The title of his thesis was *Topics in Analytic Number Theory*. For the year 2013–2014, Maynard was a CRM-ISM postdoctoral researcher at the University of Montreal. He also spent sometime at Berkeley, Princeton, and Oxford before joining the Mathematical Institute in Oxford in 2017 as a Professor of Number Theory. James's main research interest is in analytic number theory, particularly the distribution of prime numbers. In his research he uses a blend of ideas from analysis, combinatorics, and algebra to find solutions to old open problems in number theory. In November 2013, he gave a different proof of Yitang Zhang's (born 1955, China–USA) theorem that there are bounded gaps between primes and resolved a longstanding conjecture by showing that for any m there are infinitely many intervals of bounded length containing m prime numbers. Specifically, he established that there are infinitely many pairs of primes that differ by at most 600; further, he applied his approach not just to pairs of primes, but to triples, quadruples, and bigger collections (with different bounds for each). In August 2014, Maynard resolved a longstanding conjecture of Erdös on large gaps between primes, and received the largest Erdös prize, USD 10,000, ever offered. In 2016, he showed that, for any given decimal digit, there are infinitely many prime numbers that do not have that digit in their decimal expansion. In 2019, together with Dimitris Koukoulopoulos (born 1984, Greece–Canada), he proved the Duffin–Schaeffer conjecture (after Richard James Duffin, 1909–1996, USA, and Albert Charles Schaeffer, 1907–1957, USA), which asks which infinite collections of denominators produce fractions that do a good job of approximating irrational numbers. In 2020, in joint work with Thomas Bloom, he improved the best-known bound for square-difference-free sets, showing that a set $A \subset [N]$ with no square difference has size at most $N/(\log N)^{c \log\log\log N}$ for some $c > 0$. He has published more than 30 research papers and supervised three doctoral students. He has been awarded the following: SASTRA Ramanujan Prize in 2014, Whitehead Prize in 2015, EMS Prize in 2016, Cole Prize in 2020, Fields Medal in 2022, New Horizons in Mathematics Prize in 2023, and FRS of London in 2023. His partner is Eleanor Grant, a medical doctor; they have a son and a daughter.

41.4. Maryna Sergiivna Viazovska

She was born in Kyiv/Kiev, Ukraine, the oldest of three sisters. Her father was a chemist who worked at the Antonov aircraft factory, which has been leveled by a Russian airstrike (Maryna had attended kindergarten nearby), and her mother was an engineer. Maryna excelled at mathematics at school in Kiev so, in 1998, she could enter the specialized secondary school Kiev Natural Science Lyceum no. 145. At this school Maryna was influenced, in particular, by the mathematician Andrii Knyazyuk (1960–2013, Ukraine). She graduated from this school in 2001 and entered the Taras Shevchenko National University of Kiev to study mathematics. In 2002, 2003, 2004, and 2005, Maryna competed in the Mathematical Olympiad Competition and won the top awards in 2002 and 2005. In 2005, she was awarded a bachelor's degree in mathematics from the University of Kiev. In 2005, with Andriy Bondarenko (born 1987, Ukraine) she also published her first paper *Bernstein type inequality in monotone rational approximation*. Then, Maryna went to Germany to study for a master's degree at the Kaiserslautern University of Technology, which she completed in 2007. In 2010, she defended her candidate's thesis at the Institute of Mathematics of the NAS of Ukraine on the topic *Inequalities for polynomials and rational functions and quadrature formulas in the sphere*. In 2008 and 2010, with Andriy Bondarenko she published two papers *New asymptotic estimates for spherical designs* and *Spherical designs via Brouwer fixed point theorem*. In 2009, she also published her first independent paper *Estimation of the norm of the derivative of a monotone rational function in the spaces L_p*. After her candidate's degree, Maryna went to the MPIM in Bonn . In 2913, she was awarded a Doctorate of Natural Sciences, *Doctor of Science*, for her dissertation *Modular Functions and Special Cycles*, which concerns analytic number theory, written under the supervision of Don Bernard Zagier and Werner Müller (born 1949, Germany). Then, she was a postdoctoral researcher at the IHES in France, the Berlin Mathematical School, and the Humboldt University of Berlin and a Minerva Distinguished Visitor at Princeton University. Since January 2018 she has held the Chair of Number Theory as a Full Professor at the École Polytechnique Fédérale de Lausanne in Switzerland after a short stint as tenure-track Assistant Professor. In 2016, Maryna solved the sphere-packing problem in dimension 8 (how many eight-dimensional balls can fit in an eight-dimensional space?). This problem had been solved only for three or fewer dimensions, and the proof of the three-dimensional version (the Kepler conjecture, after Johannes Kepler, 1571–1630, Germany–Czechoslovakia) involved long computer calculations. In 2017, her solution also led to a solution in dimension 24. Her work has potential reverberations in several other fields, including energy minimization, free interpolation formulas, and signal processing. She has published 20 papers and supervised one doctoral student. Maryna has received several awards and honors: Salem Prize in 2016, Clay Award in 2017, SASTRA Ramanujan Prize in 2017, European Prize in Combinatorics in 2017, New Horizons in Mathematics Prize in 2018, Ruth Lyttle Satter Prize in 2019, Fermat Prize in 2019, EMS Prize in 2020, Honorary Member of the LMS in 2020, elected to the Academia Europaea in 2021, Fields Medal in 2022 (second woman to win a Fields Medal), Senior Scholar at the Clay Mathematics Institute in July 2022, and honored as one of the BBC 100 Women in December 2022. She married Daniil Evtushinsky (born 1984, Ukraine), who also works at the École Polytechnique Fédérale de Lausanne. They have two children, a son and a daughter.

41.5. *Mark Braverman*

He was born in Perm, Russia, to a mathematician mother Elena Yanovna Braverman (born 1961, Russia–Israel–Canadian) and a physicist father. Following the collapse of the Soviet Union and its resulting instability, the young family moved to Haifa, Israel, in 1992, when Mark was 8 years old. Mark showed an early talent for mathematics by winning two bronze medals and one gold at the IMO in 1998, 1999, and 2000. In 2001, he received his Bachelor of Arts degree in mathematics and computer science in 2001 from the Technion in Haifa. Later in 2001, his family moved to Canada, and in the winter semester Mark joined the graduate school at the University of Toronto. Mark received his Ph.D. in 2008 from the Department of Computer Science at the University of Toronto under the supervision of Stephen Arthur Cook. The title of his thesis was *Computability and Complexity of Julia Sets*, a topic on which he worked with Michael Yampolsky (born 1972, Russia–Canada). After his doctorate, Mark spent a month at the IAS, Princeton, two years as a postdoctoral researcher at Microsoft Research New England in Cambridge, Massachusetts, and a year as an Assistant Professor at the University of Toronto. In 2011, he joined the Princeton University Department of Computer Science as an Assistant Professor, and since 2015 he has been a Professor. His interests center on the connections between theoretical computer science and other disciplines, such as complexity theory, information theory, the theory of real computation, machine learning, algorithms, algorithmic mechanism design, and its applications (particularly in the context of healthcare). He has more than 200 research publications to his credit and has supervised seven doctoral students and over a dozen postdocs. He has been awarded the Packard Fellowship in 2013, Stephen Smale Prize in 2014, EMS Prize in 2016, Presburger Award in 2016, Waterman Award in 2019, and IMU Abacus Medal in 2022. In 2007, he married Anna, a writer and a clinical psychologist; they have three children.

41.6. *Elliott Hershel Lieb*

He was born in Boston, USA. His father came from Lithuania and was an accountant; his mother came from Bessarabia and worked as a secretary. At the age of five, his family moved to the Bronx (County in New York State), where Elliott was educated in the New York City school system, graduating from the Bronx High School of Science. At the age of 17, he moved with his parents back to Boston, where he was able to attend MIT and received his Bachelor of Science degree in physics in 1953. Then on an NSF fellowship, Elliott went to Birmingham University in England for his Ph.D. studies in the Department of Mathematical Physics under Rudolf Ernst Peierls (1907–1995, Germany–UK), Samuel Frederick Edwards (1928–2015, UK), and Gerald Edward Brown (1926–2013, USA). In 1956, he received his Ph.D. for the dissertation *Non-Linear Scalar Meson Field Theory*, written under the supervision of Samuel Edwards. During 1956–1957, Elliott was a Fulbright Fellow at Kyoto University, Japan, attached to the Yukawa Institute for Theoretical Physics. After postdoctoral appointments at Illinois and Cornell universities, he worked as a Theoretical Physicist in the newly installed IBM laboratory in Yorktown Heights, New York, from 1960 to 1963. In 1961–1962, Elliott was on leave as Professor of Applied

Mathematics at Fourah Bay College, the University of Sierra Leone. In 1963, he joined Yeshiva University in New York as an Associate Professor. In 1966, Elliott moved to Northeastern University in Boston, and in 1968 he returned to MIT as a faculty member and moved in 1975 to Princeton as a Professor. Currently he is Higgins Professor of Physics (Emeritus). Elliott has made significant contributions in several fields, including quantum and classical many-body problems, atomic structure, the stability of matter, functional inequalities, the theory of magnetism, and the Hubbard model. He has published more than 320 research papers and supervised 10 doctoral students. Elliott's main research papers were gathered in four Selecta volumes in 2002 and 204, and on the occasion of his 90th birthday the EMS published two volumes reviewing his work in more than 50 chapters. Elliott has also published several books, including *Analysis* (2001), *Inequalities* (2002), *The stability of matter in quantum mechanics* (2009), *The stability of matter in quantum mechanics* (2010), and *Studies in Mathematical Physics: Essays in Honor of Valentine Bargmann* (2015). His name appears in his several original contributions, including the Lieb conjecture, Lieb lattice, Lieb's concavity theorem, Lieb's square ice constant, Lieb's theorem, the Lieb–Liniger model (Werner Liniger, 1927–2017, Switzerland), the Lieb–Oxford inequality (Stephen Oxford, USA), Lieb–Robinson bounds (Derek William Robinson, 1935–2021, UK–Australia), the Lieb–Thirring inequality (Walter Eduard Thirring, 1927–2014, Austria), the Lieb–Yngvason entropy principle (Jakob Yngvason, born 1945, Iceland–Austria), the Affleck–Kennedy–Lieb–Tasaki model (Ian Keith Affleck, 1952–2024, Canada; Tom Kennedy; Hal Tasaki, born 1959, Japan), the Borell–Brascamp–Lieb inequality (Christer Borell, Sweden; Herm Jan Brascamp, USA), the Brascamp–Lieb inequality, the Brézis–Lieb lemma, the Carlen–Lieb extension (Eric Anders Carlen, born 1957, USA), and Temperley–Lieb algebra (Harold Neville Vazeille Temperley, 1915–2017, UK). Elliott has been awarded several prizes in mathematics and physics, including the Heineman Prize for Mathematical Physics in 1978, Birkhoff Prize in 1988, Max PlanckMmedal in 1992, Boltzmann Medal in 1998, Rolf Schock Prize in 2001, Levi Leonard Conant Prize in 2002, Henri Poincaré Prize in 2003, Erwin Schrödinger Medal in 2021, American Physical Society Medal for Exceptional Achievement in Research in 2022, Gauss Prize in 2022, Dirac Medal in 2022, and Kyoto Prize in 2023. Elliott is a member/fellow of several academies/societies, including the following: the United States NAS, Austrian Academy of Sciences, Royal Danish Academy, Chilean Academy of Sciences, AAAS, Foreign Member of the Royal Society, Academia Europaea, Fellow of the AMS, Fellow of the APS, and Fellow of the American Association for the Advancement of Science. He has been awarded honorary doctorates from the University of Copenhagen (1979), Ecole Polytechnique Fédérale Lausanne (1995), University of Munich (2004), and University of Birmingham (2007). Elliott married fellow Princeton Professor Christiane Fellbaum (born 1950, Germany–USA), a computational linguistics researcher.

41.7. Barry Charles Mazur

He was born in New York City. Barry attended the Bronx High School of Science and became interested in mathematics during his first year. He spent two years as an undergraduate at MIT, studying courses leading to a Bachelor of Science degree. He did not graduate from the university on account of failing the Reserve Officer Training

Program (a college program that prepares students to become military officers while pursuing a degree). However, based on his mathematical ability, Princeton University accepted Barry for graduate studies. In 1959, at Princeton he received his Ph.D. in mathematics for defending his dissertation entitled *On Embeddings of Spheres*, written under the supervision of Ralph Hartzler Fox and R. H. Bing (1914–1986, USA). Thus, his only academic degree is a Ph.D. In 1959, Barry published five influential research papers: *The definition of equivalence of combinatorial imbeddings, On the structure of certain semi-groups of spherical knot classes, Orthotopy and spherical knots,* and *On embeddings of spheres* in *Bull. Amer. Math. Soc.* and *On embeddings of spheres* in *Acta Math.* During the year 1958–1959, he was a Research Fellow at the IAS, Princeton. In 1959, Barry became a Junior Fellow of Harvard University. In 1963, he joined the Mathematics Department of Harvard University as an Assistant Professor, and then became an Associate Professor in 1965, Full Professor in 1969, and William Petschek Professor of Mathematics in 1982, and since 1998 he has continued as a Gerhard Gade University Professor. He has made significant contributions in the fields geometric topology, differential topology, number theory, and algebraic geometry. His work was a key ingredient in Wiles' proof of Fermat's Last Theorem in number theory. He is also known for Mazur's torsion theorem in arithmetic geometry, the Mazur swindle in geometric topology, and the Mazur manifold in differential topology. Barry has more than 150 research publications and has supervised 59 doctoral students. He has also published/edited several books, including *Etale homotopy* with Michael Artin in 1969, *Smoothings of piecewise linear manifolds* with Morris Hirsch in 1974, *Arithmetic moduli of elliptic curves* with Nicholas Katz in 1985, *Filtrations on the Homology of Algebraic Varieties* with Eric Mark Friedlander (born 1944, Santurce, Puerto Rico) in 1994, *Imagining numbers: particularly the square root of minus fifteen* in 2003, *Prime numbers and the Riemann hypothesis* with William Arthur Stein (born 1974, USA) in 2016, and *Collected works of John Tate: Parts I and II*, edited with Jean-Pierre Serre in 2016. Barry has received several awards and honors, including the Oswald Veblen Prize for geometry in 1966, Cole Prize for number theory in 1982, Chauvenet Prize for exposition in 1994, Steele Prize for Seminal Contribution to Research in 2000, and Chern Medal in 2022. In early 2013, he was presented with one of the 2011 National Medals of Science by President Barack Obama. In 1978, he was elected member of the American Academy of Sciences; in 1982, elected member of the United States NAS; and in 2001, elected member of the APS. He was awarded honorary doctorate degrees in 2004 from Colby College and in 2016 from the University of Waterloo. He is married to Grace Dane Mazur, a writer. They had one son, Zeke Mazur, who died in 2016. Barry has a brother, Joseph Conrad Mazur (born 1942, Bronx), who was a Professor Emeritus of Mathematics at Marlboro College, in Marlboro, Vermont, until the college closed in 2020 and merged with Emerson College in Boston. Joseph has written several popular mathematics books.

41.8. Nikolai Nikolayevich Andreev

He was born in Saratov, Russia. He received his Ph.D. degree from Lomonosov Moscow State University in 2000. The title of his dissertation was *Restricted approximation of individual functions and extremal problems of positioning points on a sphere*, written under the supervision of Sergey Borisovich Stechkin (1920–1995,

Russia) and Vladimir Aleksandrovich Yudin (1947–2012, Russia). Nikolai is the Head of the Laboratory for Popularization and Promotion of Mathematics at the Steklov Institute of Mathematics of the RAS (Moscow). Among his projects is the creation of the website Mathematical Etudes, which contains sketches, including entertaining popular science stories about modern problems in mathematics, and films that reveal well-known stories in a new way. He is recognized for tremendous resilience in often overcoming hardship to continue kindling enthusiasm for mathematics among a large number of people of all life circumstances via web resources, lectures, and a book. He was awarded the Prize of the President of the Russian Federation in the area of sciences and innovations for young scientists in 2010, Gold Medal of the RAS in 2017 for outstanding achievements in science popularization, and Leelavati Award in 2022 for his wondrous art of mathematical animation and of mathematical model-building.

42. Author and His Contributions to Mathematics

This is Sadhna Agarwal, wife of Ravi Prakash Agarwal; we were married on 9 December 1974. During the last 50 years, I have seen him reading, writing, and teaching mathematics for almost 12 hours daily. Ravi was born on 7 October 1948 in Moradabad, Utter Pradesh, India, to Radhey Shiam Agarwal (1919–1991, India) and Godawari Agarwal (1924–2016, India). He started going to elementary school at the age of three along with his immediate elder brother Satya Prakash Agarwal (born 1946, India), who was then five years old. Teachers in school allowed Ravi to continue until he reached sixth grade, but then due to minimum age restrictions there was a problem with allowing him to sit the final board exams, which was resolved by the Head Master (with the consent of Ravi's father), who put Ravi's date of birth officially as 10 July 1947 (during that time there were no birth certificates in India). After completing his high school and secondary school studies in local colleagues, he obtained his Bachelor of Science degree in 1967 and Master of Science degree in 1969 in mathematics (ranking in second position among all master's mathematics students, almost 500, in that year), both from Agra University. In 1969, Ravi was selected for a Ph.D. programme at the IIT Madras, India, which is one of the most prestigious institutions in India. He earned his doctorate degree in 1973 for his thesis *Boundary Value Problems for Ordinary and Functional Differential Equations*. He started his Ph.D. work with Krishna Mohan Das (India), but submitted his independent work (finding his own problems and solving them) through the Head of the Mathematics Department, Swami Dayal Nigam (1924–2009, India). During the year 1973–1974, he was a Post Doctor Fellow at the IIT, Madras. In 1974, he joined the Regional Engineering College (now the National Institute of Technology) Tiruchirappalli (Tamil Nadu, India) as a Lecturer (now Assistant Professor). On 8 December 1975 (after exactly one year of our marriage), our daughter Sheba Agarwal was born. In 2008, she completed her Ph.D. in cell biology at Erasmus University Rotterdam, the Netherlands. At the time of Ravi's appointment, he was promised a promotion within two years, but unfortunately in 1976 the Tamil Nadu Government was dismissed and President's rule was imposed, so his promotion had to wait until the new Government was formed. However, in 1977, Ravi moved to the Institute of Mathematical Sciences (Matscience) in Madras as an Assistant Professor (a drastic change from pure teaching institution to pure research institution). At Matscience Ravi learned how to stand in the mathematical world, publishing research papers in foreign leading journals, attending international conferences, and giving and listening to lectures from others on recent research works. From January 1980 to June 1981, he was awarded the world's most prestigious Alexander von Humboldt Foundation Fellowship to work with leading numerical analyst Günther Hämmerlin (1928–1997, Germany) at the Mathematisches Institut der Ludwig-Maximilian-Universitiät, Munchen, Germany. On 15 May 1980, our son Hans Agarwal was born in Munchen, Germany. He completed his Ph.D. in chemical engineering at Lehigh University, USA, in 2006. For the year July 1981–June 1982, Ravi was offered a scholarship by the Consiglio Nazionale delle Ricerche to work with

Roberto Conti (1923–2006, Italy) at the Istituto Matematico "Ulisse Dini", Universita degli Studi di Firenze, 50134 Firenze, Italy.

In July 1982, Ravi moved to Singapore, widely recognized as a city-state where the same rules and regulations are strictly enforced and followed by everyone, earning it the nickname "The Fine City" due to the hefty fines imposed for breaking even minor laws; this includes rules on cleanliness, public behavior, and even chewing gum, which is banned in the country. He joined the National University of Singapore (NUS) as a Lecturer and was promoted to Senior Lecturer after one year in 1983. His next promotion to Associate Professor was in 1991. In 1982, when Ravi joined the NUS there was only one Full Professor in the Mathematics Department, but slowly the rules changed, and now there are several Full Professors. For the academic year June 1997–May 1998, Ravi took sabbatical leave from the NUS and on the invitation of Robert Pertsch Gilbert (born 1932, USA) he joined the Mathematics Department of the University of Delaware as a Visiting Professor. In 2001, Ravi left Singapore (but continued to be a Singapore citizen until 2022) and moved to the USA to join the Florida Institute of Technology (FIT), Melbourne, Florida, as a Full Professor of Mathematics. Here he had the opportunity to work under the leadership of Vangipuram Lakshmikantham (1924–2012, India–USA). His next move was in 2011, when he joined Texas A&M University-Kingsville (TAMUK), Kingsville, Texas, as a Professor and Chairman of the Department of Mathematics. His vision and management raised both the academic and research outputs of the department. The department established itself in the world research arena, drawing many collaborating researchers and scholars to department. Ravi stepped down from the Chairmanship in 2019, and in 2024 he left TAMUK to join the FIT as an Emeritus Research Professor.

Ravi has been a Visiting Professor/Scientist for short periods (up to 3 months) at Marathwada University, Aurangabad (India, 1979); the Indian Institute of Science, Bangalore (India, 1979); the International Center for Theoretical Physics, Trieste (Italy, 1982, 1983); J. E. Purkne University Brnö (Czechoslovakia, 1983); the University of Manitoba, Winnipeg (Canada, 1983, 1986); the University of Western Australia, Perth (Australia, 1989); the Japan Society for the Promotion of Science Cooperation Programmes (Japan, 1991); the University of Saskatchewan, Saskatoon (Canada, 1991); the Politecnico di Milano, Milano (Italy, 1995, 2008); San Diego State University, San Diego (USA, 1998); the University of Queensland, Brisbane (Australia, 2000); the University of Missouri, Rolla (USA, 2000); the University of Hong Kong, (Hong Kong, 2006); the University of Roma, (Italy 2008); Seattle University (USA, 2009); Middle East Technical University, Ankara (Turkey, 2009); King Fahd University of Petroleum and Minerals, Dhahran (Saudi Arabia, 2009, 2010, 2011); King Abdulaziz University, Jeddah (Saudi Arabia, 2011); and the Institute of Mathematics Academia Sinica, Taipei (Taiwan, 2013).

In the year 1971 when Ravi was a Ph.D. student at the IIT, Madras, he read the obituary of Bertrand Arthur William Russell (1872–1970, UK). In his lifetime he published 2000 articles and 70 books, married five times, and had many adulterous affairs. He also saw Bertrand Russell with the famous Indian actor Rajendra Kumar in a Hindi movie *Aman*, which was released in May 1967. For several years Ravi wondered how in one life one human being can publish so many articles and books. It worked for Ravi as a inspiring challenge to continue working and publishing his research findings individually as well as collaboratively in more than 2050 research articles in very high-impact-factor/leading international journals, including *Advances in Mathematics, Applied Mathematics and Computation,* the *Journal of Computational and Applied Mathematics,* the *Journal of Differential Equations,* the *Journal of Geometric Analysis,* the *Journal of Fixed Point Theory and Applications,* the *Journal of the LMS,* the *Journal of Mathematical Analysis and Applications,* the *Journal of Optimization Theory and Applications, Mathematische Nachrichten, Pacific Journal of Mathematics, Proceedings of the AMS, Proceedings of the Edinburgh Mathematical Society, Proceedings of the RSE,* and *Studies in Applied Mathematics.* More than 725 of his collaborators (almost all of them Professors now) are from several countries, including Algeria, Australia, Brazil, Bulgaria, Canada, China, Croatia, Czech Republic, Egypt, Georgia, Greece, Iran, Iraq, Ireland, Israel, Italy, Korea, Malaysia, Pakistan, Poland, Portugal, Romania, Saudi Arabia, Serbia, Singapore, Spain, Taiwan, Turkey, the USA, and Vietnam. Ravi's research interests vary in several diverse fields in mathematics, including ordinary differential equations; operator theory; difference and functional equations; fractional differential equations; real functions; partial differential equations; numerical analysis; integral equations; general topology; calculus of variations and optimal control; optimization; biology and other natural sciences; approximations and expansions; systems theory; control; operations research; mathematical programming; probability theory and stochastic processes; functions of a complex variable; special functions; elementary number theory; global analysis, analysis on manifolds; history and biography; functional analysis; mechanics of deformable solids; sequences, series, and summability; abstract harmonic analysis; fluid mechanics; statistics; harmonic analysis on Euclidean spaces; differential geometry; algebraic topology; dynamical systems and ergodic theory; linear and multilinear algebra; matrix theory; game theory, economics, finance, and other social and behavioral sciences; computer science; geometry; integral transforms; operational calculus; and measure and integration. He has also supervised four doctoral students.

Ravi has written 52 books independently as well as collaboratory with leading publishing companies such as Springer, Cambridge University Press, Elsevier, and AMS Mathematical Surveys and Monographs: *Boundary Value Problems for Higher Order Differential Equations* (1986) pp. 307; *Essentials of Ordinary Differential Equations* (1991) p. 467; *Difference Equations and Inequalities: Theory, Methods and Applications* (1992) p. 777; *Uniqueness and Nonuniqueness Criteria for Ordinary Differential Equations* (1993) p. 312; *Error Inequalities in Polynomial Interpolation and Their Applications* (1993) p. 365; *Opial Inequalities with Applications in Differential and Difference Equations* (1995) p. 393; *Advanced Topics in Difference Equations* (1997) p. 507; *Focal Boundary Value Problems for Differential and Difference Equations* (1998) p. 289; *Positive Solutions of Differential, Difference and Integral Equations* (1999) p. 417; *Difference Equations and Inequalities: Second Edition, Revised and Expended* (2000) p. 980; *Fixed Point Theory and Applications* (2001) p. 170; *Oscillation Theory for Difference and Functional Differential Equations* (2000) p. 337; *Infinite Interval Problems for Differential, Difference and Integral Equations* (2001) p. 341; *Nonlinear Integral Equations and Inclusions* (2001) p. 362; *Oscillation Theory for Second Order Linear, Half-linear, Superlinear and Sublinear Dynamic*

Equations (2002) p. 672; *Oscillation Theory for Second Order Dynamic Equations* (2003) p. 404; *Singular Differential and Integral Equations with Applications* (2003) p. 402; *Nonoscillation and Oscillation Theory for Functional Differential Equations* (2004) p. 376; *Discrete Oscillation Theory* (2005) p. 1000; *An Introduction to Ordinary Differential Equations* (2008) p. 321; *Ordinary and Partial Differential Equations with Special Functions, Fourier Series and Boundary Value Problems* (2009) p. 410; *Fixed Point Theory for Lipschitzian-type Mappings with Applications* (2009) p. 368; Inequalities for Differential Forms (2009), p. 387; *Morse Theoretic Aspects of p-Laplacian Type Operators* (2010) p. 141; *An Introduction to Complex Analysis* (2011) p. 331; *π, e, ϕ with MATLAB: Random and Rational Sequences with Scope in Supercomputing Era* (2011) p. 298; *Nonoscillation Theory of Functional Differential Equations with Applications* (2012) p. 520; *Applications of q-Calculus in Operator Theory* (2013) p. 262; *Constant-Sign Solutions of Systems of Integral Equations* (2013) p. 648; *Convergence Estimates in Approximation Theory* (2014) p. 361; *Oscillation and Stability of Delay Models in Biology* (2014) p. 340; *Dynamic Inequalities on Time Scales* (2014) p. 256; *Regularity of Difference Equations on Banach Spaces* (2014) p. 208; *Creators of Mathematical and Computational Sciences* (2014) p. 495; Zero, *A Landmark Discovery, the Dreadful Void, and the Ultimate Mind* (2015) p. 157; *Functions of a Complex Variables* (2015) p. 718; *Fixed Point Theory in Metric Type Spaces* (2015) pp. 385; *Hardy Type Inequalities on Time Scales* (2016) p. 305; *Optimal Control* (2016) p. 209; *An Introduction to Linear Algebra* (2017) p. 232; *Non-Instantaneous Impulses in Differential Equations* (2017) p. 251; *An Introduction to Real Analysis* (2018) p. 277; *500 Examples and Problems of Applied Differential Equations* (2019) p. 388; *Theory of Translation Closedness for Time Scales* (2020) p. 577; *Hilbert-Type Inequalities: Operators, Compositions and Extensions* (2020), p. 403; *Lyapunov Inequalities and Applications* (2021) p. 607; *Optimal Control, Second Edition* (2021) p. 251; *Dynamic Equations and Almost Periodic Fuzzy Functions on Time Scales* (2022) p. 185; *Combined Measure and Shift Invariance Theory of Time Scales and Applications* (2022) p. 434; *Fixed Point Theory in Generalized Metric Spaces* (2022) pp. 136; *Mathematics Before and After Pythagoras* (2024) p. 658; *Sturmian Theory with Applications*; and *Fixed Point Theory: From Early Foundations to Contemporary Challenges* (in preparation).

Ravi has contributed tirelessly to the scientific and mathematical community. He has reviewed more than 10,000 articles for almost 60 leading international journals. He served as Editor-in-Chief of several journals published by Elsevier (Holland) and SpringerOpen (USA). Currently, he serves more than 40 international journals in the capacity of an Honorary, Advisory, Associate, or Assistant Editor. He has published 25 volumes and conference proceedings as an Editor for Birkhäuser Verlag, World Scientific, CRC Press, Hindawi, John Wiley & Sons, and Gordon & Breach. Ravi has also edited several special issues of journals: *Computers and Mathematics with Applications* (1994, 1998, 2001, and 2003), *Nonlinear Analysis: Theory, Methods and Applications* (1995, 2000), *Neural, Perallel & Scientific Computations* (1997), *Journal of Computational and Applied Mathematics* (1998 and 2000), *Mathematical Inequalities and Applications* (1998), *Dynamic Systems and Applications* (1999 and 2005), *Mathematical and Computational Modelling* (2000), and *Applied Mathematics and Computation* (2002). He has also organized very successful international conferences: International Conference on Numerical Mathematics (NUS, 1988), Differential and Difference

Equations and Applications (FIT, 2005), and International Conference on the Theory, Methods, and Applications of Nonlinear Equations (TAMUK, 2012).

Ravi has participated and given main lectures at several international conferences, including the Seventh Conference on Theoretical and Applied Mechanics (Ranchi, 1972, India) [he was awarded first prize for his presentation and work]; Approximate Methods for Navier–Stokes Problems (Paderborn 1979, Germany); General Inequalities 3 (Oberwolfach 1981, Germany); Operator Inequalities (Oberwolfach 1981, Germany); Ordinary Differential Equations (Oberwolfach 1983, Germany); General Inequalities 4 (Oberwolfach 1983, Germany); Int. Conf. on Qualitative Theory of Differential Equations (Edmonton 1984, Canada); Trends in the Theory and Practice of Nonlinear Analysis (Texas 1984, USA); EQUADIFF 6 (Brnö 1985, Czechoslovakia); General Inequalities 5 (Oberwolfach 1986, Germany); Int. Conf. on Optimization: Techniques and Applications (1987, Singapore); Int. Conf. on Functional Equations and Inequalities (Szczawnica, 1987, Poland); Int. Conf. on Numerical Mathematics (1988, Singapore); International Symposium on Asymptotic and Computational Analysis (Winnipeg 1989, Canada); General Inequalities 6 (Oberwolfach 1990, Germany); First World Congress of Nonlinear Analysts (Tampa, 1992, USA); Second Int. Conf. on Dynamic Systems and Applications (Atlanta 1995, USA); First Int. Conf. on Neural, Parallel and Scientific Computations (Atlanta 1995, USA); Second Int. Conf. on Difference Equations and Applications (Vesprem 1995, Hungary); General Inequalities 7 (Oberwolfach 1995, Germany); International Workshop on Difference and Differential Inequalities (Gebze, 1996, Turkey); Second World Congress of Nonlinear Analysts (Athens, 1996, Greece); Modelling and System Stability Investigations (Kiev, 1997, Ukraine); EQUADIFF 9 (Brnö 1997, Czechoslovakia); Third Midwest-Southeastern Atlantic Joint Regional Conference on Differential Equations (Nashville, TN 1997, USA); The Centennial Celebration: A Century of mathematics and Statistics at Nebraska (Lincoln 1998, USA); Third Int. Conf. on Dynamic Systems and Applications (Atlanta 1999, USA); Third World Congress of Nonlinear Analysts (Catania, 2000, Italy); Sixth Int. Conf. on Difference Equations and Applications (Augsburg, 2001, Germany); Int. Conf. on Differential, Difference Equations and their Applications (Patras 2002, Greece); Fourth Int. Conf. on Dynamic Systems and Applications (Atlanta 2003, USA); Fourth World Congress of Nonlinear Analysts (Orlando, 2004, USA); The 24th Annual Southeastern-Atlantic Regional Conference on Differential Equations (Chattanooga, 2004, USA); Fifth Int. Conf. on Dynamic Systems and Applications (Atlanta 2007, USA); Fifth World Congress of Nonlinear Analysts (Orlando, 2008, USA); Boundary Value Problems (Santiago de Compostela, 2008, Spain); Fourteenth Int. Conf. on Difference Equations and Applications (Istanbul, 2008, Turkey); EQUADIFF 12 (Brnö 2009, Czech Republic); Int. Conf. on Differential and Difference Equations and Applications in honour of Ravi P. Agarwal (Ponta Delgada 2011, Portugal); Int. Conf. on Applied Analysis and Algebra (Istanbul 2012, Turkey); 11th International Workshop on Dynamical Systems and Applications (Ankara 2012, Turkey); the Int. Conf. on Mathematical Inequalities and Nonlinear Functional Analysis with Applications (Cinju 2012, Korea); Southeastern-Atlantic Regional Conference on Differential Equations (Georgia Southern University 2012, USA); Int. Conf. on Applied Analysis and Mathematical Modelling (Istanbul 2013,

Turkey); Int. Conf. on Anatolian Communications in Nonlinear Analysis (Bolu 2013, Turkey); Peterson Conference, University of Nebraska (Lincoln 2013, USA); the Int. Conf. on Nonlinear Analysis and Optimization (Kaohsiung 2013, Taiwan); 2013 Workshop on Nonlinear Analysis, Optimization and Their Applications (Kaohsiung 2013, Taiwan); International Boundary Value Problems Workshop (Diyarbakir 2014, Turkey); Int. Conf. and Workshop on Mathematical Analysis (Putrajaya 2014, Malaysia); International Congress in Honour of Professor Ravi P. Agarwal (Bursa 2014, Turkey); Int. Conf. on Recent Advances in Pure and Applied Mathematics (Antalya 2014, Turkey); ODE-day at China University of Geosciences: Conference in honor of Professor Ravi P. Agarwal (Beijing 2015, China); the Ninth Int. Conf. on Differential Equations and Dynamical Systems (Dallas 2015, USA); the Seventh Int. Conf. on Dynamic Systems and Applications (Atlanta 2015, USA); the Fifth Int. Conf. on Neural, Parallel and Scientific Computations (Atlanta 2015, USA); Int. Conf. on Nonlinear Operators, Differential Equations and Applications (Cluj-Napoca 2015, Romania); the 11th Int. Conf. on Fixed Point Theory and Applications (Istanbul 2015, Turkey); Int. Conf. on Analysis and its Applications (Aligarh 2015, India); Int. Conf. on Applied Mathematics and Analysis (Ankara 2016, Turkey); 2nd Int. Conf. on Analysis and its Application (Kirsehir 2016, Turkey); Third Int. Conf. New Trends in the Applications of Differential Equations in Sciences (Sofia 2016, Bulgaria); Recent Trends in Pure and Applied Mathematics (Alba Iulia 2017, Romania); Int. Conf. on Mathematical Sciences and Statistics (Putrajaya 2018, Malaysia); Int. Conf. on Applied Analysis and Mathematical Modelling (Istanbul, Turkey 2019); 4th Int. Conf. on Mathematics: An Istanbul Meeting for World Mathematicians (Istanbul, Turkey 2020); Int. Conf. in Mathematics and Applications (Bangkok, Thailand, 2020); Int. Conf. on Advances in Differential Equations and Numerical Analysis (Guwahati, India, 2020); International Symposium to Celebrate the Birth Anniversary of Ramanujan (Jabalpur, India, 2020); Applied Nonlinear Analysis and Soft Computing (Guwahati, India, 2020); 86th Annual Conference of the Indian Mathematical Society (Vellore, India, 2020); International Congress on Fundamental and Applied Sciences (Prishtina, Kosovo, 2020); One Day International Webinar on Mathematics and Mathematical Sciences (Kolkata, India, 2020); Importance of Mathematics in Science and Technology (Rajam, India, 2020); National Mathematics Day-2020 (Karaikudi, India, 2020); Int. Conf. on Recent Advances and Applied Mathematics, (Bodrum in Mugla, Turkey, 2021); Fifth Int. Conf. of Mathematical Sciences (Istanbul, Turkey, 2021); 9th Int. Conf. on Applied Analysis and Mathematical Modelling (Istanbul, Turkey, 2021); 3rd International Congress on Human-Computer Interaction, Optimization and Robotic Applications (Tokat, Turkey, 2021); First Western Conference on Mathematics and Applications (Prishtina, Kosovo, 2021); 16th Int. Conf. "Dynamical Systems-Theory and Applications" (Lodz, Poland, 2021); Int. Conf. on Science and Computing (Jaipur, India, 2021); Int. Conf. on Mathematics and its Relevance to Science and Engineering (Hyderabad, India, 2022); Nonlinear Functional Analysis, Technion-Israel Institute of Technology (Haifa, Israel, 2022); Emerging Applications of Mathematics and Statistics in Engineering Science and Technology (Rourkela, India, 2022); Int. Conf. on Mathematical Analysis and Applications in Science and Engineering (Porto, Portugal, 2022); International Symposium & International Student Workshop on

Interdisciplinary Mathematics in the CiTi areas (Bucharest, Romania, 2022); 10th Int. Conf. on Applied Analysis and Mathematical Modeling (Istanbul, Turkey, 2022); Sixth Int. Conf. of Mathematical Sciences (Istanbul, Turkey, 2022); 5th Int. Conf. on Mathematical Modelling, Applied Analysis and Computation (Jaipur, India 2022); the Int. Conf.: Dynamical Systems, Modeling, and Mathematical Sciences (Abu Dhabi, 2022); Int. Conf. on Nonlinear Analysis and Applications-2022 (ICNAA-2022) (India and Mexico, 2022); Int. Conf. in Mathematics and Applications (Bangkok, Thailand, 2022); Int. Conf. on Nonlinear Applied Analysis and Optimization (Varanasi, India, 2022); 4th Int. Conf. on Mathematical Techniques and Applications (Kattankulathur, India, 2023); Int. Conf. on Applied and Industrial Mathematics (Great Noida, India, 2023); 14th Int. Conf. on Fixed Point Theory and its Applications (Brasov, Romania, 2023); and Int. Conf. (In Memory of Late Professor S. L. Singh) on Nonlinear Analysis and Applications & Symposium on Ancient Indian Mathematics (Rishikesh, India, 2024).

Ravi has given major colloquium talks all over the world: Marathwada University, Aurangabad (India, 1979); Indian Institute of Science, Bangalore (India, 1979), Universität Karlsruhe (Germany, 1979, 1981, and 1989); der Universität München (Germany, 1979, 1981, 1989, and 1995); Georg-August-Universität Göttingen (Germany, 1980, 1983, and 1989); Universität Stuttgart (Germany, 1980); Mathematisch Centrum Amsterdam (Holland, 1980); University Van Amsterdam (Holland, 1980); Universita Degli Studi Di Parma (Italy, 1980); Universita Degli Studi Di Firenze (Italy, 1980, 1982, and 1995); University of Ioannina (Greece, 1980); Technische Hochschule Darmstadt (Germany, 1981); Universität Osnabrück (Germany, 1981); Universität Hannover (Germany, 1981); Johann Wolfgang Goethe-Universität Frankfurt (Germany, 1983, 1989); Albert-Ludwigs-Universität Freiburg (Germany, 1983); der Universität Tübingen (Germany, 1983); Universita Degli Studi Di Trieste (Italy, 1983 and 1995); Universita Degli Studi Di Trento (Italy, 1983); J. E. Purkne University Brnö (Czechoslovakia, 1983); Comenius University Bratislava (Czechoslovakia, 1983); the University of Manitoba (Canada, 1983 and 1986); Scuola Normale Superiore, Pisa (Italy, 1987 and 1995); Politechnica di Milano (Italy, 1987, 1995, and 2008); Rheinisch-Westfälische Technische Hochschule Aachen (Germany, 1989); University of Western Australia (Australia, 1989); Murdoch University (Australia, 1989); University of Dundee (UK, 1989); Brunel University of West London (UK, 1989); the University of Sussex (UK, 1989); the University of Liverpool (UK, 1989); University of Manchester (UK, 1989); University of Cambridge (UK, 1989); Oxford University (UK, 1989); University of Saskatchewan (Canada, 1991); the University of Tokyo (Japan, 1991); Tohoku University (Japan, 1991); Nagoya University (Japan, 1991); Ehime University (Japan, 1991); Okayama University (Japan, 1991); Kagoshima University (Japan, 1991); Hiroshima University (Japan, 1991); RIMS at Kyoto University (1991); Universita Degli Studi Di Roma (Italy, 1995 and 2008); Universita Degli Studi Di Bologna (Italy, 1995); SISSA, Trieste (Italy, 1995); Universität Augsburg (Germany, 1995); Institute of Mathematics, Ukrainian Acad. Sci, Kiev (Ukraine, 1997); University of Nebraska, Lincoln (USA, 1997); Auburn University (USA, 1997 and 2005); Washington University, St. Louis (USA, 1997); Wake Forest University (USA, 1998); FIT (USA, 1998); University of Central Florida (USA, 1998); North Carolina State University (USA, 1998); San Diego State University, San

Diego (USA, 1998); University of Southern California, L.A. (USA, 1998); University of Missori, Rolla (USA, 2000); the University of Queensland (Australia, 2000); University of Delaware (USA, 2000); Geogia Institute of Technology (USA, 2000); the Hong Kong Polytechnic University (Hong Kong, 2006); the University of Hong Kong (Hong Kong, 2006); City University of Hong Kong (Hong Kong, 2006); University of Calgary, (Canada, 2006 and 2007); Howard University (USA, 2006); Georgetown University (USA, 2006); Western Kentucky University (USA, 2006); Michigan Technological University (USA, 2007); Seattle University (USA, 2009); King Fahd University of Petroleum and Minerals (Saudi Arabia, 2009, 2010, and 2011); Istanbul Technical University (Turkey, 2009); Middle East Technical University (Turkey, 2009); Cankaya University (Turkey, 2009); Osmangazi University (Turkey, 2009); Izmir University (Turkey, 2009); Universidade De Santiago De Compostela (Spain, 2010); King Abdulaziz University (Saudi Arabia, 2010 and 2011); American University of Sharjah (Sharjah, 2010); United Arab Emirates University (Al-Ain, 2010); Texas A&M University-Corpus Christi (USA, 2012); Panamerican University (USA, 2012); Institute of Mathematics, Academia Sinica (Taipei, Taiwan, 2013); National Changhua University of Education (Taiwan, 2013); Universitatea "Ovidius" din Constanta (Romania, 2015); Transilvania University of Brasov (Romania, 2015); Plovdiv University, (Bulgaria, 2016); Gujarat University (Ahmedabad, India, 2023); Ariel University, Drakhlin's Seminar (Israel, 2023); and Lorestan University, seminar on mathematical analysis (Iran, 2023).

Ravi has been ranked as a Highly Cited Researcher for the 15 consecutive years and was also recognized as one of the "World's Most Influential Scientific Minds" in 2014 and 2015 by Thomas Reuters/Clarivate Analytics (the world's most prestigious scientific organization). Since 2021, he has been listed among the worlds top 2% scientists by Stanford University/Elsevier. In 2024, Research.com ranked him 34th in the world ranking and 26th in the USA, and according to their listing his work has been cited 57,288 times. The world's most popular weekly science and technology magazine *New Scientist*, in the July 2003 issue, published the importance of his joint work on dynamical equations on time scales. One of his joint publications of 2002 entitled "Dynamic equations on time scales: a survey" (coauthored with Martin Bohner, born 1966, Germany–USA; Donal O'Regan, born 1959, Ireland; and Allan Clemens Peterson, born 1942, USA) has been designated an "Emerging Research Front" by Thomson ISI Essential Science Indicators. ISI Essential Science Indicators list the most prominent papers in 22 broad fields of science. This was the only paper selected in the field of mathematics in October 2007. Ravi was also nominated as a possible candidate for a BBVA Foundation Frontiers of Knowledge Award in the year 2010, an international award scheme recognizing significant contributions in the areas of scientific research and cultural creation. More than 100 established mathematicians nominated him for this award. This award of EURO 400,000 is given to awardees in each category. Many BBVA award winners are Nobel Laureates, including legendary physicist Stephen Hawkins (1942–2018, England). Ravi has received several honorable recognitions from different institutions for his contribution to mathematics, education, and research. He was honored with a Doctor Honoris Causa (Universitatea "Ovidius" din Constanta, Romania, 2015), Professor Honoris Causa (Universitatea Babeş-Bolyai Din Cluj-Napoca, Romania,

2015), honorary doctorate (University of Nis, Serbia, 2017), Doctor Honoris Causa (Plovdiv Universoty, Bulgaria, 2017), Doctor Honoris Causa ("Constantin Brancusi", University of Targu-Jiu, Romania, 2017), Doctor Honoris Causa (University of Oradea, Romania, 2017), Doctor Honoris Causa ("1 December 1918", University of Alba Lulia, Romania, 2017), honorary doctorate (Istanbul Gelisim University, Turkey, 2019), and Doctor Honoris Causa (Transilvania University of Brasov, Romania, 2019). He was appointed Adjunct Professor at the University of Delaware (USA, 2000); King Fahd University of Petroleum and Minerals Chair Professor (Saudi Arabia, 2010, 2011); Honorary Distinguished Professor at King Abdual Aziz University (Saudi Arabia, 2011–2015); Adjunct Professor at the University of Nebraska (2013, USA); and Distinguished University Professor at the FIT (2018–2024) and at King Abdual Aziz University (2019–2023). Besides these honors, Ravi has also received several plaques and gifts in recognition of his contributions from a number of universities around the world. In addition, many leading mathematicians of the world have written appreciating remarks on his work. This list includes Garrett Birkhoff, William Norrie Everitt (1924–2011, England), Lloyd Kenneth Jackson (1922–2009, USA), Steven George Krantz (born 1951, USA), Paul Erdös, Lothar Collatz (1910–1990, Germany), Hans Jörg Stetter (born 1930, Germany), Günther Hämmerlin, Paul Leo Butzer (born 1928, Germany), Karl Leberecht Emil Nickel (1924–2009, Germany), Rainer Kress (born 1941, Germany), Eric Russell Love (1912–2001, Australia), Martin Bohner (born 1966, Germany–USA), Jean Mawhin (born 1942, Belgium), Pieter Jacobus van der Houwen (born 1939, the Netherlands), Donal O'Regan (born 1959, Ireland), Juan José Nieto Roig (botn 1958, Spain), Roberto Conti (1923–2006, Italy), Maria Alessandra Ragusa (born 1966, Italy), Simeon Reich (born 1948, Poland-Israel), and Alexander Domoshnitsky (born 1957, USSR–Israel).

In conclusion, Ravi is a visionary scientist, educator, and administrator and has contributed significantly to several universities, to nations, and to the world through his long service, dedication, and tireless efforts. For him providing help to others is the most important endeavor of life.

References

1. Schappacher, N. *Framing Global Mathematics: The International Mathematical Union between Theorems and Politics*; Springer Nature: Cham, Switzerland, 2022.
2. Holden, H.; Piene, R. (Eds.) *The Abel Prize 2003–2007*; Springer: Berlin/Heidelberg, Germany, 2009.
3. Holden, H.; Piene, R. (Eds.) *The Abel Prize 2008–2012*; Springer: Berlin/Heidelberg, Germany, 2014.
4. Holden, H.; Piene, R. (Eds.) *The Abel Prize 2013–2017*; Springer: Berlin/Heidelberg, Germany, 2019.
5. Holden, H.; Piene, R. (Eds.) *The Abel Prize 2018–2022*; Springer: Berlin/Heidelberg, Germany, 2023.

Index

MDPI AG
Grosspeteranlage 5
4052 Basel
Switzerland
Tel.: +41 61 683 77 34

MDPI Books Editorial Office
E-mail: books@mdpi.com
www.mdpi.com/books

www.ingramcontent.com/pod-product-compliance
Lightning Source LLC
Chambersburg PA
CBHW040852230926
51850CB00012BA/2932
* 9 7 8 3 7 2 5 8 4 6 1 6 0 *